GAY AND LESBIAN RIGHTS

Selected Titles in ABC-CLIO's
CONTEMPORARY
WORLD ISSUES
Series

For a complete list of titles in this series, please visit
www.abc-clio.com.

Books in the Contemporary World Issues series address vital issues in today's society, such as genetic engineering, pollution, and biodiversity. Written by professional writers, scholars, and nonacademic experts, these books are authoritative, clearly written, up-to-date, and objective. They provide a good starting point for research by high school and college students, scholars, and general readers as well as by legislators, businesspeople, activists, and others.

Each book, carefully organized and easy to use, contains an overview of the subject, a detailed chronology, biographical sketches, facts and data and/or documents and other primary-source material, a directory of organizations and agencies, annotated lists of print and nonprint resources, and an index.

Readers of books in the Contemporary World Issues series will find the information they need to have a better understanding of the social, political, environmental, and economic issues facing the world today.

GAY AND LESBIAN RIGHTS

A Reference Handbook

Second Edition

David E. Newton

CONTEMPORARY WORLD ISSUES

A B C 🟢 C L I O

Santa Barbara, California
Denver, Colorado
Oxford, England

Library of Congress Cataloging-in-Publication Data

Newton, David E.
  Gay and lesbian rights: a reference handbook / David E. Newton. — 2nd ed.
      p. cm. — (Contemporary world issues)
  Includes bibliographical references and index.
  ISBN 978-1-59884-306-4 (hard copy: alk. paper) — ISBN 978-1-59884-307-1 (ebook)
    1. Gay rights—United States—Handbooks, manuals, etc. 2. Gay liberation movement—United States—Handbooks, manuals, etc. I. Title.
  HQ76.3.U5N48 2009
    323.3'2640973—dc22   2009024255

ISBN: 978-1-59884-306-4
EISBN: 978-1-59884-307-1

13 12 11 10 9   1 2 3 4 5

This book is also available on the World Wide Web as an eBook. Visit www.abc-clio.com for details.

Contemporary World Issues
An Imprint of ABC-CLIO, LLC

ABC-CLIO, LLC
130 Cremona Drive, P.O. Box 1911
Santa Barbara, California 93116-1911

This book is printed on acid-free paper ∞

Manufactured in the United States of America

For Dan,
again and always

Contents

List of Tables

Preface

Over its more than 230-year history, the United States has seen one group of citizens after another fighting for basic civil liberties, rights that they have felt were due them under the Constitution. In the 1920s, for example, women marched for, and eventually won, the right to vote. Four decades later, blacks and whites marched together for laws prohibiting discrimination based on race. At the same time, legal challenges were made against miscegenation laws that banned marriage between people of different races. In the 1980s, the Americans with Disabilities Act extended antidiscrimination laws to people with a variety of disabilities.

For more than half a century, another group of citizens has been working to gain civil rights legislation for gay men and lesbians. That effort was modest and timid until the 1980s, when gays began to be more aggressive and active in arguing for laws that would grant them the civil rights to which they thought they were entitled. Today, a multifaceted campaign is focused on eliminating discrimination in housing, employment, and public accommodation, on obtaining for same-sex couples many of the social, political, and economic benefits available to married heterosexual couples, and otherwise erasing the limitations on a person's civil rights that result from his or her sexual orientation. Over the last decade, the gay and lesbian rights movement has also expanded to include bisexuals and transgendered persons.

Given the general disapproval that many Americans have for homosexual behavior, this effort has had some remarkable successes. Today, 20 states, the District of Columbia, and more than 140 cities and counties have laws prohibiting discrimination (usually in housing, employment, and public accommodation) on the basis of sexual orientation and, in many cases, gender identity. Ten states have also adopted some form of recognition of same-sex relationships, such as marriage (Massachusetts, Iowa, Connecticut, Vermont, Maine, and New Hampshire), domestic partnership, or civil union.

But these gains have also prompted a strong response from other Americans who argue that lesbians and gay men do not qualify for civil rights legislation because of their supposedly immoral lifestyle. Groups such as the Institute for Marriage and Public Policy, the Marriage Law Project, and the Traditional Values Coalition have tried to remain one step ahead of the gay rights movement, proposing legislation that would prohibit both same-sex marriage and similar arrangements and laws banning discrimination based on sexual orientation.

These groups have been very successful in some areas. For example, the U.S. Congress passed and President Bill Clinton signed into law the Defense of Marriage Act of 1996, prohibiting the federal government from recognizing same-sex marriages approved by any individual state, and permitting the states to take similar actions. A bill to amend the U.S. Constitution to prohibit same-sex marriage, the Federal Marriage Amendment, also has strong support in the U.S. Congress. It passed the House of Representatives in 2006 by a vote of 236 to 187, enough to pass, but not enough for a proposed constitutional amendment. Antigay legislation at the state and local levels has also been very successful throughout the South, in parts of the Midwest, and in some areas of the West.

The gay civil rights movement extends throughout the world, with many nations struggling with the question as to how, if at all, they will grant gays and lesbians the same rights as those enjoyed by heterosexuals. As of late 2008, most nations in Europe, and a few nations in Asia, Africa, and South America have abolished their sodomy laws; adopted some form of same-sex marriage, civil union, domestic partnerships, or registered partnership laws; removed bans on adoption of children by same-sex couples; adopted antidiscrimination legislation; equalized the age of consent for homosexuals; and passed hate crime laws that protect lesbians and gay men. This progress has not occurred universally, with most Muslim states and African nations acting in the reverse direction, introducing stronger prohibitions against homosexual acts of all kinds for all individuals.

The first chapter of this book provides a broad general introduction to the history of the gay rights movement in the United States. It summarizes the successes and failures of the movement from the mid-20th century to the present day. Chapter 2 offers a review of some of the main issues involved in the gay civil rights movement, issues such as hate crime legislation; same-sex marriage; adoption of children by same-sex couples; and discrimination in housing, employment, and public accommodation. Chapter 3 discusses the development of the gay rights movement on an international scale. That movement had a much earlier beginning in parts of Europe then it did in the United States, and it has progressed in very different ways at very different rates than it has here. Chapter 4 gives a chronology of important events in the lesbian, gay, bisexual, and transgendered (LGBT) movement both in the United States and around the world. The chronology also includes some items that illustrate the varying attitudes about homosexual behavior held by different societies around the world. Chapter 5 provides brief biographical sketches of some of the most important figures on both sides of the gay and lesbian rights debate.

Chapter 6 consists of a number of documents dealing with the status of the gay and lesbian rights movement in the United States today. Chapter 7 is a compilation of organizations working for and against the gay and lesbian rights movement, primarily, but not exclusively, in the United States. Chapter 8 provides a list of print and electronic resources dealing with gay and lesbian rights issues. The book concludes with a glossary that introduces and explains a number of basic terms used in discussing the gay and lesbian civil rights movement.

1

Background and History

Introduction

R obin could hardly believe her eyes. The attorney general
had written to rescind the state's offer of a job with its
Department of Law. Robin had been certain that the job
was hers. She had graduated sixth in her class at one of the best
law schools in the South, been elected to Phi Beta Kappa, had
served as editor of the school's law review, and had clerked at
the state Department of Law. Upon completion of her tenure as
law clerk, the attorney general had offered Robin a permanent
position as a department attorney. The unexpected problem that
had arisen was that the attorney general had learned that Robin
is a lesbian and was planning to be married to her partner. The
attorney general decided that Robin's proposed marital status
disqualified her from working for the state, and he withdrew
his offer of a position in the Department of Law. (The details of
this case are available in *Shahar v. Bowers* [United States Court
of Appeals, Eleventh Circuit, No. 93-9345], online at: http://
caselaw.lp.findlaw.com/cgi-bin/getcase.pl?court=11th&navby=
case&no=939345opa.)

Robin eventually decided to sue the state attorney general
for discriminating against her on the basis of her sexual orientation. She lost that case in district court and again in the U.S.
Eleventh Circuit Court of Appeals. Her final appeal to the U.S.
Supreme Court was rejected in 1998.

Gay and Lesbian Rights: The Issues

For most Americans, the principle that all people are equal under the law is probably one of the cornerstones of this society. Yet, for most of its history, the United States has not always followed that principle in practice. For example, women were long consigned to a second class status, not receiving the right to vote in federal elections until 1920. And, blacks were not guaranteed equal rights under the law until passage of the Civil Rights Act of 1964. The key provisions of that act are found in sections 1981 and 2000, which say, respectively:

> All persons within the jurisdiction of the United States shall have the same right in every State and Territory to make and enforce contracts, to sue, be parties, give evidence, and to the full and equal benefit of all laws and proceedings for the security of persons and property as is enjoyed by white citizens, and shall be subject to like punishment, pains, penalties, taxes, licenses, and exactions of every kind, and to no other (U.S.C. Title 42, Chapter 21, Section 1981).
>
> No person in the United States shall, on the ground of race, color, or national origin, be excluded from participation in, be denied the benefits of, or be subjected to discrimination under any program or activity receiving Federal financial assistance (U.S.C. Title 42, Chapter 21, Section 2000d).

Even this declaration of "equal rights for all Americans" proved not truly to include all Americans. For example, the Americans with Disabilities Act of 1990 extended equal rights to all citizens with any "physical or mental impairment that substantially limits a major life activity."

At the end of the first decade of the 21st century, one major group of Americans is not yet included in the general principle of "equality under the law": gay men and lesbians. As Robin's case at the beginning of this chapter illustrates, individuals, agencies, and organizations may, in most states, still legally discriminate against gay men and lesbians in housing, employment, access to public accommodations, and other areas on the basis of their sexual orientation. For example, a landlord may refuse to rent to same-sex couples in Kansas (to mention just one state) simply because he or she knows or suspects that they are gay men or lesbians.

As of 2009, a number of states had banned this form of discrimination, either on the basis of sexual orientation (seven states) or on the basis of sexual orientation and gender identify or gender expression (13 states and the District of Columbia; The Task Force, 2008). The term *gender expression* refers to the condition in which a person feels that he or she actually belongs to a gender opposite that evidenced by physical characteristics. A man may believe that he is really a woman, or, conversely, a woman may feel that she is really a man. (People who act on these feelings and have gender reassignment surgery are known as transsexuals.) In addition, nondiscrimination provisions have been adopted by nearly 150 cities and towns. In most cases, these laws prohibit discrimination in housing, employment, and access to public accommodations, although details of the legislation may differ somewhat from state to state and city to city.

Discrimination in housing, employment, and access to public accommodations are sometimes viewed as the basic three gay and lesbian rights issues because they are so relevant to the daily lives of every gay man and lesbian. But other issues are also important. They include:

- Sodomy laws: Sodomy laws proscribe certain types of sexual behavior, such as anal and oral intercourse. In actual practice, these laws are used almost exclusively against same-sex behaviors. In 2003, the U.S. Supreme Court ruled that sodomy laws are unconstitutional, and such laws are now unenforceable in the United States. At the time of the Supreme Court's ruling, 13 states still had sodomy laws on their books.
- Hate crime laws: Hate crimes are defined as crimes that are motivated, at least in part, because of the victim's gender, race, national origin, sexual orientation, or some other characteristic. Federal law currently permits prosecution of a person who commits a crime that can be attributed to the victim's race, color, religion, or national origin. Efforts are under way to add gender, sexual orientation, gender identity, and disability to federal law. As of 2009, 45 states and the District of Columbia have some type of hate crime law on their books, the exceptions being Arkansas, Georgia, Indiana, South Carolina, and Wyoming. Of these laws, 32 also cover sexual

orientation and 11 include gender identity. One goal of the gay and lesbian rights movement is to obtain passage of federal legislation adding sexual orientation and gender identity to existing hate crimes laws. A bill with that provision passed the U.S. House of Representatives in May 2007, but did not pass in the Senate, partly because of President George W. Bush's promise to veto the bill.

- Military service: In theory, prohibitions against gay men and lesbians serving in the U.S. military have existed since the Revolutionary War. The first recorded case of a serviceman being discharged from the military occurred in 1778, when Lieutenant Gotthold Frederick Enslin was dismissed for an act of sodomy (Arnesen 1998). That penalty was assessed, however, because of a specific act committed by Lieutenant Enslin, and not because of his status as a gay man. In fact, the United States had no formal policy about gay men and lesbians serving in the military until 1942, when the armed forces instituted a policy of screening men and women at the time of their enlistment. That policy proved to be somewhat flawed as many non-gay, non-lesbian individuals claimed that they were homosexual in order to avoid serving in the military, and many gay men and lesbians were able to avoid the screening process, eventually serving (and often with considerable distinction) in the military services. Since the end of World War II, a debate has raged as to whether gay men and lesbians should be allowed to serve in the military and, if so, under what circumstances. In 1993, President Bill Clinton recommended and the U.S. Congress adopted the present policy covering this subject, a policy commonly known as "don't ask, don't tell." According to this policy, gay men and lesbians are allowed to serve in the U.S. military provided that they do not reveal their sexual orientation or discuss issues that would permit an outsider to know that they are gay or lesbian. This policy has not satisfied either the proponents or opponents of having gay men and lesbians serve in the U.S. military, and it continues to be an issue of significant interest to those on both sides of the question.
- Adoption: The issue of adoption of children by same-sex couples is relatively new in the United States (and

other parts of the world). Until recently, same-sex relationships generally met with disapproval, and the notion that a same-sex couple might seek to adopt a child was unlikely. Over the past two decades, that situation has changed; same-sex couples have become more open about their relationships, and adoption of children has become more common. Most states and the federal government have no legal framework for dealing with same-sex adoptions, and cases in which legal action is required are generally decided on a case-by-case approach by local and state courts. As of 2009, five states have some type of legal framework designed to prevent same-sex adoptions. The situations in Michigan and Nebraska rely on rulings made by the state attorneys general, prohibiting the adoption of children under one or more circumstances by two people of the same gender. Florida, Mississippi, and Utah have all passed specific laws that prohibit same-sex couples from adopting children. As same-sex relationships become more common and, in many cases, are accorded some type of legal recognition, the issue of adoption by same-sex couples is likely to become more common, and more formal legal guidelines are likely to be adopted.

- Marriage: Perhaps the single most controversial issue confronting not only gay men and lesbians, but society as a whole, is that of same-sex marriage, or some legal variation of the institution. In the early stages of the gay and lesbian rights movement, there were probably few individuals who would have predicted that marriage would eventually become a major goal of the movement. Yet today, efforts are proceeding in a number of states to obtain for gay men and lesbians the same rights associated with legal marriage that are currently available to non-gay, non-lesbian couples.

These issues constitute the core of the discussion over gay and lesbian rights in the United States today. They are the focus of Chapter 2, which deals with the problems and controversies over gay and lesbian rights, and current resolutions that have been reached over at least some of these questions. Before reviewing the current state of affairs, however, it is useful to look back into history and follow the path by which these issues have come to the forefront among gay men and lesbians and among those who support and oppose the direction of the modern movement.

The Invisible Minority

The gay and lesbian rights movement in the United States is very much a product of economic, social, and political changes that occurred in the early 20th century. Prior to 1900, the United States was still primarily a rural and agricultural nation, with just over 60 percent of its citizens living in rural areas, and just under 40 percent living in urban areas. Only 30 years later, that pattern had been reversed, with 56 percent of the population located in urban areas and 44 percent located in rural areas (U.S. Census Bureau 1995). This change had profound significance for men and women whose erotic attraction was for members of the same sex. In an agrarian society, such individuals have little opportunity to find and interact with other men and women of a similar sexual orientation, and they have essentially no opportunity to ban together to form groups that can lobby on issues of common interest. The concept of a gay and lesbian rights movement, then, has essentially no meaning at all prior to the 1930s.

At that point, however, men and women of all backgrounds had begun to move to cities, where the forces to form and maintain families were less pronounced. People began to develop social groups outside the family, centered on the working place, cultural institutions, bars and restaurants, sporting clubs, or other settings in which like-minded individuals could band together. In such locations, the possibility of same-sex relationships became much greater, and men and women could come together to share their lives with others of a similar sexual orientation (two of the best analyses of this change in society are, for the United States, D'Emilio 1983 and, for Great Britain, Weeks 1979).

This analysis does not suggest that gay men and lesbians, upon moving to the city, discovered a free and open society in which they experienced general acceptance for their "lifestyle." Indeed, homosexual behavior was almost universally renounced as sinful, criminal, "sick," or some combination of all three. The common meeting place that gay men and lesbians often found in the early 20th century was probably most often a dirty bar at the end of a dark alley in which watered drinks were served at outrageous prices with the constant threat of raids by local police who had not been paid off by the bar owner. Anyone found in such a location could count on having his or her name listed in the paper, with the consequent loss of their job and, in some cases, estrangement from parents, family, and friends. One common description of this life was the observation at the time that "The only happy homosexual is a dead homosexual." (Although the origin of this phrase is unknown, it is perhaps best known from Matt Crowley's 1968 play "Boys in the Band.") The "freedom" provided to gay men and lesbians by the urban experience came at a very high price, indeed.

Under these conditions, it is somewhat difficult to imagine a group of gay men and/or lesbians coming together to organize for equal rights. Yet, in late 1924, the first organization of gay men was formed in the United States by Henry Gerber of Chicago, Illinois. Gerber had served in Germany in World War I and had been exposed to what at the time was a burgeoning gay and lesbian movement in that country. When he returned to the United States, he could not understand why his homeland could not welcome a similar organization. Thus, he wrote a Declaration of Purpose for a new organization that he named the Society for Human Rights, and applied to the state of Illinois for a charter for the organization. Somewhat surprisingly, the state approved the charter on Christmas Eve 1924, and the organization came into existence. Gerber later wrote that he had four major objectives for the society:

- To enlist as many gay men as possible in the organization;
- To arrange a series of lectures about the attitude of society about same-sex relationships, especially stressing the need to avoid seducing adolescents;
- To publish a newsletter, "Friendship and Freedom," that would serve as a forum of discussion among gay men; and
- To educate legal authorities and legislators about the nature of same-sex relationships and about "the futility and folly of long prison terms for those committing homosexual acts, etc." (Gerber 1926).

Gerber's great plans came to nothing. He was able to find only three other men to join his new organization, one a minister who preached to blacks; a second, a laundry worker; and a third, a railroad worker whose job was already in jeopardy because he was suspected of being gay. The organization itself lasted only a few months because the wife of one of the members reported its existence to the police. After a series of trials, all four members of the organization were ruined; Gerber lost his home (the government simply took possession of it), his job, and all of his friends. Whatever other promise it might offer to gay men and lesbians, the newly urbanized United States was not yet ready for a formal organization promoting gay and lesbian rights.

Winds of Change

In fact, it was to be nearly 30 years before a successful gay rights organization was to appear in the United States. That organization, the Mattachine Foundation (later renamed the Mattachine Society), was founded by one of the great pioneers of the gay and lesbian rights movement, Harry Hay, along with a handful of friends that included Rudi Gernreich, Bob Hull, William Dale Jennings, and Chuck Rowland. (There is some possibility that one or more secret or semi-secret organizations of gay men existed before the founding of the Mattachine Society. One such group, called the Sons of Hamity, may have existed as early as the 1880s, surviving only briefly before being reorganized in the 1930s. At least one gay historian regards the group as nothing other than one gay man's fantasy. Another early group for which better documentation is available was Knights of the Clock, an organization formed in 1951 by Dorr Legg and his partner, Merton Bird, as a support group for interracial couples. Quite remarkably, the organization attempted to deal with two strong prejudices at the same time: racism and homophobia. Although the group's first meetings were held in 1951, it was not incorporated by the state of California until 1954.) The group was named after a medieval French society of unmarried men who performed dances and plays during the Feast of Fools. The men in the French group reportedly never appeared unmasked in public.

One of the first acts of the new organization was the adoption of a statement of "Missions and Purposes." It included the following four objectives:

- TO UNIFY those homosexuals isolated from their own kind in order to provide a basis on which "all of our people can ... derive a feeling of 'belonging'";

- TO EDUCATE homosexuals and heterosexuals in order
  to develop an "ethical homosexual culture paralleling
  the cultures of the Negro, Mexican and Jewish
  peoples";
- TO LEAD the "more ... socially conscious homosexuals
  [in order to] provide leadership to the whole mass of
  social deviates"; and
- TO DEVELOP a program of "political action" against
  "discriminatory and oppressive legislation" and to
  assist "our people who are victimized daily as a result
  of our oppression," and who constitute "one of the
  largest minorities in America today." (Cutler 1956, 412;
  Cutler was a pseudonym used by one of the early
  pioneers of the gay rights movement, W. Dorr Legg.)

The early structure of the Mattachine Society was determined to a large extent by the fact that most of the group's
founders were members of the Communist Party who believed
that their new organization should follow organizing principles
with which they had become familiar as a result of earlier political experiences. They organized a somewhat elaborate, five-
tiered pyramid of cells (discussion groups) in which gay men
(there were virtually no women members) could analyze their
position in society and try to understand the basis for the
oppression they all experienced. This system made it possible
for individuals to interact with a small group of like-minded
men without making themselves known to large numbers of
other members. Given the status of homosexuality in society at
the time, secrecy was a matter of primary concern, and many
members used one or more pseudonyms at meetings.

At first, this approach was very successful, as more and
more gay men heard about and began to join the Mattachines.
Before long, however, the powerful organizing skills brought to
the Mattachine Society by its Communist founders turned out
to be a serious detriment. The era in which Hay and his colleagues founded the Mattachine Society was also a period in
which conservative reactionary beliefs had begun to hold sway
in the United States. Fears of a Russian-based Communist
threat, not only in the United States, but also throughout the
world, were leading to a rising panic about the stability of
American democracy. As one indication of that fear, President
Dwight D. Eisenhower had signed an executive order in 1953

citing a number of factors, "sexual perversion" among them, as cause for dismissal or preclusion from employment from government service (Executive Order 10450, 1953). Even earlier, in February 1950, Senator Joseph McCarthy (R-Wis.) had initiated his campaign against the presence of Communists in the federal government, a campaign that was eventually to conflate Communism with homosexuality (Johansson and Percy 1994, 81–85).

The linking of homosexuality with Communism struck terror into the hearts of gay men who had begun to associate themselves with the Mattachine Society. Such an association could only intensify the hatred and oppression that they already experienced simply by having their sexual orientation known. Members of the society began to disassociate themselves from Hay and the other founders with a Communist background. In response to these concerns, Hay and Hull withdrew from the Mattachines, and the organization itself reassessed its goals and objectives. Rather than trying to mobilize gay men to bring about social change, the association chose to work for the assimilation of gay men and lesbians into the general society. Instead of striking out to demand equal rights for everyone, regardless of sexual orientation, the Mattachines determined to dress in suits and ties (and, later, to have women dress in conservative dresses) to show that they were "just like all other Americans," worthy of the respect and consideration of heterosexuals. This theme was to dominate much (if not all) of the gay and lesbian organizations that developed over the next decade.

On October 15, 1952, one of the Mattachine discussion groups considered the possibility of producing a newsletter and, in conjunction with that effort, creating a new organization for homosexuals independent of the Mattachine Society. Both the newsletter and the new organization were to be called ONE. The articles of incorporation for the new organization, ONE, Inc., were signed on November 15, 1952, while the first issue of the newsletter, *ONE: The Homosexual Magazine*, appeared in January 1953. One of the unique features of One, Inc., in comparison with the parent Mattachine Society, was the new organization's openness to women. For the first time among major homosexual organizations, women were as welcome to join the new group as were men. In fact, a number of women—including Joan Corbin, Irma Wolf, Stella Rush, Helen Sandoz, and Betty Perdue (all of whom used pseudonyms)—were instrumental in organizing the new group and contributing to its early successes.

More than a year after the appearance of its first issue, *ONE* magazine was to become embroiled in one of the first legal challenges involving a gay or lesbian organization. That challenge arose because, in October 1954, the U.S. Post Office declared the magazine to be "obscene," and refused to distribute the publication. One, Inc., chose to challenge that ruling and brought suit in Los Angeles district court against the Los Angeles postmaster, Otto K. Olesen. The trial court found in favor of the defendant, as did the U.S. Court of Appeals for the Ninth District (*One v. Olesen*, 241 F.2d 772 1957). One, Inc., then appealed to the U.S. Supreme Court which, on January 13, 1958, made a ruling that surprised all observers in the magazine's favor. In a brief *per curiam* (for the court as a whole) statement, the court reversed the appellate court's decision and stated simply that "The petition for writ of certiorari is granted and the judgment of the United States Court of Appeals for the Ninth Circuit is reversed" (*One, Incorporated, v. Olesen* 1958). This decision is of special interest since it is the first instance in which the U.S. Supreme Court ruled on a gay and lesbian rights issue in history.

By 1955, the Mattachine Society had reached the nadir of its short history. At that point, its turn toward a more conservative and more accommodationist philosophy had the effect of, once again, attracting gay men (and a few lesbians) to its cause. Membership in the Los Angeles chapter began to grow, and new chapters were established in San Francisco, New York, and Chicago. In addition, contacts with gay men in other cities throughout the nation had been initiated. In January 1955, two members of the San Francisco chapter began publication of the *Mattachine Review*, a journal that included scholarly articles, reviews, fiction, poetry, reports of chapter activities, reports from the national convention, and other items of interest to gay men and lesbians. The journal ceased publication in 1966. Mattachine itself, as a national organization, survived only until 1961, when it was dissolved as a corporate entity. Local chapters in New York, Los Angeles, and San Francisco lasted for a few more years, and organizations with the same or similar names (such as Mattachine Midwest, in Chicago) appeared from time to time thereafter. But, for the most part, the brief revolutionary days envisioned by Harry Hay and his colleagues had, by the early 1960s, largely died out. (Probably the most complete history of the Mattachine Society readily available to readers is that found in D'Emilio, Chapters 4 and 5.)

One, Inc. has had a longer history than has the Mattachine Society. It eventually focused its attention on publishing and educational programs. In addition to *ONE*, the organization began publication of a scholarly journal, the *ONE Institute Quarterly*, which has evolved into today's *Journal of Homosexuality*. In 1965, the organization divided into two parts as the result of a somewhat acrimonious dispute among the group's members. One of the two spinoff organizations continued as One, Inc. It merged with the Institute for the Study of Human Resources, an organization that continues to exist. The other spinoff organization eventually became the Homosexual Information Center, which also survives today.

In addition to the Mattachine Society and One, Inc., the third organization that formed the heart of the early gay and lesbian rights movement was the Daughters of Bilitis (DOB), the female counterpart of the Mattachine Society and One, Inc. DOB was formed in October 1955 by Phyllis Lyon and Del Martin who, at the time, had been partners for three years. Lyon and Martin were interested primarily in finding a mechanism by which lesbians could socialize with one another. The group they formed for this purpose was named after a fictional lesbian character created by the French poet Pierre Louÿs in his 1894 work *The Songs of Bilitis*. The name was chosen at least partly because it was obscure enough to have little meaning to non-gays and non-lesbians (and, as it turned out, to Lyon and Martin, at first), providing the security that lesbians (as well as gay men) so desperately needed at the time.

DOB had not been in existence very long before its founders and some of its members realized that lesbians faced greater challenges than finding a place to socialize. They were also confronted with the same problems of oppression as those faced by gay men, compounded by the double stigma of being female in a male-dominated society. In its 1958 statement of purpose, DOB defined its mission as:

- Education of the variant . . . to enable her to understand herself and make her adjustment to society . . . this to be accomplished by establishing . . . a library . . . on the sex deviant theme; by sponsoring public discussions . . . to be conducted by leading members of the legal psychiatric, religious, and other professions; by advocating a mode of behavior and dress acceptable to society.

- Education of the public ... leading to an eventual break-down of erroneous taboos and prejudices.
- Participation in research projects by duly authorized and responsible psychologists, sociologists, and other such experts directed towards further knowledge of the homosexual.
- Investigation of the penal code as it pertains to the homosexual, proposal of changes, ... and promotion of these changes through the due process of law in the state legislatures. ("Purposes of the Daughters of Bilitis" 1956)

As the previous statement suggests, DOB at first chose the road to accommodation and assimilation, attempting to show heterosexuals that lesbians are really no different from non-gay women, except for their erotic interests. The story is told that at the organization's 1960 convention, Del Martin escorted San Francisco police officers into the meeting hall to prove that participants were all "properly" dressed, with "dresses, stockings, and heals" (Gallo 2006, 62–63). But, as with the Mattachine Society and One, Inc., there were other viewpoints about the group's proper mission. In response to increasingly aggressive raids on gay bars across the nation, for example, some members called for a more radical agenda for the Daughters, working to achieve freedom from harassment and civil equality. This clash of views was to continue at some level or another for the remaining period of the organization's existence.

Almost certainly, the most important single achievement of the Daughters of Bilitis was its magazine, *The Ladder*, first published in October 1956. It appeared quarterly for most of its 14-year history, and monthly in 1971 and 1972. Its circulation was never very large—seldom more than a few hundred—but its impact among lesbians in the United States was enormous. It was the first publication through which large numbers of lesbians could exchange ideas of common interest. As with its male counterpart, *ONE*, *The Ladder* provided a grab bag of articles for its readers, ranging from fiction and poetry, to book reviews, to historical essays, to biographical sketches, to news of interest to the lesbian community, to advice on legal issues.

By the late 1960s, DOB and *The Ladder* had become victims of dramatic changes in U.S. society that affected gay men and lesbians at least as much as it did their heterosexual counterparts. A debate raged within the organization and on the pages of the journal about the role of lesbians in the feminist movement (which often rejected any connection with lesbians), as well as the ongoing dispute over accommodation versus revolution. By 1972, exhausted by these debates and devoid of financial resources, the magazine ceased publication; DOB had gone out of existence two years earlier. As with the Mattachine Society and One, Inc., DOB's relatively short lifetime does not begin to express its significance in the history of the gay and lesbian rights movement. All three organizations established a new framework by which gay men and lesbians could view themselves, express their concerns, and begin to engage the non-gay community in understanding and dealing with its problems and challenges.

The Storm Breaks

The 1960s were one of the great decades of turmoil in modern U.S. history. The period was marked by the powerful antiwar movement in opposition to the Vietnam conflict, the rise of modern feminism, the growth of the civil rights movement, the appearance of a new Chicano movement, and the first hints of a gay and lesbian rights movement. At the beginning of the decade, there was relatively little indication that gay men and lesbians were interested in disrupting society; they had, for the most part, concluded that the best course of action was to try to fit into the general culture, obtain popular acceptance for their way of life, and hope for relief from the oppression and disapproval that largely defined their lives.

That view was not, however, universal among gay men and lesbians. A relatively small number of men and women believed that strong action against social standards and institutions was the only way for gay men and lesbians to achieve true freedom and equality as American citizens. One of the best known of these individuals was Franklin Kameny, who had been fired in 1957 from his post as an astronomer in the Army Map Service in Washington, D.C., because of his homosexuality. Kameny has spent the rest of his life in a battle against policies and agencies that deny equal rights to all Americans, regardless of their sexual orientation.

In early 1962, a group of gay men and lesbians representing four organizations—the Daughters of Bilitis, the Janus Society of Philadelphia, the New York Mattachine Society, and the Washington Mattachine Society—met in Philadelphia to consider the possibility of forming an umbrella group that would take a more militant approach to solving social and political problems faced by gay men and lesbians. The result of that meeting was the formation of the East Coast Homophile Organizations (ECHO), which held its first national convention in Philadelphia in January 1963. The theme of that conference was "Homosexuality—Time for Reappraisal." The group met twice more, in Washington in 1964 ("Homosexuality—Civil Liberties and Social Rights"), and in New York City in 1965 ("The Homosexual Citizen in the Great Society"). Perhaps equal in importance to the conference was the informal network of militant gay men and lesbians that formed after the Philadelphia meeting. These men and women carried their campaign back to their parent organizations, challenging them to abandon their accomodationist philosophies and to become more aggressive in battling for their rights. Needless to say, this campaign proved destructive to many, if not all, of the gay and lesbian groups then in existence, contributing to at least some extent to the demise of some of them.

The success of ECHO suggested the possibility of an even more ambitious step—a national coalition of militant gay and lesbian leaders. In August 1966, that possibility came to fruition with a meeting in Kansas City of representatives from 15 gay and lesbian groups called the National Planning Conference of Homophile Organizations (NPCHO). In addition to representatives from the five ECHO organizations, there were attendees from the Midwest, South, and West, resulting in the first truly national organization of gay men and lesbians to form in the United States. Representatives called for a national conference also to be held in Kansas City later in the year, at which time the organization's name was changed to the North American Conference of Homophile Organizations (NACHO).

NACHO remained a small, but influential, element in the gay and lesbian movement over the next four years. It held three more national conferences after the Kansas City meeting, conducted and reported on research on the legal status of gay men and lesbians and on discrimination in housing and employment, organized demonstrations in a variety of cities over injustices based on sexual orientation, and established a legal defense fund to be used in court cases involving gay men and lesbians. Probably the most important long-term effect of the organization's existence was the opportunity for increasingly radicalized gay men and lesbians to push for a militant approach to the common problems they faced. At the 1970 convention, for example, members of the NACHO Youth Committee decided to abandon a "respectable" approach to dealing with gay and lesbian issues and agreed to a "radical manifesto" that they entitled "The Homophile Movement Must Be Radicalized!" Among the 12 points in the manifesto were the following:

- We see the persecution of homosexuality as part of a general attempt to oppress all minorities and keep them powerless. Our fate is linked with these minorities; if the detention camps are filled tomorrow with blacks, hippies and other radicals, we will not escape that fate, all our attempts to dissociate our-selves from them notwithstanding. A common struggle, however, will bring common triumph.
- Our enemies, an implacable, repressive governmental system; much of organized religion, business and medicine, will not be moved by appeasement or appeals to reason and justice, but only by power and force.
- We regard established heterosexual standards of morality as immoral and refuse to condone them by demanding an equality which is merely the common yoke of sexual repression.
- We declare that homosexuals, as individuals and members of the greater community, must develop homosexual ethics and esthetics independent of, and without reference to, the mores imposed upon heterosexuality.
- We call upon the churches to sanction homosexual liaisons when called upon to do so by the parties concerned. (Teal 1971, 55)

The manifesto was not adopted by the conference as a whole—it was too radical for even the members of NACHO—but its appearance presaged a new outlook on the gay and lesbian movement that had already begun to appear.

The Stonewall Riots and Beyond

On June 27, 1969, a group of plainclothes New York City police officers raided the Stonewall Inn, a popular gay bar in the city's

Greenwich Village neighborhood. Such raids were not uncommon in New York, nor in almost any other large city in the United States at the time. During such a raid, law enforcement officers routinely removed some patrons of the bar to a local police station, where they often spent the night. Names, addresses, and occupations of the bar customers were routinely taken and often released to the local newspapers. Occasionally, the police physically assaulted patrons. Most gay men and lesbians accepted this practice as just one of the hazards of having a somewhat open social life. For reasons that will probably never be completely clear, the night of June 27, 1969, was an aberration in this pattern. As police began to remove patrons from the bar for transfer to a police paddy wagon, other customers began to fight back. They used whatever weapons they could find, including an uprooted parking meter, to resist police activities, to the point that some police officers were eventually trapped inside the bar. Customers then set fire to the bar. No lives were lost, nor were there any serious injuries as a result of this action. (Two excellent resources on the Stonewall riot and subsequent actions are Carter 2004 and Duberman 1993.)

As indicated in earlier parts of this chapter, the Stonewall riot did not mark the beginning of a gay and lesbian rights movement. It did, however, mark a striking transformation in the nature of that movement. The event was propitious, of course, because it took place in the midst of general upheaval and revolution throughout the United States, driven partly by an ongoing civil rights movement for people of color, a rapid upsurge of the feminist movement, and violent protest against the ongoing war in Vietnam. There was hardly a group of any kind that considered itself oppressed that had not begun to do battle with traditional American society to obtain what it regarded as their due rights under the U.S. Constitution. For gay men and lesbians, the defining event in that effort was the Stonewall riot of 1969.

Rioting continued for four more nights, with gay men and lesbians roaming the streets of New York, making themselves more visible than ever before, and laying out a challenge to the heterosexual society. Within weeks, 37 men and women had gathered together to form the Gay Liberation Front (GLF), the first organization of gay men and lesbians in the United States to actually use the word *gay* in its name. GLF was a classic revolutionary organization that saw its goal not only as ending the oppression of gay men and lesbians, but also on a broader scale, fighting social, economic, and political injustices wherever they might occur. As is the case with most "front" groups, GLF saw a responsibility to join arms with other liberation groups, such as those fighting against racism and sexism. Unfortunately, like most groups of the type, progress was hindered by internal squabbles, often over points that were sometimes obscure and unimportant in the broader scheme of things.

Within months of the formation of GLF, a number of its members, frustrated at infighting and lack of progress on gay rights issues, abandoned the group to form a new organization, more moderate in its political views and more eager to move forward on an agenda of improving the social and political status of gay men and lesbians. That group was the Gay Activists Alliance (GAA). GAA members made clear the focus of their new organization in the mission statement included within its constitution. The type of organization envisioned in the constitution was to be a "single issue," politically neutral organization, that would scrupulously avoid endorsing candidates for public office, or involvements in causes not directly related to gay rights. By doing so, it hoped to avoid internal, partisan disputes among its members, and to attract persons of all political persuasions. By focusing its energies on gay rights, it hoped to avoid what it regarded as the mistake of other organizations such as the Gay Liberation Front, which embraced a variety of New Left causes unrelated to the gay liberation movement. By the term *activist*, it wished to emphasize its commitment to the use of more aggressive tactics than those employed by the homophile movement before the Stonewall riots of 1969 (International Gay Information Center, Inc. 2008).

In its 12-year existence, GAA promoted a remarkable number of activities aimed at improving the social, economic, and political lives of gay men and lesbians. On the one hand, it sponsored a host of social activities—dances, films, musical events, theatrical performances, fashion shows, and consciousness-raising meetings—that had almost never been available to lesbians and gay men and that provided the social setting in which they could come together and interact on an informal level. GAA also carried out an almost endless series of political events, including rallies, sit-ins, public demonstrations, and "zaps" to push for an end to police harassment and entrapment of gay men and lesbians, elimination of discriminatory policies in housing and employment, and repeal of state and local laws that prohibited same-sex related crimes. (A "zap" was an unannounced public confrontation of a public official that called attention to an issue of importance to gay men and lesbians, such as interrupting a press conference by the mayor on construction of a new public housing project.)

GAA also worked for two important pieces of legislation, a sexual orientation nondiscrimination act in the New York state legislature that would have outlawed discrimination against same-sex couples (the first bill of its kind in the United States) and a civil rights ordinance in the New York City Council, which would have banned discrimination in housing and employment in the city. Both pieces of legislation failed (and were not to pass for at least 10 more years), although GAA's activities brought the issue of civil rights for lesbians and gay men to the forefront of public attention for the first time in history.

The rise of a new and more militant gay and lesbian rights movement taking place in New York City was mirrored in hundreds of other cities and towns, large and small, liberal and conservative, throughout the United States. Historian John D'Emilio has estimated that by the mid-1970s, there were more than a thousand gay and lesbian groups throughout the United States, as well as growing numbers of such organizations in almost every developed nation of the world (D'Emilio 1983, 2). Some groups were small, interested in focusing largely or entirely on social events and issues. Others formed primarily to promote an activity of interest to gay men and lesbians—a publication, sporting activity, or cultural project, for example. But most had at least some interest in political issues, such as the overthrow of sodomy laws, efforts to reduce police entrapment and harassment, and legislation to ban discrimination against gay men and lesbians in housing and employment.

As lesbian and gay organizations grew throughout the nation, the unity of purpose that appeared so strongly in some of the early groups, such as the Gay Activists Alliance, began to fray. Some of the oldest and largest groups were among the first to feel these ruptures. At GAA, for example, lesbians began to feel that they were being treated as second-class citizens at the organization by gay men, just as non-lesbian women were so treated in the general society by non-gay men. Increasingly, open disputes broke out at GAA and other gay and lesbian events between men and women, leading in 1973 to the withdrawal from the alliance of a number of strongly feminist women, who formed their own organization, Lesbian Feminist Liberation (LFL; Stonewall Library and Archives 2008). Members of the new group and their allies chose not to use the term *gay* to define themselves, but adopted women-centered terms, such as lesbian, dyke, and woman-loving-woman. The trend that led to the formation of LFL in New York City soon spread across the nation with the formation of women-only groups to which men, either gay or non-gay, were generally not admitted. (As an illustration of this philosophy and its practice in one region of the country, see Sandilands 2002, 131–163.)

New activist gay and lesbian organizations also encountered opposition internally from their more conservative members. In 1973, for example, Bruce Voeller, a research biochemist and then president of GAA, sought to modify the philosophy and activities of the organization, weaning it loose from what he referred to as its "blue-jeans elitism" approach to street activism and leading it toward a more moderate course of action on national issues of critical importance to gay men and lesbians. He was unable to make his case to GAA members and, with a number of leading figures in the movement, established a new organization, the National Gay Task Force (NGTF; later renamed the National Gay and Lesbian Task Force [NGLTF] and widely known simply as The Task Force). Among those joining Voeller in the new organization were Franklin Kameny, once the firebrand of the early gay rights movement; Howard Brown, formerly health sciences administrator for the city of New York; Martin Duberman, then professor of history at the Lehman Graduate Center of the City University of New York; Barbara Gittings, long-time gay and lesbian activist and then chair of the gay caucus of the American Library Association; and gay activist Ron Gold.

The Task Force has had a major role in the battle over almost all of the social and political issues of interest to lesbians and gay men in the United States over the past 35 years. It convinced the American Psychiatric Association to remove homosexuality from its list of mental disorders in 1973; persuaded the U.S. Civil Service Commission to remove its ban on employing lesbians and gay men in federal positions; worked with members of the U.S. Congress to introduce the first federal antidiscrimination legislation in 1975; led a 1981 campaign to defeat an anti-gay/lesbian bill called the Family Protection Act; formed the Privacy Project in 1986 to work for revocation of state sodomy laws; and established the Military Freedom Project in 1988 to work against bans on gay men and lesbians in the military. Along with the Human Rights Campaign (founded in 1980), The Task Force has been one of the largest, best funded, most highly respected, and most effective national agencies working for the civil rights of lesbians and gay men.

Changing Minds, Changing Laws

One consequence of the explosion of gay and lesbian organizations in the late 1960s and early 1970s was a changing perception of public attitudes toward gay- and lesbian-related issues. Scientific data on public attitudes about homosexuality are not generally available prior to the late 1970s (probably representing to some extent the invisibility of gays and lesbians prior to that time). But the Gallup Organization has been including questions about homosexual behavior and related issues in some of its polls for more than 30 years. Changes in public attitudes reflected in these polls are instructive. For example, public opinion was evenly divided in Gallup's first poll on the question as to whether or not same-sex relationships should be legal, with 43 percent on each side of the question (and 14 percent with no opinion or no response). By 2007, opinion had shifted, with 59 percent of Americans polled agreeing that such relationships should be legal, and 37 percent disagreeing (this, and subsequent results, from Gallup Polls 2007). A similar trend is apparent on questions about equal rights for lesbians and gay men. A majority of subjects contacted in a 1977 poll (56 percent to 33 percent) agreed with the proposition that homosexuals should have equal rights in terms of job opportunities. By 2007, that majority had increased to 89 percent for equal rights and 8 percent opposed. Finally, with regard to one of the most important issues involving gay men and lesbians today, a 1996 survey found that 27 percent of respondents approved of same-sex marriages with full rights and responsibilities comparable to those for heterosexual marriages, and 68 percent opposed that concept. By 2007, nearly half of all respondents (46 percent) now approved of same-sex marriages, and 53 percent opposed.

Identifying the reasons for these trends is difficult. On the one hand, the vigorous activity of groups like the Gay Activists

Alliance, The Task Force, the Human Rights Campaign, and countless other national, regional, state, and local groups must have had some impact on public knowledge about and attitudes toward same-sex relationships and related issues. But visibility must also be an important factor in the change. Prior to the 1960s, "coming out" (revealing one's sexual orientation to others) was an act that required enormous courage. It is likely that very few Americans knew very many gay men and lesbians personally. After 1970, that situation changed dramatically as it turned out that Uncle Bob, Cousin Helen, the postmaster, and the family's minister were gay or lesbian. Hatred for and oppression of the ambiguous "fag" or "dyke" was one thing; but maintaining those same attitudes toward a favorite relative, friend, or coworker was something quite different. These changes in public attitudes, then, may explain in part the sweeping changes in local and state laws and regulations regarding lesbians and gay men that began in the 1970s. The chronology provided in Chapter 4 summarizes some of the most important of these changes. The 1970s were also a period during which a number of states repealed their sodomy laws, laws that were used primarily to punish sexual acts between gay men. Prior to 1962, those laws were in effect throughout the United States and commonly included rather harsh penalties such as long terms of imprisonment and large fines. In 1962, the state of Illinois became the first state to repeal its sodomy laws. Five years later, Connecticut joined Illinois in abandoning its sodomy laws, and before the end of the 1970s, 19 more states had taken similar actions. The issue of sodomy laws was not finally resolved until 2003, when the U.S. Supreme Court ruled in *Lawrence et al. v. Texas* that that state's sodomy law was an unconstitutional invasion of privacy and, therefore, null and void (U.S. Supreme Court 2003). At the time of the court's ruling, all but 14 states had already repealed their sodomy laws. Since the ruling, all but three of those states—Kansas, Oklahoma, and Texas—have taken the *pro forma* act of abolishing their sodomy laws (Gay and Lesbian Archives of the Pacific Northwest 2007).

Reaction and Disaster

An observer of the landscape of the gay and lesbian rights movement in 1980 might well be forgiven for expressing optimism about the direction of the movement. States had begun to repeal long-standing sodomy laws; some states and communities were adopting antidiscrimination legislation for gay men and lesbians; federal agencies had begun to treat lesbians and gay men as they would other job applicants and employees; and some courts had begun to accept the principle that gay men and lesbians deserve equal treatment under the law. Such an optimistic view, however, would not have taken into account two forces that cast a dark shadow on future prospects for the movement: one a growing and powerful reaction to the goals and activities of the gay and lesbian campaign for equality, primarily by religious groups; and the other, the appearance of arguably the worst epidemic in modern history, the onset of the HIV/AIDS disease.

Reaction against the Gay and Lesbian Civil Rights Movement

By the end of 1976, 36 cities and towns across the United States had adopted some type of antidiscrimination law protecting lesbians and gay men in housing, employment, and/or access to public accommodations. While this trend encouraged gay men and lesbians, it aroused concern among many Americans who disapproved of homosexual behaviors and those who engaged in such acts. Slowly, a reaction began to build against the expansion of civil rights to the homosexual community. A critical event in this reaction occurred in 1977, when former beauty queen, popular singer, and evangelical Christian Anita Bryant led a campaign to overturn a nondiscrimination ordinance adopted by the Dade (now Miami-Dade) County commission on January 28, 1977. Four weeks after the commission's action, Bryant and her allies (including the Roman Catholic Archdiocese of Miami and the Florida Conservative Union) had collected 64,000 signatures (significantly more than the 10,000 names required) on a petition calling for the repeal of the ordinance. Bryant framed the argument against granting civil rights to gay men and lesbians in the following terms:

> I don't hate homosexuals. But as a mother, I must protect my children from their evil influence. Defending the rights of my children and yours. Militant homosexuals want their sexual behavior and preference to be

considered respectable and accepted by society. They want to recruit your children and teach them the virtue of becoming a homosexual.... [We] must not give them the legal right to destroy the moral fiber of our families and our nation. (As quoted in Eisenbach 2006, 280)

In a special election held on June 7, the citizens of Dade County voted to overturn the antidiscrimination ordinance by an overwhelming 69 percent to 31 percent majority. In voter surveys, the two most powerful arguments against the ordinance turned out to be the threat posed by the gay and lesbian movement to children and the belief that antidiscrimination laws for lesbians and gay men were "special" rights, not a matter of providing equal protection under the law (Kanowitz 2007).

Bryant and her supporters saw the Dade County vote as a message about the growing gay and lesbian "threat." She said that she would

now carry our fight against similar laws throughout the nation that attempt to legitimize a lifestyle that is both perverse and dangerous to the sanctity of the family, dangerous to our children, dangerous to our freedom of religion and freedom of choice, dangerous to our survival as one nation, under God. (as cited in Baker 1977, 6)

True to their word, opponents of lesbian and gay rights succeeded in repealing antidiscrimination ordinances in Eugene, Oregon; Wichita, Kansas; and St. Paul, Minnesota in the next few months. They were also emboldened to take a more proactive stance against gay and lesbian rights in a variety of settings around the United States. The most important of those campaigns took place in California in 1977, where a conservative Republican legislator from Orange County, John Briggs, proposed putting an initiative on the state ballot that would prohibit lesbians and gay men from teaching in California's public schools. The initiative went even further, requiring the firing of *any* teacher "advocating, soliciting, imposing, encouraging, or promoting" public or private acts of homosexuality (California Voters Pamphlet 1978). When sufficient signatures were obtained to put the initiative on the November 1978 ballot, it appeared to have overwhelming support, with about two-thirds of voters expressing approval. Opponents of the initiative mounted an aggressive campaign against the proposal, obtaining the support of Governor Ronald Reagan. In a speech about the initiative, Reagan warned that the Briggs amendment had "the potential for real mischief.... What if an overwrought youngster, disappointed by bad grades, imagined it was the teacher's fault," Reagan asked, "and struck out by accusing the teacher of advocating homosexuality? Innocent lives could be ruined" (Log Cabin Republicans [n.d.]). Reagan's opposition to the initiative was probably pivotal; the proposition was defeated on November 7, 1978, by a two-to-one margin, just the reverse of public attitudes on the issue less than a year earlier.

Defeat of the Briggs initiative in California by no means meant the end of efforts to curtail the rights of gay men and lesbians in the United States. At nearly the same time that Californians were considering the fate of homosexual teachers, an almost identical bill was being introduced into the Oklahoma legislature by state senator Mary Helm. Under the bill, public schools in the state would be required to fire or refuse to hire any person who engaged in "public homosexual conduct" or "public homosexual activity." The latter term was defined as "advocating, soliciting, imposing, encouraging, or promoting public or private homosexual activity in a manner that creates a substantial risk that such conduct will come to the attention of schoolchildren or school employees" (Cited in Murdock and Price 2001, 252). The bill received widespread support throughout the state, including a favorable comment from future chief justice of the U.S. Supreme Court, William Rehnquist, who compared homosexual behavior to a contagious disease that needed to be quarantined (Murdock and Price 2001, 253). The bill passed the Oklahoma house of representatives by a vote of 88 to 2, and the state senate unanimously. It went into effect in April 1978 and remained on the books until it was declared unconstitutional by the U.S. Supreme Court in 1984 (U.S. Supreme Court 1985). In an ironic sidebar to this story, as the bill was being considered, Oklahoma City was being swept by a surge of hate crimes directed against lesbians and gay men by a group of teenage Ku Klux Klan members. Educators in the city who spoke out against these crimes would, under provisions of the Helm Act, have been subject to dismissal from their jobs (Murdock and Price 2001, 252).

One of Oklahoma's neighbors also sought to limit job opportunities of gay men and lesbians at about the same time that the Oklahoma legislature was considering the Helm bill. The Arkansas legislature began consideration of a bill that, like the Briggs and Helm acts, would ban gay and lesbian teachers from public schools in the state. However, the bill also included prohibitions against the certification of lesbians and gays in the state in the fields of pediatrics, psychiatry, child psychology, and youth counseling. Anyone found to be lying about his or her sexual orientation in one of these fields was to be subject to a prison term of five years (Shilts 1982, 212–213).

The AIDS Epidemic

In 1981, the U.S. Centers for Disease Control (now the Centers for Disease Control and Prevention; CDC) started receiving reports of an unusual new disease pattern developing in selected cities on the east and west coasts. The reports concerned a disease known as Kaposi's sarcoma (KS), a type of cancer typically seen only in older men of Mediterranean extraction. The unusual feature of these reports was that KS was showing up in young American men and was especially virulent. Men who contracted the disease often become very ill very quickly, often dying within a few months of diagnosis. At the same time, the CDC was receiving reports on the spread of another disease, pneumocystis carinii pneumonia (PCP), typically seen only in patients with severely compromised immune systems. Again, PCP patients were young men who had otherwise been in good health. A number of the PCP patients also died relatively soon after diagnosis. At first, experts in the field and members of the media referred to these unusual disease patterns as "gay cancer." But by the end of the year, the CDC had begun to call the condition "gay-related immune deficiency disease" (GRID) and were declaring GRID an epidemic in the United States. It took three years for medical researchers to isolate the causative organism responsible for the disease, a virus that was named the human immunodeficiency virus (HIV), and to agree on a name for the disease, acquired immunodeficiency syndrome (AIDS). (Arguably the best single resource on the development of HIV/AIDS in the United States, including a review of the political response to the disease and its effect on the gay and lesbian community, is Shilts 1987.)

Most people today know at least something about the spread of HIV/AIDS, first across the United States, and eventually throughout the world. For the first decade after its appearance, HIV/AIDS was essentially incurable; only a small fraction of individuals survived a diagnosis of AIDS by more than a few months or a few years. The annual diagnosis and death rates from AIDS mushroomed from 100 and 30, respectively, in 1981, to 12,044 and 6,996 five years later, and to 49,546 and 31,836 in 1990. During the peak year of 1993, 79,879 new cases of HIV/AIDS were recorded, and 45,733 deaths occurred. As of the end of 2006, the last year for which data are available, 1,014,797 Americans had been diagnosed with HIV/AIDS and 565,927 had died of the disease (Avert 2008).

The carnage produced in the gay community by the HIV/AIDS epidemic was a personal, social, and political disaster for the gay and lesbian movement. Until a successful treatment was devised for the disease, a diagnosis of HIV/AIDS was usually a death sentence. In these circumstances, nearly all of the political energies of gay men and lesbians shifted from advocating for political reforms to developing support systems for people with HIV/AIDS. Organizations grew up throughout the nation, from the country's largest cities to its most rural areas, with the goal of educating men and women about the nature of HIV/AIDS, working to change the sexual behavior of individuals so as to prevent the spread of HIV/AIDS, raising money to support research on the causes and possible cures for the disease, and providing support services for people who had contracted the disease. As of early 2009, there were at least 600 organizations nationwide whose sole or primary purpose was providing services to men and women with HIV/AIDS disease (The Body 2008). This number, of course, almost certainly represents a significant decrease in the number of organizations that were functioning during the 1990s, when the disease was raging at its worst throughout the nation. The disease not only distracted the attention of the leaders of the gay and lesbian civil rights movement but, in many cases, also took the lives of those leaders.

As disastrous as the HIV/AIDS epidemic was for the gay and lesbian community, it did have a few bright spots. One such spot was that gay men and lesbians were forced to take responsibility for dealing with this epidemic largely on their own; the federal government for many years played almost no role in supporting research on the disease, promoting educational programs to prevent its occurrence, or providing support for people living with the disease. President Ronald Reagan, whose tenure in the White House corresponded neatly with the first decade of the epidemic, is famously known for not even having spoken the word *AIDS* in public until six years into the epidemic. More important, of course, had been his consistent refusal to commit federal funds to doing battle with the epidemic (see, for example, Lazarus 2004). For gay men and lesbians, then, one lesson of the HIV/AIDS crisis was a reaffirmation of Friedrich Nietzsche's famous quotation, "That which does not kill me makes me stronger" (Nietzsche 1888). In this case, organizing to deal with the HIV/AIDS crisis forced gay men and lesbians to learn about and develop a whole host of new tools for dealing with important social and political issues, tools that they were to put to use in the years after health issues had become less centrally crucial to the gay and lesbian community.

New Horizons

In the first decade of the 21st century, the face of the gay and lesbian civil rights movement has begun to undergo a significant change. One issue, sodomy laws, has essentially been resolved by the U.S. Supreme Court's ruling in 2003 declaring all such laws unconstitutional. Laws dealing with hate crimes against lesbians and gay men have also been adopted by all but three states. (Although efforts are still being made in the U.S. Congress to adopt federal legislation that would provide uniform protection across the nation.) Legislation banning discrimination in housing, employment, and access to public accommodation has also continued to spread through the states, with nine more states having passed such laws between 2000 and 2007 (The Task Force 2008). But two new and closely related issues have moved to the forefront of the gay and lesbian rights movement: same-sex marriage and adoption of children.

Prior to 2000, the number of lesbian and gay couples seeking to adopt a child *as a couple* was probably very small. No statistics are available on this point. The latest estimate available (2007) is that about 65,500 adopted children are currently living with same-sex parents in the United States (Gates, Badgett, Macomber, and Chambers 2007). However, a number of scattered legislative actions and court cases have focused on efforts by lesbian or gay couples to adopt children. These actions and cases have gradually begun to clarify the status of same-sex adoptions in the United States. In 1999, for example, New Hampshire repealed its existing law prohibiting same-sex couples from adopting children (Marriage Law Project 2000, 2). One might assume that this action would resolve the status of same-sex adoptions in at least one state; it didn't. Instead, various counties in the state interpret state law in different ways, such that same-sex couple adoption is permitted in some counties, but not in others (Boston.com 2006). State courts throughout the nation have also taken very different positions on same-sex adoptions. Alabama courts, as an example, have allowed some types of same-sex adoptions, but have not as yet ruled on all possible kinds of such adoptions (Marriage Law Project, 4). As in New Hampshire, different counties in the state interpret state law and higher court rulings in different ways, such that same-sex adoptions may or may not be allowed, depending on the county in which an application is filed.

At the present time (2009), state laws and policies tend to fall into one of three categories: adoption of a child by one member of a same-sex couple; adoption by a same-sex partner of the partner's child; and adoption by both members of a same-sex couple. In many cases, a state's policy on one or more of these options is not expressly stated in law, so that an option may not be specifically forbidden or allowed. For example, some states permit the adoption of a child by any responsible adult, but make no special provision for the sexual orientation of that adult. Currently, four states—Arkansas, Florida, Mississippi, and Utah—have a specific legal restriction against the adoption of a child by a gay man or lesbian, whether coupled or not. In four other states—Missouri, Nebraska, North Dakota, and Ohio—the law is unclear as to whether or not such adoptions are permitted. All other states allow adoption by a responsible adult man or woman. The adoption by both members of a same-sex couple is permitted in 11 states and the District of Columbia and explicitly prohibited in five states. For the remaining 34 states, same-sex adoption is either not explicitly addressed in the law (24 states) or its legal status is unclear or variable within the state (10 states; Human Rights Campaign 2008).

Of all current issues involving the civil rights of gay men and lesbians, none is probably as widely debated as same-sex marriage. It seems unlikely that the protestors at the Stonewall riot could have imagined that their descendants would one day be fighting not for individual liberties or protection from police harassment or the right to work without discrimination, but the right to be legally married to someone of the same sex. Yet, today, that debate rages across the country. Probably the most significant event in the debate over same-sex marriage came in February 2004 when the Massachusetts Supreme Judicial Court ruled that there was no impediment in the state constitution against the marriage of two individuals of the same gender (Massachusetts Supreme Judicial Court 2004). That decision was followed by similar rulings four years later by supreme courts in California and Connecticut. The most recent developments in this field, along with arguments for and against same-sex marriage, as well as the debates over other civil rights for lesbians and gay men, are the subject of the next chapter.

References

Arnesen, Cliff. 1998. "A Veteran Grows in Brooklyn." *International Journal of Sexuality and Gender Studies* 3 (4): 319–327.

Avert. 2008. "United States AIDS Cases and Deaths by Year." http://www.avert.org/usastaty.htm. Accessed October 31, 2008.

Baker, Joe. 1977. "Miami: The Message Was Loud and Clear: Stay in the Closet!" *The Advocate*, July 13.

Boston.com. 2006. "Gay Adoption Policies Vary by County in N.H." April 10. http://www.boston.com/news/local/new_hampshire/articles/2006/04/10/gay_adoption_policies_vary_by_county_in_nh/. Accessed October 31, 2008.

California Voters Pamphlet. 1978. General Election, November 7, 1978, 29. Available online at: http://library.uchastings.edu/ballot_pdf/1978g.pdf. Accessed October 29, 2008.

Carter, David. 2004. *Stonewall: The Riots That Sparked the Gay Revolution.* New York: St. Martin's Press.

Cutler, Marvin. 1956. *Homosexuals Today, a Handbook of Organizations and Publications.* Los Angeles: ONE, Inc., as cited in Jonathan Katz. *Gay American History: Lesbians and Gay Men in the U.S.A.* New York: Thomas Y. Crowell, 1976.

D'Emilio, John. 1983. *Sexual Politics, Sexual Communities: The Making of a Homosexual Minority in the United States, 1940–1970.* Chicago: University of Chicago Press.

Duberman, Martin. 1993. *Stonewall.* New York: Penguin Books.

Eisenbach, David. 2006. *Gay Power: An American Revolution*. Cambridge, MA: Da Capo Press.

Executive Order 10450—Security Requirements for Government Employment, April 27, 1953. Available online at: http://www. presidency.ucsb. edu/ws/index.php?pid=59216. Accessed on October 30, 2008.

Gallo, Marcia. 2006. *Different Daughters: A History of the Daughters of Bilitis and the Rise of the Lesbian Rights Movement*. New York: Carroll & Graf Publishers.

Gallup Polls. 2007. "Tolerance for Gay Rights at High-Water Mark." http://www.gallup.com/poll/27694/Tolerance-Gay-Rights-High Water-Mark.aspx#2. Accessed October 30, 2008.

Gates, Gary J., M. V. Lee Badgett, Jennifer Ehrle Macomber, and Kate Chambers. 2007. "Adoption and Foster Care by Gay and Lesbian Parents in the United States." Los Angeles: The Williams Institute, March (Executive Summary; unpaginated).

Gay and Lesbian Archives of the Pacific Northwest. 2007. "Sodomy Laws." http://www.glapn.org/sodomylaws/index.htm. Accessed October 30, 2008.

Gerber, Henry. 1926. "The Society for Human Rights—1925." *One*. September. Available online at: http://www.glapn.org/sodomylaws/ usa/illinois/ilnews02.htm.

Human Rights Campaign. 2008. "Adoption Laws: State by State." http://www.hrc.org/issues/parenting/adoptions/2375.htm. Accessed October 31, 2008.

International Gay Information Center, Inc. 2008. "Gay Activists Alliance: Historical Note." http://microformguides.gale.com/Data/ Introductions/20240FM.htm. Accessed October 30, 2008.

Johansson, Warren, and William A. Percy. 1994. *Outing: Shattering the Conspiracy of Silence*. London: Routledge Press.

Kanowitz, Saul. 2007. "Whatever Happened to Anita Bryant? 30 Years after the Dade County Struggle for LGBT Rights." *Socialism and Liberation*. June. Available online at: http://socialismandliberation.org/ mag/index.php?aid=807. Accessed October 30, 2008.

Katz, Jonathan. 1976. *Gay American History: Lesbians and Gay Men in the U.S.A.* New York: Thomas Y. Crowell.

Lazarus, David. 2004. "Downside of Reagan Legacy." SFGate. http:// www.sfgate.com/cgi-bin/article.cgi?f=/c/a/2004/06/09/BUGBI72U8Q1. DTL. Accessed October 31, 2008.

Log Cabin Republicans. [n.d.] "A Proud History." http://online.logcabin. org/about/history.html. Accessed October 30, 2008.

Marriage Law Project. 2000. "Adoption by Homosexuals and Same-Sex Couples: A Legal Memorandum." http://www.marriagewatch.org/ publications/adoption.PDF. Accessed October 31, 2008.

Massachusetts Supreme Judicial Court. 2004. Opinions of the Justices to the Senate. SJC-09163. Available online at: http://news.findlaw. com/hdocs/docs/conlaw/maglmarriage20304.html. Accessed October 31, 2008.

Murdock, Joyce, and Deb Price. 2001. *Courting Justice: Gay Men and Lesbians v. the Supreme Court*. New York: Basic Books.

Nietzsche, Friedrich. 1888. *Twilight of the Idols*. http://users.compaqnet. be/cn127103/Nietzsche_twilight_of_the_idols/the_twilight_of_ the_Idols.htm. Accessed October 31, 2008.

One v. Olesen, 241 F.2d 772. 1957. Available online at: http://bulk. resource.org/courts.gov/c/F2/241/241.F2d.772.15139_1.html. Accessed on October 29, 2008.

"Purposes of the Daughters of Bilitis." 1956. *The Ladder* 3 (2): 2. As cited in Katz. *Gay American History*, 426.

Sandilands, Catriona. 2002. "Lesbian Separatist Communities and the Experience of Nature." *Organization and Environment* 15 (2): 131–163.

Shilts, Randy. 1987. *And the Band Played On: Politics, People, and the AIDS Epidemic*. New York: St. Martin's Press.

Shilts, Randy. 1982. *The Mayor of Castro Street*. New York: St. Martin's Press.

Stonewall Library and Archives. [n.d.] "Pride: Party or Protest?" http://www.stonewall-library.org/prideexhibit/09-panel.htm. Accessed October 29, 2008.

The Body. 2008. "United States HIV/AIDS Organizations." http:// www.thebody.com/index/hotlines/other.html. Accessed October 31, 2008.

The Task Force. 2008. "State Nondiscrimination Laws in the U.S." http://www.thetaskforce.org/downloads/reports/issue_maps/ non_discrimination_7_08_color.pdf. Accessed on October 29, 2008.

Teal, Donn. 1971. *The Gay Militants: How Gay Liberation Began in America, 1969–1971*. New York: St. Martin's Press.

U.S. Census Bureau. 1995. "Urban and Rural Population: 1900 to 1990." http://www.census.gov/population/www/censusdata/files/ urpop0090.txt. Accessed on October 29, 2008.

U.S. Supreme Court. 2003. *Lawrence et al v. Texas*. 2003. 539 U.S. 558. Available online at: http://caselaw.lp.findlaw.com/scripts/getcase.pl? court=US&vol=000&invol=02-102#opinion1. Accessed October 30, 2008.

U.S. Supreme Court. 1985. *National Gay Task Force v. Board of Education of City of Oklahoma City*. 1985. 470 U.S. 903.

U.S. Supreme Court. 1985. *One, Incorporated, v. Olesen*, 355 U.S. 371 (1958). Available online at http://caselaw.lp.findlaw.com/scripts/ getcase.pl?navby=CASE&court=US&vol=355&page=371. Accessed on October 29, 2008.

Weeks, Jeffrey. 1979. *Coming Out: Homosexual Politics in Britain.* London: Quartet Books.

2

Problems, Controversies, and Solutions

All social and political movements evolve. As some objectives are achieved, new goals are set and new actions taken to accomplish those goals. In this respect, movements are organic entities, constantly growing and changing and, in many cases, withering and dying. The gay and lesbian rights movement is no different in this respect from the women's suffrage movement, the civil rights movement, the movement for Native American rights, and other movements throughout American history.

In the United States, the emphasis of the early gay and lesbian movement was on liberation: the right and ability of people to be open about their sexual orientation; to be free from harassment just because of their sexuality; and the opportunity to enjoy the same basic rights of employment, housing, and public accommodation available to all non-gay, non-lesbian Americans. To an extent, the modern gay and lesbian rights movement continues to embrace those objectives. But a shift in emphasis has occurred. For many lesbians and gay men, the most important challenge in their lives is not just to "come out" to relatives, friends, neighbors, and coworkers, as it was for their predecessors in the 1960s. Today, the emphasis of the gay and lesbian rights movement is for equality, the demand that they no longer be treated as second-class citizens in the United States just because of their sexual orientation.

This campaign has, of course, met with enormous resistance from critics who say that homosexual behaviors are

35

immoral, and those who practice such behaviors do not qualify for the same rights as "decent" Americans. They argue that just as criminals lose their civil rights because of their crimes, so lesbians and gay men are not worthy of the same legal protections as other Americans. Other critics of the gay and lesbian rights movement suggest that all Americans are already guaranteed their civil rights by existing laws and statutes and, of course, by the U.S. Constitution. There is no need, they say, to provide "special rights" to people just because of their sexual orientation.

This chapter focuses on the main points of contention raised by a lesbian and gay civil rights movement:

- Should gays and lesbians be included in special legislation on hate crimes?
- Should there be special legislation to guarantee nondiscrimination of gays and lesbians in employment, housing, and access to public accommodations?
- Should gay men and lesbians be allowed to serve openly in the military forces of the United States?
- Should gay and lesbian couples be allowed to adopt children and, if so, under what circumstances?
- Should same-sex marriage be allowed in the United States and, if not, should comparable arrangements (domestic partnerships or civil unions, for example) be permitted instead?

The pros and cons of each of these issues will be discussed, and an analysis presented of the current state of affairs in each case.

The Power of Language

You have just met Marco for the first time. He has just described to you his recent trip to visit relatives in Salerno. Like most people, you may want to fit Marco into some class of individuals about which you know something. Is Marco an Italian-American? A spic? Dago? Wop? Guinea? Perhaps affiliated with the Mafia? The first of these terms is probably the most value-neutral; it simply describes a person's ethnic background. (Although why it may be necessary to do so in the melting pot called the United States of America is not clear.) The other terms all include value judgments. They refer to groups of people who are less decent, less worthy than white Americans.

For well over a century, people have struggled to find appropriate terms to use in describing men and women who are attracted to others of the same sex. Today, a common generic term is *homosexual* for the person or a same-sex act and *homosexuality* for a condition of same-sex attraction. These terms are derived from the Greek word *homos*, meaning "same," and not from a similar Latin term, *homo*, meaning "man." They probably first appeared in print in 1869 in a series of pamphlets written by the Hungarian journalist Károly Mária Kertbeny. As will become clear, both terms have advantages and disadvantages.

When same-sex attraction first became an issue of interest to scientists at the end of the 19th century, a number of new terms were suggested for the phenomenon of same-sex attraction. For example, German lawyer Karl Heinrich Ulrichs suggested the term *uranism* for the condition of same-sex attraction and *uranian* for those with such feelings. The important point about these terms is that they did not carry criminal or sinful connotations as did other terms in general use, such as deviance and deviants, pedophilia and pedophiles, and sodomy and sodomites. Ulrichs believed and wrote that same-sex attraction was a normal variant of human sexuality; it was neither good nor bad in and of itself, but simply another form of human sexual expression (Celebration 2009: Karl Heinrich Ulrichs). Ulrichs's contemporaries and successors suggested a number of other supposedly value-free terms to describe same-sex attraction, such as third sex or third gender, intermediate or intermediary sex, and inversion and inverts (Norton 2008).

The efforts of Kertbeny, Ulrichs, and other scientists to develop value-free language to talk about same-sex attraction had virtually no effect on everyday conversations on the subject. Throughout most of Western civilization from the late 19th century until well into the 20th century, same-sex acts were anything but value free; they were almost always regarded by the general public as sinful, criminal, or abnormal (and sometimes all three at the same time). As a consequence, a number of terms evolved to describe these acts and the individuals who engaged in them, terms such as *gay, lesbian, faggot* (or *fag*), *queer, pansy, poof, queen, lezzie, nance, fairy, fruit, auntie, butch* (for women), *femme, flit*, and *homo*. All of these terms combined a description of a sexual behavior and a value judgment about that behavior.

Gay and lesbian activists have always been very conscious of the importance of language in presenting their case to the general public. Many early groups, for example, chose to adopt the term *homophile* to describe their activities. Examples of such groups include the East Coast Homophile Organization (ECHO), the North American Conference of Homophile Organizations (NACHO), the Homophile Action League of Philadelphia, the Homophile Youth Movement in Neighborhoods (New York City), and the Student Homophile League (Columbia University). The term *homophile*, again from the Greek, literally means "same love," implying "a person who loves someone of the same gender." Members of these groups wanted to deemphasize the sexual aspects of their lives (as in homo*sexual*) and stress a deeper sense of love for others of the same sex (Wikipedia 2008a).

As the gay and lesbian movement became more emboldened during the 1960s and 1970s, groups were more likely to describe themselves as *gay*, a term that has probably become the most popular single word by which gay men and lesbians, as well as the general public, describe people who are attracted to others of the same sex. The term was first widely adopted by gay men and lesbians themselves in the days following the Stonewall riots of 1969. The Gay Liberation Front and the Gay Activists Alliance, both formed in 1969, are generally thought to be the first organizations to use the term *gay* in their names.

As a synonym for *carefree, happy, exuberant*, and similar words, the term *gay* probably dates to the 14th century (*Merriam Webster's Collegiate Dictionary* 1994, 483). Early on, the term appears to have become associated with illicit sexual activities. One source suggests that this association may date to 1637 (Online Etymology Dictionary 2008). By the end of the 19th century, it was certainly being used to describe female prostitutes, who were sometimes said to be working in "gay houses" (Wikipedia 2008b). Some authorities suggest that the term *gay* was being used by homosexual men to describe others of their own kind as early as the 1890s, although evidence for that belief is thin. In any case, it is clear that the term had been adopted by the gay underground in the United States by the 1920s. The term *gay cat*, for example, was sometimes used to describe the younger member of a same-sex male couple (Aitken 2007).

Following the Stonewall riots, those individuals whom the general society was still calling *homosexuals* had begun to start referring to themselves as *gay men and women*. Before long, a number of women began to reject that generic term, feeling that it was too strongly associated with men. They preferred to call themselves *lesbians*. Within the gay and lesbian community, the term *homosexual* was rather quickly abandoned as being too clinical and, in many cases, too derogatory.

In the 21st century, the language of same-sex relationships has taken yet another turn. Today, many political action groups refer to themselves as lesbian, gay, bisexual, and transgendered (LGBT) organizations. That term acknowledges that four classes of individuals share common political objectives and try to work together to achieve those objectives: gay men, lesbians, bisexuals, and persons who have chosen sex reassignments (transgendered persons). Other groups have adopted a term that was once among the most pejorative of all names for homosexuals: *queer*. This choice has been similar to that made by some black individuals and groups who refer to one another as *niggers* (although non-blacks may not do so). The practice throws back into the face of oppressors the very terminology once used in derision. Thus, some colleges and universities now have departments of courses in queer studies; there are journals of queer studies; and queer organizations have been formed to deal with social and political issues of interest to gay men and lesbians (and, often, bisexuals and transgendered people).

Language is an important factor in political debates over gay and lesbian issues. In the first place, it can be used to define or to deny the social and political status of minority groups. Non-gays can use the term *faggot* for gay men as a way of indicating their low worth in society. Gay men and lesbians can use the term *queer* in referring to themselves to show that they have enough self-confidence to reject the stereotyping suggested by terminology. Lesbians and gay men have also used language to educate the non-gay world about themselves. One reason for rejecting the term *homosexual* is to point out that people who are attracted to others of the same sex have full and complete lives that go far beyond their sexual experiences. No non-gay man would want to be defined as a *heterosexual*, suggesting that he can be understood entirely on the basis of his attraction to women. So lesbians and gay men want to demonstrate the same principle about their own lives. To the extent to which they are successful in that endeavor, to that extent the general society is more likely to look upon them as complex humans rather than one-dimensional sexual beings.

Hate Crimes

In May 2007, the Gallup organization conducted a poll on hate crime legislation. Pollsters asked respondents if they would approve the inclusion of "sexual orientation" in any hate crime law passed in their home state. Seventy-eight percent of respondents indicated that they would favor the inclusion of gay men and lesbians in such laws; 13 percent opposed doing so. This trend was consistent with every subgroup included in the poll, with conservatives (57 percent "yes" and 37 percent "no") and Republicans (60 percent "yes" and 34 percent "no") providing the lowest levels of support for the proposition (Gallup 2007). At the time this poll was conducted, all but five of the 50 states had already adopted hate crime legislation that included sexual orientation (The Task Force 2008).

These data would suggest that inclusion of lesbians and gay men in state hate crime laws is a non-issue in American society today. Such, however, may not be the case. In spite of widespread public and legislative support for hate crime laws, the actual number of hate crime incidents against lesbians and gay men has been essentially constant over the past decade. Between 1995 and 2006, about 1,100 hate crimes against gay men and lesbians were reported to the Federal Bureau of Investigation (FBI) every year. These numbers rise and fall, from a low of 1,016 in 1996 to a high of 1,393 in 2001 (PublicEye.org 2008). (Some experts point out the unreliability of these numbers since so many hate crimes go unreported and since a number of governmental jurisdictions do not submit reports for their region.)

Concerns about ongoing hate crimes based on sexual orientation have prompted some federal legislators to call for an extension of existing federal hate crimes legislation to include the area of sexual orientation (as well, in most cases, as gender identity and gender). The first such bill was introduced into the U.S. Congress in 1999, where it became popularly known as the Matthew Shepard Act. Matthew Shepard was a student at the University of Wyoming who was assaulted late on the night of October 6, 1988, violence that continued into the early morning hours of October 7. He had been picked up by two non-gay men at a local bar, robbed, pistol whipped, tortured, tied to a fence in a remote area near Laramie, and left to die, which he did five days later. The Matthew Shepard Act was introduced in every session of Congress from 1999 through 2007, at which point it was finally acted upon. On May 3, 2007, the U.S. House of Representatives passed the most recent version of the bill, entitled the Local Law Enforcement Hate Crimes Prevention Act of 2007 (HR 1592). The vote was 237 yeas (212 Democrats and 25 Republicans) and 180 nays (14 Democrats and 166 Republicans). The bill was then sent to the U.S. Senate.

The Senate took no action on the Matthew Shepard Act until late September 2007, at which time Majority Leader Harry Reid (D-Nev.) attached the bill as a rider to an unrelated defense appropriations bill. The bill as a whole, including the rider, passed the Senate on September 27 by a vote of 60 (50 Democrats, 9 Republicans, and 1 Independent) to 39 (all Republicans). The apparent success of the bill was illusionary, however, as nearly all Republicans and some Democrats refused to vote for the defense authorization bill as long as it contained the hate crimes rider. In addition, President George W. Bush promised to veto the act if it contained the Shepard rider. In the end, Senator Reid withdrew the rider, and the unencumbered bill passed the Senate. As a consequence, no federal hate crimes legislation protecting individuals on the basis of sexual orientation, gender, or gender identity has yet been adopted.

The most outspoken objections to including gay men and lesbians in federal hate crimes legislation come from religious groups. (For an excellent collection of comments about the federal hate crimes bill from a variety of individuals, see Religious Tolerance 2007a.) Those groups have raised two primary concerns about such legislation. In the first place, they believe that legislation like the Matthew Shepard Act will limit the freedom of speech of anyone who raises objections to homosexual behavior based on their religious convictions. In a publication on the topic released in mid-2007, the Traditional Values Coalition (TVC) argued that adoption of the Matthew Shepard Act by the U.S. Senate would lay the legal foundation and framework to investigate, prosecute, and persecute pastors, business owners, and anyone else whose actions are based upon and reflect the truths found in the Bible, which have previously been protected by the First Amendment. This will result in a chilling effect on religious liberties (Traditional Values Coalition 2007b).

In response to this concern, Representative Artur Davis (D-Ala.) introduced an amendment to HR 1592 that read: "Nothing in this Act, or the amendments made by this Act, shall be construed to prohibit any expressive conduct protected from legal prohibition by, or any activities protected by the free speech or free exercise clauses of, the First Amendment to the Constitution (GovTrack.us. [n.d.])." This attempt at assuaging the concerns of some religious leaders failed, however, as they continued to oppose the bill even in its amended form.

Objections were also raised to the effect that the revised hate crimes act provided gay men and lesbians with "special rights." As the Traditional Values Coalition pamphlet cited here points out,

> The main purpose of this legislation is to add the categories of "sexual orientation" and "gender identity," "either actual or perceived," as new classes of individuals receiving special protection by federal law. . . . Once "sexual orientation" is added to federal law, anyone with a bizarre sexual orientation will have total protection for his or her activities by claiming that Congress sanctions their appearance, behavior or attitudes. (Traditional Values Coalition 2007b)

Among the "bizarre sexual orientations" the pamphlet identifies as earning protection under the law are incest, necrophilia, pedophilia, prostitution, bestiality, and voyeurism.

In addition to these major objections, religious leaders have also raised other concerns about the passage of hate crimes protection for gay men and lesbians. They argue, further, that such protection is not really needed since only a tiny handful of such crimes are committed every year, only 0.000205 percent of all aggravated assaults by their calculation (Traditional Values Coalition 2007b). The response to this concern is that hate crimes tend to be notoriously underreported, and that some studies have shown that as many as 41 percent of all lesbians and gay men reported having been assaulted at some time in their lives (Religious Tolerance [n.d.]).

Finally, some religious leaders have suggested that sufficient protection is already available for anyone who is the victim of a hate crime. The Traditional Values Coalition points out that "[l]ocal police and sheriffs are already effectively dealing with these crimes as a routine part of their jobs." Of much greater concern, the coalition suggests, is the fake hate crimes that gay men and lesbians report in order to get attention for themselves or for some other purpose of self-aggrandizement (Traditional Values Coalition 2007b).

Issues of Discrimination in Employment, Housing, and Access to Public Accommodations

In 2008, Harris Interactive, Inc., conducted a poll on behalf of Out & Equal Workplace Advocates (commonly known as "Out & Equal") to determine attitudes of gay men and lesbians and non-gay and non-lesbians persons on workplace issues related to sexual orientation and gender identity in the period from 2002 to 2008. One of the findings of that poll was that 65 percent of gay and lesbian respondents reported that they had been subjected to some form of harassment by coworkers. The harassment took the form of anti-gay comments, denial of promotion or job advancement, fired or forced to resign, or having a partner excluded from workplace functions. About one third of all respondents (36 percent) indicated that they remained closeted at work (that is, they had not revealed their sexual orientation to coworkers). Just over half of all gay and lesbian respondents knew that it was legal for their employee to fire a person on the basis of his or her sexual orientation, while a quarter of heterosexuals were aware of this fact. A large majority of lesbians and gay men (83 percent) supported federal legislation to ban discrimination in the workplace, while just over half (51 percent) of all heterosexual respondents expressed a similar view (Harris Interactive, Inc. 2008).

Data of the kind reported in the Harris poll suggest that discrimination based on sexual orientation still exists in the workplace and that state and federal legislation might be helpful in eliminating such discrimination. Interestingly, the corporate world seems significantly advanced over the political world in this regard. Over the past dozen years, the number of large corporations that have added sexual orientation to their nondiscrimination policies has grown from 5 percent in 1996 to 98 percent in 2008. About half of those businesses also include gender identity in their nondiscrimination policies (Out & Equal Workplace Advocates 2008). More and more companies are accepting the proposition that discrimination based on sexual orientation does not belong in their workplace and that they may need to become active in the campaign to pass nondiscrimination legislation. In 2005, for example, a group of gay and lesbian workers at Microsoft, Gay and Lesbian Employees at Microsoft (GLEAM), convinced management to support antidiscrimination legislation then being considered in the Washington state legislature. Microsoft CEO Steve Ballmer said in an e-mail to employees that "Diversity in the workplace is such an important issue for our business that it should be included in our legislative agenda" (Gunther 2006).

Opposition to nondiscrimination legislation based on sexual orientation, like that against hate crime legislation, comes largely (but not exclusively) from evangelical and Roman Catholic religious groups. For example, the Traditional Values Coalition has published newsletters and appeals that use arguments against nondiscrimination legislation that mirror those against hate crimes legislation. An appeal for donations mailed to members by TVC in September 2007 listed two reasons for concerns about nondiscrimination legislation, both of which had also been given for the group's opposition to hate crimes legislation. First, the appeal said, the proposed Employment Nondiscrimination Act (ENDA) being considered in Congress would force private sector employers across America to hire cross-dressers, transgenders, "she-males," and many other people with "bizarre sexual practices." This bill brings sexual behavior into the workplace or be sued for discrimination (Traditional Values Coalition 2007a).

In this letter, TVC leaders Lou Sheldon and Andrea S. Lafferty again cited "30 sexual orientations" that they said would be covered by ENDA (see the previous discussion of hate crimes legislation). There is no discussion of the status of gay men and lesbians in this letter, which focuses entirely on the problems that religious organizations would have in being forced to hire "she-males" who are "female from the waist up and male from the waist down" (Traditional Values Coalition 2007a).

The letter's second argument against ENDA is that its "real purpose is to silence people of faith." It claims that in spite of an exception provided for religious organizations, the act offers protection only to the leader of a religious group, and not to the host of other individuals working with and for that group, individuals such as religious school teachers, publishers of religious materials, and church volunteers (Traditional Values Coalition 2007a; for other statements of opposition to ENDA, see Barber 2007, Adams 2007. and Focus on the Family 2007).

The arguments presented by TVC and similar groups have, themselves, been subjected to some criticisms. For example, the group Religious Tolerance has pointed out the skewed definition of the term *sexual orientation* used by TVC and some other groups. It suggests that the meaning of the term is fairly clear within the bill and that, in any case, protection for transgendered persons was removed from the bill before its final passage in the Senate. Religious Tolerance also points out that critics have sometimes misrepresented the scope of the bill, suggesting it applies only to homosexuals. In fact, the bill offers protection to individuals of all sexual orientations, including homosexuals, heterosexuals, and bisexuals (Religious Tolerance.org 2007b).

While resistance to ENDA remains, public opinion polls, the actions of state and federal legislators, and endorsements by a wide variety of social and political groups suggest that the battle over nondiscrimination legislation based on sexual orientation appears to be largely over, and that the passage of ENDA may occur in the not-so-distant future. (For a list of organizations that have expressed support for ENDA, see Leadership Conference on Civil Rights 2007.)

Discrimination against lesbians and gay men in areas other than employment has also long been a civil rights issue. Robin's story at the beginning of Chapter 1 might also be told about discrimination in housing and access to public accommodations. In 2003, physician Fred Sternbach visited the Royal Colonial apartments in Boca Raton, Florida, looking for a temporary rental for himself and his partner of 16 years, Stephen Miller, while their home was being rebuilt. Having completed an application form, Dr. Sternbach was shown a number of apartments by manager Peggy Watson. He found one that he liked and indicated that he would like to rent it. A short time later, Watson called to check on the listing of Miller's name as "partner" on the rental application. When she discovered that Miller was Sternbach's domestic partner, she withdrew the offer of a rental, saying the complex rented only to married couples (Lambda Legal 2003).

Had Sternbach and Miller lived in most parts of the United States, that would have been the end of the story. There is no federal legislation prohibiting discrimination in housing on the basis of sexual orientation. The Fair Housing Act of 1968 (Title VIII of the Civil Rights Act of 1964) prohibits discrimination in the sale, renting, financing, or other related transactions on the basis of race, color, national origin, religion, gender, family status, or disability . . . but not sexual orientation or gender identity. Palm Beach County, in which Boca Raton is located, does have legislation prohibiting discrimination on the basis of sexual orientation. On the basis of this law, Sternbach and Miller were able to obtain a settlement from the owners of the Royal Colonial. The settlement included a requirement that the owners place a statement of nondiscrimination in their office and on their rental application forms. In addition, the owners agreed to pay Sternbach and Miller $75,000 in damages and legal fees (Lambda Legal 2003).

As of early 2009, 18 states and the District of Columbia, as well as more than 180 communities, had adopted legislation banning discrimination in housing on the basis of sexual orientation. The specific provisions of the laws in each state and community vary somewhat, which is one argument for the adoption of a federal law. A handful of the state laws also apply to gender identity (Nolo Press 2008a). In contrast with the issue of discrimination in employment on the basis of sexual orientation (see previous discussion), there is no federal legislation pending on the problem of discrimination in housing.

For proponents of legislation prohibiting discrimination in housing, the issue is fairly straightforward. The Constitution, the Civil Rights Act of 1964, and a great deal of additional federal and state legislation are all based on the premise that all Americans are equal under the law. It simply is not acceptable that some people can be denied the right to buy a home, rent an apartment, apply for a loan, obtain redress from an insurance company, and carry out other business transactions simply because of their sexual orientation. Even more significant, perhaps, is the fact that such actions are almost without exception based on a person's identity (gay man, lesbian, bisexual, etc.) rather than on specific acts that may or may not be legal, moral, or acceptable in society.

More to the point, perhaps, is the fact that the experience of Fred Sternbach and Stephen Miller in Boca Raton was hardly unique. In a 2001 study of attitudes about issues related to sexual orientation, the Kaiser Family Foundation found that 34 percent of gays and lesbians surveyed had either experienced some form of discrimination in housing themselves or knew of someone who had (Kaiser Family Foundation 2001). In addition, 63 percent of the general public believed that gay men and lesbians experienced discrimination in renting an apartment or buying a home "often" (23 percent) or "sometimes" (40 percent; Kaiser Family Foundation 2001).

Opponents of nondiscrimination legislation in housing based on sexual orientation have raised a number of specific objections. One of the most common arguments is that civil rights protections have traditionally been offered to groups that meet three qualifications: (1) they had experienced a long history of discrimination; (2) they were economically disadvantaged; and (3) their identifying features (such as skin color) were "immutable characteristics" (American Civil Liberties Union 2008). Gay men and lesbians certainly do not exhibit two of these three qualities (being economically disadvantaged and having immutable characteristics), and their claim of being the subject of discrimination is doubtful, according to one critic. Therefore, they are not eligible for civil rights protection, and granting them such protection would be providing them with "special rights" (American Civil Liberties Union 2008).

Proponents of nondiscrimination legislation have responded that there is something "legally wrong" with arguments against such legislation. It is not a "special right" at all for gay men and lesbians to expect that they be able to receive equal treatment in housing, employment and other areas of public interaction. Opposition to nondiscrimination legislation simply "requires the government to treat gay and lesbian people differently from all other people" (American Civil Liberties Union 2008).

In comparison with other issues of concern to the gay and lesbian civil rights movement, discrimination in housing (and to an even greater extent, access to public accommodations) has often not been a matter of vital concern. Very few, if any, court cases dealing specifically with the topic have been heard (Nolo Press 2008b), and state and local legislation to ban such discrimination has progressed slowly, but surely, across the nation. After the first two such laws were passed in Wisconsin and Massachusetts in 1982 and 1989, respectively, eight more states (Hawaii, Connecticut, New Jersey, Vermont, California, Minnesota, Rhode Island, and New Hampshire) and the District of Columbia adopted such laws in the 1990s. Since then, eight more states have joined the bandwagon (Maryland, 2001; New York, 2002; New Mexico, 2003; Illinois, 2005; Maine, 2005; Washington, 2006; Oregon, 2007; and Iowa, 2007; DeWitt 2007).

Lesbians and Gay Men in the Military

Historically, the United States armed forces have had a policy of excluding men and women who engage in homosexual acts since the earliest days of the republic. A service member found guilty of committing such an act was subject to discharge (usually a dishonorable discharge), with loss of veteran benefits. After World War I, the military began to make a change in that policy. It decided to exclude individuals not because of specific acts, but because of their (often perceived) sexual orientation. For example, the U.S. Army issued new standards for admission in 1921 in which interviewers were instructed to be alert for "the stigmata of degeneration," which might include in men features such as "sloping narrow shoulders, broad hips, excessive pectoral and pubic adipose . . . scant and downy beard . . . or . . . a female figure." These features, the army directive said, would be an indication of "internal glandular disturbances" of the male homosexual (Bérubé 1990, 14; Bérubé's book is generally regarded as the primary source for information about the issue of gay men and lesbians in the U.S. military during the 20th century). Thus, a man or woman applying for service in the army or navy was judged by his or her erotic interests, not on the basis of sexual acts he or she may have performed. This policy in and of itself is somewhat unusual in that the law normally punishes a person for the acts he or she performs, not the kind of person he or she is.

Given the modest role played by the military in the United States in the period between the two world wars, this policy was of relatively little concern to most people. That situation changed as World War II broke out. Untold numbers of men and women volunteering for or having been drafted into the military services were assessed on the basis of the 1921 policy, expressed in 1942 in somewhat different terms. That policy was, however, unsatisfactory for a variety of reasons. Since it was based on a preinduction psychological interview, accurate information about a recruit's sexual orientation was difficult to obtain. Some gay men and lesbians lied to interviewers and were inducted into the services. Some men and women who were not gay or lesbian also lied about their sexual orientation, claiming to be homosexual, when they were not, thus avoiding military service. In addition, as World War II progressed, the policy for admitting gay men and lesbians to the military varied, depending in part on the military's need for new recruits. As places in the army, navy, and other services were more readily filled, the policy was more strongly enforced. As a need for recruits grew, enforcement of the policy diminished (Herek [n.d.]).

Although official policy about the admission of lesbians and gay men to the U.S. military has remained relatively constant over the past half century, internal debates about that policy have continued throughout that period. The army, navy, Department of Defense, and other military agencies have commissioned and/or conducted a number of studies designed to investigate the suitability of having gay men and lesbians serving in the armed forces. In 1952, for example, the Department of Defense appointed a committee to review policy on the inclusion of gay men and lesbians in the armed services. The committee was unable to agree on its recommendations and issued two reports. One argued that there was no reason to exclude homosexuals from military service, while the minority report claimed that gay men and lesbians were security risks and should, therefore, not be allowed to serve (Bérubé 1990, 277).

Perhaps the most famous of these early reports was one prepared for the U.S. Navy under the direction of Captain S. H. Crittenden Jr., and was popularly known, therefore, as the Crittenden Report. That report assumed at the outset that navy policy on the exclusion of homosexuals was not in question, and focused instead on their status as potential security risks. The report concluded that "The concept that homosexuals pose a security risk is unsupported by any factual data . . . The number of cases of blackmail as a result of past investigations of homosexuals is negligible. No factual data exist to support the contention that homosexuals are a greater risk than heterosexuals" (Rimmerman 1966, 272–273).

The navy declined to release this report, explaining that it was only a draft. Twenty years later, a federal judge ordered the release of this and other reports dealing with Department of Defense policy on homosexuals in the military forces. (For a review of efforts by the U.S. military establishment to prevent the release of unfavorable reports on this topic, see Bérubé 1990, 359. For a discussion of efforts to obtain suppressed reports on the topic, see Gibson 1978, 356–367.) This ruling ignored the military services' own statements that they had "no evidence of special studies pertaining to homosexuals" (the army) or that they could locate no such studies (the navy; Bérubé 1990, 278).

In 1981, the Department of Defense issued an updated version of its policy on the inclusion of lesbians and gay men in the military services. DOD directive 1332.14, issued on January 28, 1982, said that:

> Homosexuality is incompatible with military service. The presence in the military environment of persons who engage in homosexual conduct or who, by their statements, demonstrate a propensity to engage in homosexual conduct, seriously impairs the accomplishment of the military mission. The presence of such members adversely affects the ability of the Military Services to maintain discipline, good order, and morale; to foster mutual trust and confidence among servicemembers, to ensure the integrity of the system of rank and command; to facilitate assignment and worldwide deployment of servicemembers who frequently must live and work under close conditions affording minimal privacy; to recruit and retain members of the Military Services; to maintain the public acceptability of military service; and to prevent breaches of security. (U.S. Department of Defense 1982)

DOD's promulgation of this new policy statement did not extinguish the debate about homosexuals serving in the armed forces, although it did remain in effect for another decade. During that time, military personnel, politicians, and the general public continued to argue over the justice and validity of this policy. In the 1992 presidential campaign, Democratic candidate Bill Clinton promised that one of his first acts as president would be to discontinue this policy and allow homosexuals to serve in the military. Upon his election, he found that it would not be easy to fulfill this promise and, instead, asked a number of his advisors to suggest an alternative approach to the issue. The compromise that was reached was called "don't ask, don't tell," (DADT) and has remained official U.S. policy concerning the presence of gay men and lesbians in the military ever since. According to this policy,

> Applicants for military service will no longer be asked or required to reveal if they are homosexual or bisexual, but applicants will be informed of the conduct that is proscribed for members of the armed forces, including homosexual conduct.

> **Discharge Policy**
> Sexual orientation will not be a bar to service unless manifested by homosexual conduct. The military will discharge members who engage in homosexual conduct, which is defined as a homosexual act, a statement that the member is homosexual or bisexual, or a marriage or attempted marriage to someone of the same gender. ("Gay Rights in the Military" 1993)

Pros and Cons of "Don't Ask, Don't Tell"

In spite of its longevity, the U.S. military's policy of DADT appears to be acceptable and satisfactory to almost no one. The armed forces still seem strongly opposed to including lesbians and gay men in the military. Since the policy was implemented in 1993, a total of 11,694 men and women have been discharged under its regulations (Servicemembers Legal Defense Network [n.d.]a); additional data are available from Burrelli and Dale 2005, CRS-11.) Supporters of the "don't ask, don't tell" policy have provided a number of arguments in favor of their position. These include:

- Military officers are unable to maintain discipline if gay men and lesbians are present in a unit.

- Unit morale suffers from the presence of gay men and lesbians.
- Fighting men and women lose trust in one another and confidence in their ability to carry out a mission when lesbians and gay men are part of a unit.
- Men and women are worried about being in close living contact with gay men and lesbians.
- The general public will lose confidence in the military if gay men and lesbians serve in the armed forces.
- Lesbians and gay men are security threats because they are subject to blackmail because of their sexual orientation. (These arguments are inferred from DOD Directive 1332.14, mentioned previously.)

Opponents of DADT have listed a number of reasons that the current policy is ineffective and unfair and should be repealed. The Servicemembers Legal Defense Network, for example, has listed 10 arguments in opposition to this policy. They are:

- The policy is discriminatory in that there are no other laws in the United States that mandate firing of a person because of his or her sexual orientation.
- The policy damages military readiness because so many otherwise qualified individuals are forced to leave the military.
- The policy is expensive. By one estimate, the Department of Defense has spent more than $360 million between 1994 and 2003 in administering the policy.
- The service of more than a million gay men and lesbians should be honored by repealing the policy.
- Asking lesbians and gay men to hide the truth about who they are is contrary to the military's ideals of honesty and integrity.
- Women suffer disproportionately as a result of this policy; they are excluded at twice the rate of the portion of the military as a whole.
- Military and national security forces from a number of other nations include lesbians and gay men, with no apparent damage to their functions.
- DADT can be applied hypocritically, as the policy is ignored when the need for military personnel is greatest (as during the Iraq and Afghanistan wars).

- Every report commissioned on the involvement of lesbians and gay men in the military has concluded that DADT could be repealed without damage to military readiness. (Servicemembers Legal Defense Network [n.d.]b. For another analysis of the current DADT policy from a legal standpoint, see Scott 2004.)
- Recent polls show that as many as three-quarters of all Americans believe that lesbians, gay men, and bisexuals should be allowed to serve in the military.

A number of public surveys have now confirmed the last of these points, an important consideration, perhaps, in determining the fate of DADT. In one of the earliest of these polls, sponsored by NBC and the *Wall Street Journal* in July 1993, 40 percent of respondents said that they favored allowing openly gay men and lesbians to serve in the U.S. military, 52 percent were opposed, and 8 percent had no opinion. Only a decade later, those numbers had changed significantly. A 2004 CNN/Gallup poll found 63 percent in favor of allowing gay men and lesbians to serve and 32 percent opposed (Burrelli and Dale 2005, CRS-6). That trend has continued to the current day, with a 2008 *Washington Post*-ABC News poll finding that 75 percent of respondents approved of having lesbians and gay men who are open about their sexuality serving in the U.S. military. That approval rate held true for most subgroups, including Democrats (83 percent), Republicans (64 percent), independents (76 percent), liberals (90 percent), moderates (80 percent), conservatives (64 percent), men (66 percent), women (83 percent), Protestants (69 percent), and Catholics (83 percent). The only exception to the trend was among veterans of the armed forces—50 percent of whom approved of allowing openly gay men and lesbians to serve, although that approval rate rose to 71 percent for homosexuals who were not "out" about their sexual orientation ("3/4 Support Gays in Military Whether They 'Tell' or Don't" 2008).

In spite of these poll results, the future of the nation's "don't ask, don't tell" policy is not clear. The U.S. military establishment has shown a strong reluctance to allow openly gay men and women to serve in the armed forces, and legislators have traditionally been disinclined to oppose this position.

Same-Sex Adoption

In March 2007, researchers at The Williams Institute of the University of California at Los Angeles School of Law and the Urban Institute in Washington, D.C., published what is probably the most current and most exhaustive study of the adoption and fostering of children by same-sex couples in the United States (Gates, Badgett, Macomber, and Chambers 2007). Among the findings reported by these researchers are the following:

- More than one-third of all lesbians and one in six gay men are biological parents or parents of an adopted child.
- About 40 percent of all lesbians and more than half of all gay men have expressed the desire to have a child, leading to a total of more than 2 million gay men, lesbians, and bisexuals interested in adopting.
- At present, an estimated 65,500 adopted children are already living with gay or lesbian parents.
- Gay and lesbian parents are currently raising an estimated 4 percent of all adopted children in the United States.
- An estimated 14,100 foster children are living with lesbian or gay parents, accounting for about 3 percent of all children being fostered in the United States. (Gates, Badgett, Macomber, and Chambers 2007, Executive Summary)

For some Americans, these data may be a surprise. One of the most common pejorative statements used by anti-gay crusaders in the 1970s, for example, was that "homosexuals cannot reproduce; therefore they must recruit." This statement was used to warn parents of the danger of gay men and lesbians preying on their children (see, for example, reference to Anita Bryant's comment on this point in Mariner 2004). But evidence has long existed that many men who now identify themselves as gay (about 13 percent, by one estimate) and many women (about 28 percent) as lesbian, were once legally married to someone of the opposite sex (Carpenter and Gates 2006, Table 6, 27 and Table 7, 28). They were, thus, capable of having children

TABLE 2.1
Public Opinion on Same-Sex Adoption

Poll	Support	Oppose
Princeton Survey Research Associates (1994)[a]	29	–
Princeton Survey Research Associates (1996)[a]	36	–
Harris Interactive (1996)[b]	16/15[c]	61/65[c]
Princeton Survey Research Associates (1997)[a]	40	–
Princeton Survey Research Associates (1998)[a]	36	–
Pew Research Center for the People and the Press (1999)[d]	38	57
Harris Interactive (2000)[b]	22/21[c]	55/57[c]
Gallup (2003)[e]	49	48
Harris Interactive (2004)[b]	36/33[c]	43/45[c]
Pew Research Center for the People and the Press (3/2006)[a]	46	48
Pew Research Center for the People and the Press (7/2006)[a]	42	52

Note: Percentages may not add to 100 because of additional answers, such as "no attitude" or "no response/decline to respond."
[a]Alan Yang, "From Wrongs to Rights, 1973–1999: Public Opinion on Gay and Lesbian Americans Moves toward Equality" (Washington, DC: Policy Institute of the National Gay and Lesbian Task Force, n.d.), p. 15.
[b]Harris Interactive, "Support for Adoption by Same-Sex Couples Has Increased Substantially, But Plurality of Public Still Opposes It," http://www.harrisinteractive.com/harris_poll/index.asp?PID=455, accessed November 3, 2008.
[c]Female couple adopting/male couple adopting.
[d]Pew Research Center for the People and the Press, "Pragmatic Americans Liberal and Conservative on Social Issues," http://pewforum.org/publications/surveys/social-issues-06.pdf, p. 22, accessed November 3, 2008.
[e]Jennifer Robison (Gallup News), "Homosexual Parenting Evenly Divides Americans," http://www.gallup.com/poll/8740/Homosexual-Parenting-Evenly-Divides-Americans.aspx, accessed November 3, 2008.

within a traditional heterosexual marriage, and are reasonably likely to have done so. The more fundamental point, of course, is that absent some abnormality of the reproductive system, any man or any woman, regardless of sexual orientation, is capable of producing children.

Public opinion polls about same-sex adoption have seldom, if ever, found a majority of Americans supporting this action. In some of the earliest polls on this question, conducted in the early 1990s, the number of supporters of same-sex adoption was close to 30 percent. In the late 1990s, public support for same-sex adoptions increased somewhat, but has remained essentially constant since that time. Table 2.1 summarizes some of the polls conducted on this question.

As of early 2009, four states had specific laws prohibiting adoption by same-sex couples: Arkansas, Florida, Mississippi, and Utah. The laws in these states differ slightly from one another. Florida's law is the earliest, passed in 1977, shortly after the brouhaha raised by repeal of the Dade County ordinance banning discrimination against lesbians and gay men. That law banned adoption by "any homosexual person," whom the state later defined as "anyone known to engage in current, voluntary homosexual activity" (*Florida Department of Health and Rehabilitation. Services. v. Cox.* 1993). In 2008, the state legislature somewhat simplified that prohibition in a revised article on adoption that reads: "No person eligible to adopt under this statute may adopt if that person is a homosexual" (Florida Senate 2008). The Mississippi law states simply that: "Adoption by couples of the same gender is prohibited" (Mississippi Code of 1972, as amended 2008). Utah's version of the prohibition reads that: "A child may not be adopted by a person who is cohabiting in a relationship that is not a legally valid and binding marriage under the laws of this state" (Utah State Legislature 2008). Arkansas' law was approved by voters on November 4, 2008, by a vote of 57 percent to 43 percent. The measure (Initiative 1) had been placed on the ballot in response to a ruling of the Arkansas Supreme Court invalidating the state's earlier ban on same-sex adoption (see following discussion). The vast majority of states have either expressly permitted same-sex adoption under some circumstances or have not yet adopted legislation clarifying the status of same-sex adoptions. (For a summary of state adoption laws, see Human Rights Campaign 2008 and Lambda Legal 2008).

A number of arguments have been presented in support of same-sex adoption. Perhaps the most fundamental argument may be that many same-sex couples wish to adopt children and are able to provide them with stable homes and families. In addition, same-sex adoptions are needed because there are so many children in the United States and the rest of the world waiting to be adopted. According to the most recent statistics available, there were about 510,000 children in foster care in the United States as of September 30, 2006. Of this number, about 129,000 children were considered "adoptable," that is, parental rights had been terminated and no other options for unification with family members were available. On average, those children had been in foster care for just over two years (28.9 months). They ranged in age from infants to adults 20 years of age (U.S. Department of Health and Human Services. Administration for Children & Families 2008). The number of heterosexual couples qualified to adopt these foster children appears to be very small. Although current data are sparse, earlier research suggests that there may be only one qualified heterosexual couple for six available foster children (Petit and Curtis 1997, 72, 124).

The debate over the adoption of children by same-sex couples is one that involves both sloganeering and reliance on scientific data. Opponents of same-sex adoption argue that the primary purpose of adoption is to meet the needs of children, not the needs of adopting adults. They believe that children do not grow up normally unless they live in a home with one mother and one father; same-sex couples cannot, of course, provide that setting. A typical description of this position is available in publications of the organization Focus on the Family (FOF). FOF claims that its reason for existence is "to spread the Gospel of Jesus Christ through a practical outreach to homes" (Focus on the Family 2008a). In one of its policy statements about same-sex adoption, FOF writer Kristin Darr says that:

> Evidence shows that for proper child development to occur, children should have daily access to the different and complementary ways that mothers and fathers parent. Mothers and fathers have distinct styles of interacting with others, unique ways of playing with children, different styles of communication, distinct means of showing children care and affection, and unique ways of behaving in general. These differences teach children crucial lessons and better equip them with life skills. In light of the unique contributions made by the mother and the father, it is no wonder that children with a married mom and dad are much less likely to live in poverty and to suffer from depression and much more likely to do well in school and to experience future relationship success. In fact, children do best in every important measure when raised by two married, biological parents. (Darr 2008; footnotes omitted)

Darr documents these claims with references to a number of sources that review the scientific evidence regarding the effects of same-sex adoptions on children. One such source is an "issue analysis" published by FOF entitled "Why Children Need Father-Love and Mother-Love" by Glenn T. Stanton. Stanton is director of Global Family Formation Studies at Focus on the Family, with a master's degree in interdisciplinary humanities with an emphasis in philosophy, history, and religion (Focus on the Family 2008b). Stanton cites *Psychology Today, USA Today*, a number of popular books on parenting, and a small number of scholarly journals to support his claims that men and women bring differing skills and attitudes to a family that are not available in a single-gender family. These skills include differing methods of parenting, differing methods of playing, differing methods of communication, and differing ways of preparing children for the world. In addition, fathers are able to introduce children to the world of men, and mothers to the world of women. Finally, fathers (but not mothers) are the conduit through which children are introduced to the world of work (Stanton 2008).

Proponents of same-sex adoption also look to scientific studies to support their views on the issue. In 2004, for example, the Council of Representatives of the American Psychological Association (APA) adopted a resolution supporting the right of same-sex couples to adopt children. The resolution listed a number of reasons raised by opponents of same-sex adoption for their stand and explained why each of these reasons lacked scientific standing. It pointed out that:

- Homosexual behavior itself is not a mental disorder and there is no evidence that same-sex attraction impairs psychological functioning in any way.
- No scientific evidence exists to support the argument that gay men and lesbians are unfit to be parents.
- Lesbians and heterosexual women do not differ from the way they function as members of a family or in the raising of children.
- Some studies suggest that gay and lesbian couples may actually be better parents than heterosexual couples matched for a number of characteristics.
- Children raised by same-sex couples develop sexual identities and gender identities in essentially the same way as those raised by opposite-sex parents. In other words, children raised by same-sex couples are no more likely to become gay or lesbian than are children raised by heterosexual couples.
- Research has found no differences in personality development or social adjustment among children raised in same-sex families and children raised in opposite-sex homes.

- There is no scientific evidence that children raised in same-sex families are more likely to experience abuse than are those raised in heterosexual families. (American Psychological Association Council of Representatives 2004).

Based on its findings, the APA Council of Representatives concluded its resolution with seven "Whereas" statements and six "Therefore Be It Resolved" statements that included the following:

WHEREAS There is no scientific evidence that parenting effectiveness is related to parental sexual orientation: lesbian and gay parents are as likely as heterosexual parents to provide supportive and healthy environments for their children;

WHEREAS Research has shown that the adjustment, development, and psychological well-being of children is unrelated to parental sexual orientation and that the children of lesbian and gay parents are as likely as those of heterosexual parents to flourish; . . .

THEREFORE BE IT RESOLVED That the APA opposes any discrimination based on sexual orientation in matters of adoption, child custody and visitation, foster care, and reproductive health services;

THEREFORE BE IT FURTHER RESOLVED That the APA believes that children reared by a same-sex couple benefit from legal ties to each parent;

THEREFORE BE IT FURTHER RESOLVED That the APA supports the protection of parent-child relationships through the legalization of joint adoptions and second parent adoptions of children being reared by same-sex couples.[endnotes omitted] (American Psychological Association. Council of Representatives 2004)

Perhaps the most comprehensive review of scientific research on same-sex adoption is that reported in a 2005 publication of the American Psychological Association, *Lesbian and Gay Parenting* (Committee on Lesbian, Gay, and Bisexual Concerns; Committee on Children, Youth, and Families; Committee on Women in Psychology 2005). That report reviewed 107 studies dealing with all aspects of same-sex adoptions. The authors of the report concluded that there is no evidence to suggest that lesbian women or gay men are unfit to be parents or that psychosocial development among children of lesbian women or gay men is compromised relative to that among offspring of heterosexual parents. Not a single study has found children of lesbian or gay parents to be disadvantaged in any significant respect relative to children of heterosexual parents. Indeed, the evidence to date suggests that home environments provided by lesbian and gay parents are as likely as those provided by heterosexual parents to support and enable children's psychosocial growth. It should be acknowledged that research on lesbian and gay parents and their children, though no longer new, is still limited in extent. Although studies of gay fathers and their children have been conducted, less is known about children of gay fathers than about children of lesbian mothers. Although studies of adolescent and young adult offspring of lesbian and gay parents are available, relatively few studies have focused on the offspring of lesbian or gay parents during adolescence or adulthood. Although more diverse samples have been included in recent studies, many sources of heterogeneity have yet to be systematically investigated. Although two longitudinal studies have been reported, longitudinal studies that follow lesbian- and gay-parent families over time are still needed. Thus, although a considerable amount of information is available, additional research would further our understanding of lesbian and gay parents and their children [citations omitted] (Committee on Lesbian, Gay, and Bisexual Concerns; Committee on Children, Youth, and Families; Committee on Women in Psychology 2005).

A number of professional associations have joined the APA in supporting the principle of same-sex adoptions, including the American Academy of Child and Adolescent Psychiatry, American Academy of Pediatrics, American Bar Association, American Medical Association, American Psychoanalytic Association, Child Welfare League of America, National Adoption Center, National Association of Social Workers, and North American Council on Adoptable Children (Belge 2008). In some cases, these organizations may simply include sexual orientation among the categories that are acceptable for adoptive parents (National Adoption Center 2008). In other cases, an organization or association may present a position paper stating and explaining its support of same-sex adoption. For example, the

Committee on Psychosocial Aspects of Child and Family Health of the American Academy of Pediatrics (AAP) adopted a policy statement in 2002 supporting the right of same-sex couples to adopt children. The main thrust of the policy statement was that:

> Children who are born to or adopted by 1 member of a same-sex couple deserve the security of 2 legally recognized parents. Therefore, the American Academy of Pediatrics supports legislative and legal efforts to provide the possibility of adoption of the child by the second parent or coparent in these families.
>
> Children deserve to know that their relationships with both of their parents are stable and legally recognized. This applies to all children, whether their parents are of the same or opposite sex. The American Academy of Pediatrics recognizes that a considerable body of professional literature provides evidence that children with parents who are homosexual can have the same advantages and the same expectations for health, adjustment, and development as can children whose parents are heterosexual. When 2 adults participate in parenting a child, they and the child deserve the serenity that comes with legal recognition. [endnotes omitted] (Committee on Psychosocial Aspects of Child and Family Health 2002)

The release of policy statements like those from the APA and AAP cited earlier commonly elicits vigorous responses from groups opposed to same-sex adoption. For example, the AAP policy statement led to James Dobson, president of Focus on Family, to reply that the association's stand was "NOT supported by the research." Dobson presented his own case against same-sex adoption by citing a survey conducted by Robert Lerner and Althea Nagai, individuals he identified as being "professionals in the field of quantitative analysis" (Dobson 2002; Lerner and Nagai are currently listed as resident fellows at the Center for Equal Opportunity, a conservative think tank in Falls Church, Virginia). Dobson said that Lerner and Nagai criticized existing studies on same-sex adoption because they were all methodologically flawed. Dobson concluded his note on the subject by repeating essentially the same arguments that have traditionally been presented by opponents of same-sex adoption, namely that children adopted by same-sex couples are more likely to experience gender and sexual confusion; such children are less healthy, physically and mentally, commit more crimes, do less well academically, and experience more poverty than children raised in heterosexual homes; and they suffer from not having both a father and mother in the home (Dobson 2002).

These back-and-forth arguments as to what science actually has to say about same-sex adoptions can become confusing for the layperson. In 2006, a spokesperson for the Arizona American Civil Liberties Union attempted to summarize the history of this dispute. He reviewed the American Psychological Association's first statement about same-sex adoption in 1995, and the responses and counterresponses offered to that statement. His own conclusion about this debate was:

> Essentially, the attack on decades of research of same-sex parenting can be seen as part of the overall package currently being distributed by the religious right that aims to confuse and muddy the terms over research outcomes that are not in sync with specific religious ideology. Most lay people do not have a background in research so when someone like Redding [a researcher cited in the article] throws out terms like "small sample sizes, non-representative and self-selected samples" general audiences may be taken in by what is basically scientific jargon. A close reading of Redding's critique, however, reveals that his argument has little substance as it obscures facts and distorts principles: it accomplishes the very strategy that he accuses other researchers of utilizing. (Lewellen 2006)

Attitudes about same-sex adoption appear to be in flux in the United States today. In general, state laws tend to be somewhat ambiguous on the subject, and the general public appears to be rather evenly divided on the acceptability of same-sex adoption. One trend does appear to be a greater willingness on the part of courts to accept the validity of same-sex adoption. In 2005, for example, Judge Robin J. Cauthron of the U.S. District Court for the Western District of Oklahoma struck down a 2004 amendment to the state constitution of Oklahoma banning the adoption of a child by a same-sex couple. The judge wrote that the amendment "targets an unpopular group and singles them out for disparate treatment," and that action "violates the Equal

Protection Clause of the Constitution and must be set aside" (*Finstuen, et al. v. Drew Edmondson, et al.* 2005).

Faced with the question of same-sex adoption in 2006, the supreme court of Arkansas reached a similar decision. It struck down an administrative rule promulgated by the Arkansas Child Welfare Agency Review Board in 1999 that banned the adoption of children by same-sex couples. The court reviewed and approved a set of 47 scientific propositions about same-sex couples, gay men, and lesbians, earlier accepted by a lower circuit court. Those propositions included statements such as:

- Being raised by gay parents does not increase the risk of problems in adjustment for children.
- Being raised by gay parents does not increase the risk of psychological problems for children.
- Being raised by gay parents does not increase the risk of behavioral problems.
- Being raised by gay parents does not prevent children from forming healthy relationships with their peers or others.

TABLE 2.2
Attitudes of Americans with Regard to Same-Sex Marriage

Date of Poll	Favor	Oppose	Unsure/No Response
January 1996	27	65	8
March 2001	35	57	8
July 2003	38	53	9
October 2003	30	58	12
November 2003	30	62	8
February 2004	30	63	7
March 2004	32	59	9
August 2004	29	60	11
December 2004	32	61	7
July 2005	36	53	11
March 2006	39	51	10
June 2006	33	55	12
July 2006	35	56	9
August 2007	36	55	9
May 2008	38	49	13

Source: Pew Forum on Religion and Public Life, "A Stable Majority: Most Americans Still Oppose Same-Sex Marriage," 2008, http://pewforum.org/docs/?DocID=290, accessed November 5, 2008; Pew Research Center for the People and the Press, "May Political/Believability Survey," 2008, http://people-press.org/reports/questionnaires/425.pdf, accessed November 5, 2008; PollingReport.com, "Law and Civil Rights," 2008, http://www.pollingreport.com/civil.htm, accessed November 5, 2008.

- Being raised by gay parents does not cause academic problems.
- Being raised by gay parents does not cause gender identity problems.
- Children of lesbian or gay parents are equivalently adjusted to children of heterosexual parents.
- There is no factual basis for making the statement that heterosexual parents might be better able to guide their children through adolescence than gay parents.
- There is no factual basis for making the statement that the sexual orientation of a parent or foster parent can predict children's adjustment.
- There is no factual basis for making the statement that being raised by lesbian or gay parents has a negative effect on children's adjustment.
- There is no evidence that gay people, as a group, are more likely to engage in domestic violence than heterosexuals.
- There is no evidence that gay people, as a group, are more likely to sexually abuse children than heterosexuals. (*Department of Human Services and Child Welfare Agency Review Board v. Howard, et al.* 2006)

(Largely in response to this ruling, an initiative vote was held in Arkansas on November 4, 2008, attempting to change the state constitution to ban the adoption of children by same-sex couples. The initiative was approved by voters by a wide margin.)

Same-Sex Marriage

Probably the most contentious issue involving the civil rights of lesbians and gay men in recent years has been that of same-sex marriage. Polling organizations have been asking Americans for over a decade about their attitudes about same-sex marriage. These polls often focus on attitudes among special groups of individuals, such as residents of a single state or region, members of religious organizations, students, and members of professional organizations. (For a summary of many of these polls, see ReligiousTolerance.org 2008a.) In general, national polls tend to show very little change in the percentage of Americans who favor allowing lesbians and gay men to marry, and a correspondingly slow decrease in those who oppose same-sex marriage. Table 2.2 shows the changes over time in a series of polls taken by the Pew Research Center for the People & the Press.

Other polling organizations have found similar trends. The Gallup organization, for example, has conducted more than a dozen polls since 1996 on this topic and found that the percentage of respondents favoring same-sex marriage has fluctuated very slightly above and below about 30 percent, with the highest and lowest levels of support all falling with the polls' margin of error (PollingReport.com 2008).

Interestingly enough, Americans seem to be willing to allow gay men and lesbians to enter into a legal marriage-like relationship that is not called a "marriage." In the United States, such relationships have been called domestic partnerships or civil unions. In states where such options exist, same-sex couples have essentially all of the legal rights as do heterosexual married couples. About the only difference between a domestic partnership or a civil union and a legal marriage is the name given to the legal entity. When Americans are asked if they approve of domestic partnerships or civil unions, they tend to respond significantly more favorably than they do for same-sex marriages. For example, the Pew Research Center has asked respondents in their surveys the following question: "Do you strongly favor, favor, oppose, or strongly oppose allowing gay and lesbian couples to enter into legal agreements with each other that would give them many of the same rights as married couples?" Presented with this option, respondents consistently say they support such arrangements at a rate 10 to 15 percentage points higher than they do for a corresponding question on same-sex marriage. Other polling organizations have found a similar trend when they offer respondents a question on domestic partnerships and civil unions (PollingReport.com 2008).

Legal Status of Same-Sex Relationships

The first state having to deal with the issue of same-sex relationships was Hawaii. In 1991, three same-sex couples sued the state for refusing to grant them marriage licenses, saying that the state's action amounted to illegal discrimination (a case ultimately known as *Baehr v. Lewin*). The trial court found in favor of the defendants, and the plaintiffs then appealed that ruling to the Hawaii Supreme Court. On May 27, 1993, that court remanded the case to the original court, saying that it had erred in not considering the possibility that the defendants' constitutional rights may have been abridged by the state's refusal to issue a marriage license. The case then passed to the First Circuit Court for the State of Hawaii, which issued its ruling on December 3, 1996. In that ruling, the court said that the HRS 572–1, the law governing the issuance of marriage licenses, was unconstitutional because it violated the equal protection clause of Article I, Section 5 of Hawaii's constitution (*Baehr v. Miike* 1996).

At that point, it was clear to all legal observers that the state of Hawaii could not refuse to issue marriage licenses to same-sex couples under existing constitutional provisions. As a result, the state legislature offered an amendment to the state constitution to be voted on at the general election in November 1998. That amendment restricted marriage in Hawaii to one man and one woman. The amendment passed by a wide margin and became part of the state constitution. When an appeal of the circuit court's ruling in *Baehr v. Lewin* reached the Hawaii Supreme Court in 1999, that court declined to hear the appeal because adoption of the constitutional amendment had rendered the issue moot. (In recognition of the issues raised by the defendants in *Baehr v. Lewin*, the Hawaii legislature also passed a bill creating a marriage-like status called a *reciprocal beneficiary relationship*. Similar to a civil union or a domestic partnership, a reciprocal beneficiary relationship gives to same-sex couples some of the legal rights enjoyed by opposite-sex couples, including inheritance rights, the right to make health care decisions, health insurance and pension benefits for state workers, and the right to own property jointly (State of Hawaii Department of Health 2008).

The next state to deal with same-sex marriage was Vermont. In December 1999, the Vermont Supreme Court ruled that denial of marriage benefits to same-sex couples was unconstitutional under the state constitution. It suggested that the legislature had to create some type of entity that remedied this situation. It did not specifically require the state to issue marriage licenses to same-sex couples, but it did insist on some type of equal treatment for them.

After a long and contentious debate, the state legislature created a new marriage-like category that it called a *civil union*.

Two people joined in a civil union have all the rights and responsibilities of any married couple in the state, except that their relationship has a different name. As of June 2008, more than 1,490 couples had formed civil unions in the state. Those civil unions are not recognized in other states, and their dissolution may present some serious problems for the partners involved (Office of the Vermont Secretary of State 2008). The status of civil unions in Vermont became moot in April 2009, however, when the state legislature adopted legislation, over the veto of Republican governor Jim Douglas, legalizing same-sex marriage in the state. As of early 2009, Connecticut, New Hampshire, and New Jersey had also adopted laws establishing entities known as civil unions (although Connecticut's law also became moot with the state supreme court's subsequent ruling on same-sex marriage; see following discussion).

A second type of marriage-like arrangement for same-sex couples is known as a *domestic partnership*. The first governmental body to create a domestic partnership option for same-sex couples was the District of Columbia in 1992. However, the U.S. Congress, which controls funding for the district, refused to authorize funds to implement this program until 2002. Since that time, the district program has slowly expanded, adding an ever-increasing array of benefits for same-sex couples (DC Department of Health 2008). California became the first state to create a domestic partnership option in 1999, followed by Oregon in 2007 (effective in 2008). There are essentially no substantive differences between civil unions and domestic partnerships, except for the name by which they are called.

The most important breakthrough in the debate over same-sex marriage came in November 2003 when the supreme judicial court of Massachusetts ruled that it was unconstitutional under the state constitution for Massachusetts to prohibit same-sex couples from civil marriages. The Massachusetts legislature then asked the court for an advisory opinion as to whether the creation of a civil union or domestic partnership category would satisfy the conditions of constitutional guarantees. It asked the court:

> Does Senate, No. 2175, which prohibits same-sex couples from entering into marriage but allows them to form civil unions with all "benefits, protections, rights and responsibilities" of marriage, comply with the

equal protection and due process requirements of the Constitution of the Commonwealth and articles 1, 6, 7, 10, 12 and 16 of the Declaration of Rights? (Massachusetts Supreme Judicial Court 2004)

After a lengthy analysis of the legal issues involved, the court answered that question, "No." It said:

We are of the opinion that Senate No. 2175 violates the equal protection and due process requirements of the Constitution of the Commonwealth and the Massachusetts Declaration of Rights . . . The bill maintains an unconstitutional, inferior, and discriminatory status for same-sex couples, and the bill's remaining provisions are too entwined with this purpose to stand independently. (Massachusetts Supreme Judicial Court 2004)

For three years after the court's decision, opponents of same-sex marriage, led by the Roman Catholic Church in Massachusetts, attempted to have the state constitution amended to ban marriage between two men or two women. Partly because of the complex procedure required for amending the constitution, those efforts failed. Under the provisions of that process, efforts to amend the state constitution cannot be successful until the year 2012 at the earliest (ReligiousTolerance.org 2008b; see especially page for year 2007).

The second state to overturn a ban on same-sex marriage was California. On May 15, 2008, the state's supreme court ruled in a 4-to-3 decision that the state's constitution guaranteed the same substantive constitutional rights as opposite-sex couples to choose one's life partner and enter with that person into a committed, officially recognized, and protected family relationship that enjoys all of the constitutionally based incidents of marriage (Supreme Court of California 2008).

Opponents to the court's decision immediately put into action an effort to amend the state's constitution to ban same-sex marriage. That effort appeared on the November 4, 2008, general election as Proposition 8. The proposition passed by a vote of 52 percent to 48 percent. (On the same day, voters in Florida and Arizona also passed bans on same-sex marriage.) Exit polls indicated that the vote was very close among almost every racial, ethnic, and gender group with the exception of black women, who voted in favor of the proposal 74 percent to 26 percent (CNN.com 2008). As of early 2009, the status of more than 18,000 same-sex couples who had been married between the supreme court's May 15 decision and the November 4 vote had not been determined.

The third state to embrace same-sex marriage was Connecticut, whose supreme court ruled in a 4-to-3 decision on October 10, 2008, that the state's existing ban on same-sex marriage was unconstitutional, and that same-sex couples were entitled by the state's constitution to exactly all the same rights as those accorded opposite-sex couples (Connecticut Supreme Court 2008). That decision came as the result of a suit filed in August 2004 by Gay and Lesbian Advocates and Defenders (GLAD), a nonprofit legal rights organization that works to end discrimination based on sexual orientation.

A new issue with which the Connecticut court had to deal was the fact that during the time the GLAD case was working its way through the courts, the Connecticut legislature had approved civil unions for same-sex couples. At one point, a trial court ruled that the availability of civil unions invalidated the GLAD claims because same-sex couples now had precisely the same legal rights in the state as did opposite-sex couples. In its decision, the supreme court disagreed. It said:

> We do not see how the recently created legal entity of civil union possibly can embody the same status as an institution of such long-standing and overriding societal importance as marriage. If proof of this obvious fact were necessary, it would suffice to point out that the vast majority of heterosexual couples would be unwilling to give up their constitutionally protected right to marry in exchange for the bundle of legal rights that the legislature has denominated a civil union. (Connecticut Supreme Court 2008)

The court's decision came too late to permit opponents to place an initiative petition on the November 4, 2008, general election ballot, as had occurred in California. Instead, they suggested that passage of Proposition 1, calling for a new state constitutional convention, might provide the opportunity to add a ban on same-sex marriage to a new constitution. That proposition failed, however, by a vote of 59 percent to 41 percent (Keating 2008).

Following the general election of November 2008, the status of same-sex marriages in the United States was as follows:

- 41 states have some type of statute banning same-sex marriage;
- 30 states have constitutional amendments banning same-sex marriage;
- 5 states—Massachusetts, New Jersey, New Mexico, New York, and Rhode Island—have neither statutory nor constitutional bans on same-sex marriage. (National Conference of State Legislatures 2008)

Federal Actions

Opponents of same-sex marriage have been concerned for over a decade that state legislatures and courts might soon begin to recognize the legality of same-sex marriages and that other states would be required to acknowledge the validity of those marriages. The latter concern rests in the so-called Full Faith and Credit Clause of the U.S. Constitution (Article IV, Section 1), which says: "Full Faith and Credit shall be given in each State to the public Acts, Records, and judicial Proceedings of every other State. And the Congress may by general Laws prescribe the Manner in which such Acts, Records and Proceedings shall be proved, and the Effect thereof."

In order to clarify the federal government's stand on same-sex marriage and its status under the Full Faith and Credit Clause, the U.S. Congress passed and President Bill Clinton signed the Defense of Marriage Act (DOMA) in 1996. That act contained two major provisions. One stated that the federal government was not required to acknowledge the legality of any type of same-sex relationship, even if it had been approved by one or more of the states. The second provision specifically abnegated any application of the Full Faith and Credit Clause for such laws—that is, no state would be required to accept the validity of a same-sex marriage, civil union, domestic partnership, or other entity accepted by another state (the act is codified in 1 U.S.C. § 7 and 28 U.S.C. § 1738C).

Since passage of DOMA, opponents of same-sex marriage have been working to strengthen federal provisions against that possibility. They have been working for the adoption of an amendment to the U.S. Constitution that would define marriage as a legal relationship between one man and one woman. A resolution to that effect has been introduced into the U.S. Congress every year since 2002, except for 2007. The text of these resolutions has differed very little. The 2003 version, for example, said:

> Marriage in the United States shall consist only of the union of a man and a woman. Neither this Constitution or the constitution of any State, nor state or federal law, shall be construed to require that marital status or the legal incidents thereof be conferred upon unmarried couples or groups. (Library of Congress [Thomas] 2008)

In each year that it has been considered, the resolution has received a majority vote in the House of Representatives and either a small majority or a tie in the Senate. Since a two-thirds vote is required in both houses to adopt resolutions related to amending the Constitution, the proposal has, as yet, proceeded no further.

Pros and Cons of Same-Sex Marriage

Proponents of same-sex marriage often begin their arguments with what might appear to be a simple premise. In the United States, marriage is a civil act that is conducted within state and local laws. If one is asked to prove in a court of law that one is married, for example, the evidence required is usually a license issued by a state, county, or local governmental unit (USLegal 2008). Without question, many people choose to place marriage within a religious tradition, conducting a church wedding; having the blessing of a minister, rabbit, priest, or imam; and/or including other ceremonies with religious roots. But those religious connections are extraneous to the civil contract. If such is the legal status of a marriage, then, proponents ask, why should a marriage license not also be available to two people of the same sex, just as it is to people of the opposite sex.

Certainly, marriage has involved a single man and a single woman in most cultures at most times in history. But other arrangements have been sanctioned in some cultures at some times. Marriages between members of the same sex have, under some circumstances, been sanctioned even by the Roman

Catholic Church (Boswell 1994). Many people have no problem in acknowledging the essential role that religion plays in many marriages. But they dispute the contention that religious beliefs should define the conditions under which marriage should be allowed in the United States today.

Proponents of same-sex marriage also argue that excluding gay men and lesbians from entering into a marriage contract is a clear form of discrimination. People who are legally married in the United States receive a great many economic and social benefits from their status. A 1997 report by the General Accounting Office (GAO; now the U.S. Government Accountability Office) found that, at the time, heterosexual couples received 1,049 special federal benefits by virtue of their being legally married, benefits that are not available to unmarried individuals or couples (United States General Accounting Office 1997). These benefits cover a wide range of categories, including Social Security, Medicare, Medicaid, and related programs; housing; food stamps; veterans' benefits; taxation; federal civilian and military service benefits; employment benefits; immigration, naturalization, and alien status; trade, commerce, and intellectual property; financial disclosure and conflict of interest; crimes and family violence; loans, guarantees, and payments in agriculture; and federal natural resources and related laws. By denying lesbians and gay men the right to marry, they are excluded from having those benefits on no basis other than their sexual orientation.

Same-sex marriages also tend to encourage the establishment of stable families in contrast to shifting, short-term alliances. This argument is particularly ironic for those people who remember the early days of gay liberation. At the time, critics of gay men and lesbians argued that such individuals were sexually promiscuous and unable to "settle down" into a heterosexual-style stable relationship with another individual. Now, three decades later, the same groups and individuals who were making that argument in the 1960s and 1970s are suggesting that lesbians and gay men not be allowed to enter into the one institution designed to solidify relationships among individuals—civil marriage.

Opponents to same-sex marriage often begin their case with the fundamental view that they (and many other Americans) regard homosexuality as a sin and that society should not validate sinful behavior by allowing sinners to have access to civil marriage. They say that allowing same-sex marriage would be an insult to their religious beliefs. It is not clear from this argument as to whether or what kinds of sinners—adulterers or felons, for example—should also be prohibited from marrying, although most laws now in effect do not carry such restrictions.

One of the most commonly heard arguments against same-sex marriage is that the primary purpose of marriage is procreation. Thus, lesbians and gay men should not be allowed to marry because they cannot or will not produce children. One flaw in this argument is that it is not also applied to opposite-sex couples who, for whatever reason cannot or choose not to have children. The implication of the argument is that all couples, homosexual or heterosexual, should have to pass some type of test to see whether they plan to and are able to have children. If they fail either of these tests, they would then not be eligible for a civil marriage certificate.

Opponents of same-sex marriage also believe that marriages among lesbians and gay men would damage or destroy the traditional institution of marriage. Again, it is not entirely clear how the marriage of two men or two women must or even might have deleterious effects on heterosexual marriages or the families on which they are based.

Concerns about same-sex marriage may also be based on the "slippery-slope" factor. The term *slippery slope* refers to the fact that some action may lead to other actions that cause more damage than the original action itself. For example, critics worry that allowing two men or two women to marry might eventually lead to the relaxation of marriage laws that would permit a man and a goat, a woman and monkey, or two men and three women to enter into a marriage. Proponents of same-sex marriage generally do not have a good response to this argument since, of course, such arrangements might conceivably be possible at some time in the future. They do point out that there do not appear to have been many requests for such arrangements in the past, however.

Those opposed to same-sex marriage tend to be exasperated when gay men and lesbians point to the antimiscegenation laws that survived in the United States until 1967, when they were declared unconstitutional by the U.S. Supreme Court. (Antimiscegenation laws prohibit marriage between two individuals of different races.) Proponents of same-sex marriage argue that their campaign corresponds to the long efforts to rid the United States of similarly discriminatory antimiscegenation laws. Critics of that argument point out that members of ethnic or racial groups are discriminated against on the basis of genetic characteristics (such as skin color) over which they have no control, while gay men and lesbians have *chosen* a particular type of sexual lifestyle. The question remains whether a discriminatory policy (such as banning same-sex couples from marrying) is valid, no matter whether it is based on predetermined or chosen factors.

Second-Class Citizens, Still?

In the fall of 2008, U.S. District Court Judge Thelton Henderson ordered the state of California to explain how and when it was going to pay $250 million to fix medical care problems in state prisons. That payment would have been only the first step in about $8 billion that Judge Henderson said the state was obligated to pay to solve this problem. Judge Henderson had ruled in 2005 that the medical care provided to inmates in the state's 33 prisons was so poor that it violated their rights under the Eighth Amendment to the U.S. Constitution, which prohibits cruel and unusual punishment. The state responded by indicating that the only way it could abide by Judge Henderson's order was to cut spending in other fields, such as schools, state police, and welfare programs (Warren 2005, A1).

The United States has long struggled to ensure that all citizens receive equal rights under the law. The nation has not always been successful in that effort. At one time or another, equal rights have been withheld from American citizens because of the color of their skin; the country from which they emigrated to the United States; their religious affiliation; their gender; their physical and/or mental health; and, as indicated in the previous case, their criminal status. Any number of reasons have been offered for limiting the rights of minority groups in the United States. At one time, for example, religious leaders justified the practice of slavery because of the biblical story of Ham, a character whose descendants were said to have black skins because they were inherently sinful people and, therefore, not worthy as being treated as equal before the law (Goldenburg 2003). Even into the 19th century, some white ministers were teaching that blacks did not qualify for civil rights because, as the descendants of Ham, they were genetically inferior and inherently immoral (Price 2005).

Throughout the long struggle for equal civil rights for all people, organizations and individuals who were otherwise kind, decent, considerate people were not troubled by signs that warned, "No Irish need apply"; by separate eating facilities for blacks and whites; by laws that prohibited the places where Chinese railroad workers could live; by the ban on women from the most basic right of all in a democracy, the ballot box; by laws that prohibited a man and woman from being married because of the color of their skin; and by the prevention of access to public buildings because a person was in a wheelchair. Over time, essentially all of these issues were resolved, often after long and impassioned battles lasting many decades. Today, a panoply of federal, state, and local laws, along with a host of court decisions at every level of jurisdiction, have wiped out nearly all forms of discrimination against all classes of individuals in the United States. One of the very few exceptions to that situation is the class of sexual orientation. At the dawn of the 21st century, it is still legal to deny lesbians and gay men employment, housing, access to public accommodation, an opportunity to serve in the armed forces, and the right to wed someone of the same gender and/or to adopt children. Almost certainly, the driving force behind this denial of equal civil rights is a moral judgment, namely that gay men and lesbians are sinful and, therefore, they do not deserve to have the same rights as other people. The argument is a familiar one that has been discredited in relation to most minority groups, but it still holds sway in reference to sexual orientation.

When Proposition 8, banning same-sex marriage in California, was adopted on November 4, 2008, some observers wondered if the gay rights movement had hit a roadblock, whether lesbians and gay men had gone as far as they could in the battle for equal rights (McKinley and Goodstein 2008, A1). The answer is, of course, that at this juncture no one really knows the fate of the gay and lesbian rights movement. Other civil rights movements have been characterized by periods of fits and starts, times during which progress was clearly being made and times during which the movement appeared to have come to an end.

Faced with the California ballot results (along with similar results in Florida and Arizona), some gay and lesbian activists saw some reason for hope. In all three elections, the contrast between voting patterns among young voters and older voters was clear, and often striking. In California, for example, exit polls indicated that 61 percent of voters between the ages of 18 and 29 opposed the ban on same-sex marriage, while 39 percent approved the measure. By contrast, the vote in favor of the measure among older Californians ranged from about 55 percent among those ages 30 to 64, and 61 percent for voters over the age of 65. Similar patterns held true in both Arizona and Florida, with younger voters more likely to oppose a ban on same-sex marriage, and older voters more likely to support such a ban (CNN.com 2008). Whether these results presage an evolving electorate that will be more receptive to civil rights for lesbians and gay men in the future is not yet clear. What is clear is that the debate over such issues is likely to permeate the public discourse for many years to come.

References

Adams, Stephen. 2007. "ENDA: Workplace is the Wrong Place for Sexual Politics." http://www.citizenlink.org/CLtopstories/A000005542.cfm. Accessed November 2, 2008.

Aitken, Paul. 2007. "The Appropriation of 'Gay.'" http://www.altpenis.com/penis_news/gay.shtml. Accessed November 1, 2008.

American Civil Liberties Union (ACLU ProCon.org). 2008. "Should Homosexuals Have 'Equal Protection' Rights Based on Their Sexual Orientation?" (Response of Matthew D. Staver). http://aclu.procon.org/viewanswers.asp?questionID=706. Accessed November 3, 2008.

American Psychological Association. Council of Representatives. 2004. "Resolution on Sexual Orientation, Parents, and Children." http://www.apa.org/pi/lgbc/policy/parentschildren.pdf. Accessed November 4, 2008.

Baehr v. Miike. 1996. 74 Haw. 530, 852 P.2d 44. Available online at: http://people.umass.edu/leg450/Cases%20and%20statutes/Baehr.pdf. Accessed November 5, 2008.

Barber, J. Matt. 2007. "'Gay' Conquest Spells the ENDA Reason." http://www.cwfa.org/articledisplay.asp?id=13852&department=CFI&categoryid=freedom. Accessed November 2, 2008.

Belge, Kathy. 2008. "Who Supports Lesbian and Gay Adoption?" http://lesbianlife.about.com/od/families/f/SupportAdoption.htm. Accessed November 4, 2008.

Bérubé, Alan. 1990. *Coming Out Under Fire: The History of Gay Men and Women in World War Two.* New York: The Free Press.

Boswell, John E. 1994. *Same-Sex Unions in Premodern Europe.* New York: Villard Books.

Burrelli, David F., and Charles Dale. 2005. "Homosexuals and U.S. Military Policy: Current Issues." Washington, DC: Congressional Research Service.

Carpenter, Christopher, and Gary Gates. 2006. "Gay and Lesbian Partnership: Evidence from Multiple Surveys." University of California at Los Angeles. California Center for Population Research.

"Celebration 2009: Karl Heinrich Ulrichs." http://www.angelfire.com/fl3/celebration2000/. Accessed November 1, 2008.

CNN.com. 2008. "Ballot Measures." http://www.cnn.com/ELECTION/2008/results/ballot.measures/. Accessed November 7, 2008. Click on "Exit Polls."

CNN.com. 2008. "Election Center 2008." http://www.cnn.com/ELEC TION/2008/results/polls/. Accessed November 5, 2008.

Committee on Lesbian, Gay, and Bisexual Concerns; Committee on Children, Youth, and Families; Committee on Women in Psychology. 2005. *Lesbian & Gay Parenting.* Washington, DC: American Psychological Association.

Committee on Psychosocial Aspects of Child and Family Health. 2002. "Coparent or Second-Parent Adoption by Same-Sex Parents." *Pediatrics* 109 (2): 339–340.

Connecticut Supreme Court. 2008. *Elizabeth Kerrigan et al. v. Commissioner of Public Health et al.* SC 17716. Available online at: http://www.jud.state.ct.us/external/supapp/Cases/AROcr/CR289/289CR152.pdf. Accessed November 6, 2008.

Darr, Kristin. 2008. "Adoption: Meeting the Needs of Children through Mother-Father Parenting." http://www.citizenlink.org/FOSI/bioethics/adoptionpolicy/A000007974.cfm#_ftn1. Accessed November 4, 2008.

DC Department of Health. 2008. "Vital Records Division: Domestic Partnership." http://dchealth.dc.gov/doh/cwp/view,a,3,q,573324,dohNav_GID,1787,dohNav,/33110/33120/33139/.asp#6. Accessed November 5, 2008.

Department of Human Services and Child Welfare Agency Review Board v. Howard, et al. (05–814). 2006. http://courts.state.ar.us/opinions/2006a/20060629/05-814.pdf. Accessed November 4, 2008.

DeWitt, Brian. 2007. "Over Half the Nation Will Be Covered by an Equality Law." http://www.gaypeopleschronicle.com/stories07/may/0511071.htm. Accessed November 3, 2008.

Dobson, James C. 2002. "Focus on the Family Gives Facts on Gay Adoption; Pro-Family Organization Reaffirms Importance of Traditional Family." http://www.scienceblog.com/community/older/archives/K/2/pub2294.html. Accessed November 4, 2008.

Finstuen, et al. v. Drew Edmondson, et al. (CIV-04–1152-C). 2005. Available online at: http://lawprofessors.typepad.com/family_law/files/oklahoma_adoption_ruling.pdf. Accessed November 4, 2008.

Florida Department of Health and Rehabilitation. Services. v. Cox, 627 So.2d 1210, 1215 (Fla.Dist.Ct.App.1993).

Florida Senate. 2008. "The 2008 Florida Statutes, Title VI, Chapter 63: Civil Practice and Procedure." Available online at: http://www.flsenate.gov/statutes/index.cfm?App_mode=Display_Statute&Search_String=&URL=Ch0063/SEC042.HTM&Title=-%3E2004-%3ECh0063-%3ESection%20042. Accessed November 3, 2008.

Focus on the Family. 2007. "Focus on the Family Action Applauds Bush's Decision to Veto ENDA." http://www2.focusonthefamily.com/press/pressreleases/a000000962.cfm. Accessed November 2, 2008.

Focus on the Family. 2008a. "About Focus on the Family." http://www.focusonthefamily.com/about_us.aspx. November 4, 2008.

Focus on the Family. 2008b. "Balancing Faith, Family, & Practice." http://go.family.org/images/medicalConf/mcBrochure.pdf, 11. Accessed November 4, 2008.

Gallup. 2007. "Public Favors Expansion of Hate Crime Law to Include Sexual Orientation." http://www.gallup.com/poll/27613/Public-Favors-Expansion-Hate-Crime-Law-Include-Sexual-Orientation.aspx. Accessed November 1, 2008.

Gates, Gary J., M. V. Lee Badgett, Jennifer Ehrle Macomber, and Kate Chambers. 2007. "Adoption and Foster Care by Gay and Lesbian Parents in the United States." Los Angeles: The Williams Institute, and Washington, DC: The Urban Institute. Available online at: http://www.law.ucla.edu/williamsinstitute/publications/FinalAdoptionReport.pdf. Accessed November 3, 2008.

"Gay Rights in the Military: The Pentagon's New Policy Guidelines on Homosexuals in the Military." 1993. *New York Times*, July 20. http://query.nytimes.com/gst/fullpage.html?res=9F0CE5D81F30F933A15754C0A965958260&sec=&spon=&pagewanted=all. Accessed November 2, 2008.

Gibson, Edward Lawrence. 1978. *Get Off My Ship: Ensign Berg vs. the U.S. Navy.* New York: Avon.

Goldenburg, David M. 2003. *The Curse of Ham: Race and Slavery in Early Judaism, Christianity, and Islam.* Princeton, NJ: Princeton University Press.

GovTrack.us. [n.d.] "Text of H.R. 1592: Local Law Enforcement Hate Crimes Prevention Act of 2007." http://www.govtrack.us/congress/billtext.xpd?bill=h110-1592. Accessed November 1, 2008.

Gunther, Marc. 2006. "Queer Inc.: How Corporate America Fell in Love with Gays and Lesbians. It's a Movement." *Fortune*, November 30, 93–110.

Harris Interactive, Inc. 2008. "Out & Equal: Workplace Culture Report: Survey of Workplace Attitudes, 2002–2008." [Rochester, NY]: Harris Interactive, Inc. Available online at: http://www.outandequal.org/news/headlines/documents/OE_workplace_culture_report.pdf. Accessed November 2, 2008.

Herek, Gregory M. [n.d.] "Lesbians and Gay Men in the U.S. Military: Historical Background." http://psychology.ucdavis.edu/rainbow/HTML/military_history.html. Accessed November 2, 2008.

Human Rights Campaign. 2008. "Adoption." http://www.hrc.org/issues/parenting/adoptions/adoption_laws.asp. Accessed November 3, 2008. Summarized in convenient format at Wikipedia. 2008. "LGBT Adoption." http://en.wikipedia.org/wiki/LGBT_adoption. Accessed November 3, 2008.

Kaiser Family Foundation. 2001. "Inside-OUT: A Report on the Experiences of Lesbians, Gays and Bisexuals in America and the Public's Views on Issues and Policies Related to Sexual Orientation," Chart 4. http://www.kff.org/kaiserpolls/upload/New-Surveys-on-Experiences-of-Lesbians-Gays-and-Bisexuals-and-the-Public-s-Views-Related-to-Sexual-Orientation-Chart-Pack.pdf. Accessed November 3, 2008.

Keating, Christopher. 2008. "Constitutional Convention Rejected." *Hartford Courant*. November 5. Available online at: http://www.courant.com/news/politics/hc-2conquest.artnov05,0,779871.story. Accessed November 6, 2008.

Lambda Legal. 2003. "Lambda Legal Files Lawsuit on Behalf of Couple Who Were Denied Housing in Boca Raton Because They're Gay." http://www.lambdalegal.org/news/pr/housing-apartment-couple-gay-discrimination.html. Accessed November 3, 2008.

Lambda Legal. 2008. "Overview of State Adoption Laws." http://www.lambdalegal.org/our-work/issues/marriage-relationships-family/parenting/overview-of-state-adoption.html. Accessed November 3, 2008.

Leadership Conference on Civil Rights. 2007. "Dear Member of Congress." http://prideatwork.org/files/public/documents/leg.issues/Coalition%20Sign-On%204-24-07.pdf. Accessed on November 2, 2008.

Lewellen, Denver. 2006. "Lesbian and Gay Parenting: A Research Summary." http://www.equalityarizona.org/LinkClick.aspx? fileticket= tWwVXesydHU%3D&tabid=138&mid=510. Accessed November 4, 2008.

Library of Congress. Thomas. 2008. "Proposing an Amendment to the Constitution of the United States Relating to Marriage." http:// thomas.loc.gov/cgi-bin/query/z?c108:H.J.RES.56. Accessed November 6, 2008.

Mariner, Joanne. 2004. "Anita Bryant Lives: Florida's Continuing Assault on Gay Adoption." http://writ.news.findlaw.com/mariner/ 20040202.html. Accessed November 3, 2008.

Massachusetts Supreme Judicial Court. 2004. "Opinions of the Justices to the Senate." SJC-09163. Available online at: http://news.findlaw. com/hdocs/docs/conlaw/maglmarriage20304.html. Accessed November 6, 2008.

McKinley, Jessie, and Laurie Goodstein. 2008. "Bans in 3 States on Gay Marriage." *New York Times*. November 5.

Merriam Webster's Collegiate Dictionary, 10th ed. 1994. "Gay," 483.

Mississippi Code of 1972, as amended. 2008. Section 93–17–3. Available online at: http://www.mscode.com/free/statutes/93/017/0003.htm. Accessed November 3, 2008.

National Adoption Center. 2008. "Our Policies for Providing a Free Adoption Service." http://www.adopt.org/assembled/policies.html. Accessed November 4, 2008.

National Conference of State Legislatures. 2008. "Same Sex Marriage, Civil Unions and Domestic Partnerships." http://www.ncsl.org/ programs/cyf/samesex.htm. Accessed November 6, 2008. (Updated by author.)

Nolo Press. 2008a. "Sexual Orientation Discrimination." http:// articles.directorym.net/Sexual_Orientation_Discrimination-a935917.html. Accessed November 3, 2008.

Nolo Press. 2008b. "Tenant Rights against Sexual Orientation Discrimination." http://www.nolo.com/article.cfm/pg/2/objectId/ 7126BF6B-F282-4DAF-A85B2EB809E9C827/catId/64C2C325-5 DAF-4BC8-B476140 9BA0187C3/118/304/190/ART/. Accessed November 3, 2008.

Norton, Rictor. 2008. "A Critique of Social Constructionism and Postmodern Queer Theory: The Term 'Homosexual.'" http://www. rictornorton.co.uk/social14.htm. Accessed November 1, 2008.

Office of the Vermont Secretary of State. 2008. "The Vermont Guide to Civil Unions." Montpelier: Office of the Secretary of State. Available online at: http://www.sec.state.vt.us/otherprg/civilunions/ Civil_Union_Guide.pdf. Accessed November 5, 2008.

Online Etymology Dictionary. 2008. "Gay." http://www.etymonline. com/index.php?search=gay&searchmode=none. Accessed November 1, 2008.

Out & Equal Workplace Advocates. 2008. "Out & Equal Hosts First Annual Dinner." http://www.outandequal.org/news/headlines/ GalaDinner08.asp. Accessed November 2, 2008.

Petit, Michael R., and Patrick A. Curtis. 1997. *Child Abuse and Neglect: A Look at the States, 1997 CWLA Stat Book.* Washington, DC: Child Welfare League of America. As cited in American Civil Liberties Union of Utah. 2008. "Overview of Lesbian and Gay Parenting, Adoption and Foster Care." http://www.acluutah.org/dcfsfacts.htm#3. Accessed November 3, 2008.

PollingReport.com. 2008. "Law and Civil Rights." http://www.poll ingreport.com/civil.htm. Accessed November 5, 2008.

Price, Frederick, K. C. 2005. "The Gospel of Division in the Church." http://www.black-collegian.com/issues/30thAnn/division2001-30th. shtml. Accessed November 7, 2008.

PublicEye.org. 2008. "Hate Crime Statistics, 1995–2006." http://www. publiceye.org/hate/Statistics.html. Accessed November 1, 2008. The data reported here are summarized from the annual FBI Uniform Crime Report for each year included in the chart.

Religious Tolerance. 2007a. "Comments on Bill H.R. 1592 Law by Social and Religious Conservatives." http://www.religioustolerance. org/hom_hat16.htm. Accessed November 1, 2008.

Religious Tolerance.org. 2007b. "Opposition and Misinformation about ENDA: Federal Employment Non-Discrimination Act." http://www. religioustolerance.org/hom_empl7.htm. Accessed November 2, 2008.

ReligiousTolerance.org. 2008a. "Same-sex marriages and civil unions." http://www.religioustolerance.org/hom_marp.htm. Accessed November 5, 2008.

ReligiousTolerance.org. 2008b. "Same-sex marriage; Massachusetts: Lawsuit *Goodridge v. Dep't of Public Health.*" http://www.religioustoler ance.org/hom_marm.htm#menu. Accessed November 6, 2008. See especially page for year 2007.

Religious Tolerance. [n.d.] "U.S. Hate Crimes Statistics." http://www. religioustolerance.org/hom_hat14.htm#acc. Accessed November 1, 2008.

Rimmerman, Craig A., ed. 1966. *Gay Rights, Military Wrongs.* New York: Garland Publishing, Inc.

Scott, Gavin W., Jr. 2004. "Queer Eye for the Military Guy: Will 'Don't Ask, Don't Tell' Survive in the Wake of Lawrence v. Texas?" *St. John's Law Review*, Summer, 897–932.

Servicemembers Legal Defense Network. [n.d.]a "A Guide to 'Don't Ask, Don't Tell'." http://sldn.3cdn.net/43b1d9fec919b5918b_ 1zm6bxv9l.pdf, 2. Accessed November 2, 2008.

Servicemembers Legal Defense Network. [n.d.]b "Top 10 Reasons to Repeal 'Don't Ask, Don't Tell'." http://www.sldn.org/pages/top-10-reasons-to-repeal-don't-ask-don't-tell. Accessed November 2, 2008.

Stanton, Glenn T. 2008. "Why Children Need Father-Love and Mother-Love." http://www.citizenlink.org/FOSI/marriage/A000000993.cfm. November 4, 2008.

State of Hawaii Department of Health. 2008. "About Reciprocal Beneficiary Relationships." http://hawaii.gov/health/vital-records/vital-records/reciprocal/index.html. Accessed November 5, 2008.

Supreme Court of California. 2008. "In re Marriage Cases." 43 Cal.4th 757, 79. Available online at: http://www.courtinfo.ca.gov/opinions/archive/S147999.pdf. Accessed November 6, 2008.

The Task Force. 2008. "Hate Crime Laws in the U.S." http://www.thetaskforce.org/downloads/reports/issue_maps/hate_crimes_7_08_color.pdf. Accessed November 1, 2008.

"3/4 Support Gays in Military Whether They 'Tell' or Don't." 2008. http://abcnews.go.com/images/PollingUnit/1066a5GaysinMilitary.pdf . Accessed November 2, 2008.

Traditional Values Coalition. 2007a. "Dear Friend of TVC." http://www.traditionalvalues.org/xt/tvc_supporters_09_05_07.php. Accessed November 2, 2008.

Traditional Values Coalition. 2007b. "S. 1105—The So-Called Hate Crimes Bill." http://www.traditionalvalues.org/pdf_files/S1105_Hate CrimeReport2007July18075.php. Accessed November 1, 2008.

U.S. Department of Defense. 1982. Extract From DOD Directive 1332.14—January 28, 1982. Enlisted Administrative Separations. http://dont.stanford.edu/regulations/regulation41.pdf. Accessed November 2, 2008.

U.S. Department of Health and Human Services. Administration for Children & Families. 2008. "The AFCARS Report." http://www.acf.hhs.gov/programs/cb/stats_research/afcars/tar/report14.htm. Accessed November 3, 2008.

United States General Accounting Office. 1997. "Letter to Henry J. Hyde," 2. Available online at: http://www.gao.gov/archive/1997/og97016.pdf. Accessed November 6, 2008.

USLegal. 2008. "Legal Definitions: Marriage Licenses Law & Legal Definition." http://definitions.uslegal.com/m/marriage-licenses/. Accessed November 6, 2008.

Utah State Legislature. 2008. Section 78B-6–117. Available online at: http://www.livepublish.le.state.ut.us/lpBin22/lpext.dll?f=templates& fn=main-j.htm&2.0. Accessed November 3, 2008.

Warren, Jenifer. 2005. "U.S. to Seize State Prison Health System." *Los Angeles Times*. July 1, A1; Richman, Josh. 2008. "Judge Demands $250 Million from California, Stat." *Oakland Tribune*. October 6.

Wikipedia. 2008a. "Gay." http://en.wikipedia.org/wiki/Gay# cite_note-etymonline-0. Accessed November 1, 2008.

Wikipedia. 2008b. "Homophile." http://en.wikipedia.org/wiki/ Homophile. Accessed November 1, 2008.

3

Worldwide Perspective

To the extent that Americans know much about the history of the gay and lesbian rights movement, they are likely to associate the Stonewall riots of 1969 with the beginnings of that movement. As indicated in Chapter 1, the movement in the United States actually began about two decades earlier, with the formation of the Mattachine Society and the Daughters of Bilitis in the early 1950s. But the international gay and lesbian rights movement began even earlier than that, dating to the last decade of the 19th century in Germany.

Sodomy Laws throughout History

Many countries throughout the world have had sodomy laws at one time or another in their history. The term *sodomy* is an ambiguous phrase that generally refers to any sexual act that does not result in procreation. Anal sex, oral sex, and bestiality are often regarded as forms of sodomy. The term comes from the Biblical story of Sodom and Gomorrah, in which the residents of those cities were thought to have engaged in a host of perverse sexual acts, for which the cities were destroyed (Genesis 19: 4–11). Although the sexual acts inferred by the term *sodomy* can as easily be performed by heterosexual couples as by homosexual couples, sodomy laws have often been applied more stringently against the latter (Pallone 1999, 143).

For the first 15 centuries of Western civilization, acts of sodomy were judged and punished by the Christian Church, whose view of the practice was based on Biblical teachings found in the book of Leviticus. The relevant passage in Leviticus says that "You shall not lie with a male as with a woman. It is an abomination" (Leviticus 18:22 KJV). The first secular sodomy law in the Western world was promulgated by King Henry VIII in England in 1533, when the Church of England was established as independent from the Roman Catholic Church. That law, the Buggery Act, established hanging as the penalty for sodomy. The last known case in which that penalty was assessed was 1836, and the law itself was abolished in 1861. The English government changed its mind about the legality of sodomy in 1886, recriminalizing sodomy among men in an amendment to the Offences Against the Person Act of 1885. (The law made no reference because, according to one possibly apocryphal story, Queen Victoria refused to believe that two women could or would have sexual relations with each other (Khaitan [n.d.]). The 1885 act remained in force until 1967, when the Sexual Offences Act of that year decriminalized homosexual acts.

Essentially all Western European nations had sodomy laws until almost the end of the 18th century. Then, in 1791, the revolutionary French government established after the overthrow of the monarchy adopted a new penal code that removed penalties for sodomy. In doing so, France became the first government in Western Europe to take such an action (Merrick and Ragan 1996, 82). Over the next century, most Western European nations, as well as nations in other parts of the world, abandoned sodomy laws and decriminalized sexual acts between men and, sometimes, women. Such actions were taken by Luxembourg in 1795, the Netherlands in 1811, Brazil in 1830, Portugal in 1852, Guatemala and Mexico in 1871, Japan in 1880, and Italy in 1889. Other countries waited longer to decriminalize homosexual acts. Denmark acted in 1930, Poland in 1932, Uruguay in 1934, Iceland in 1940, Switzerland in 1942, Sweden in 1944, Greece in 1951, and Thailand in 1956. Sodomy laws were declared unconstitutional in the United States in 2003 (Gay & Lesbian Archives of the Pacific Northwest 2008b).

In view of events described in the following discussion, the position of the German government with regard to sodomy laws is of special interest. Homosexual acts were first criminalized in Germany in 1871 with the passage of the so-called Paragraph 175 of the Reich Criminal Code. That law prohibited sexual acts between men and between men and animals, the penalty for which was imprisonment and possible loss of civil rights.

In October 1929, a committee of the Reichstag, the German Parliament, voted to repeal Paragraph 175, a step that never took place because of the imminent assumption of the National Socialist (Nazi) party to power in Germany. Instead, the Nazis greatly expanded the law to include not only physical acts, but also such behaviors as "looking" or "touching." Penalties for conviction under the law included commitment to a mental institution, castration, and imprisonment, often in the rapidly growing concentration camps established by the Nazis (United States Holocaust Memorial Museum 2008). By some estimates, more than 100,000 men were arrested under the expanded law, and as many as 10,000 may have died in concentration camps (United States Holocaust Memorial Museum 2008).

After World War II, Paragraph 175 remained in force in both West and East Germany. West Germany maintained the more severe form of the law, as adopted in the early 1930s, while East Germany's version of the law reverted to its original, milder form. Both laws remained in effect until 1968, in East Germany, and 1969, in West Germany, although the law was not enforced after 1957 in East Germany (Blasius 1997, 134).

Today, sodomy laws have been abolished in most first-world nations. According to Gay & Lesbian Archives of the Pacific Northwest, virtually all existing sodomy laws as of early 2009 occur in Africa, the Middle East, and Southeast Asia. In the Western Hemisphere, nations with sodomy laws include Barbados, Cuba, Grenada, Guyana, Jamaica, Nicaragua, Saint Lucia, and Trinidad and Tobago. Penalties in these countries range from imprisonment for one year (Cuba) to life (Guyana). Similarly, the severity of the punishment for acts of sodomy ranges widely in countries that have such laws, from a misdemeanor conviction in Liberia to death in Afghanistan, Iran, Mauritania, Nigeria, Pakistan, Saudi Arabia, Sudan, United Arab Emirates, and Yemen. By contrast, no sodomy laws remain in Europe, North America, or South and Central America (with the exception of Guyana, Nicaragua, and most Caribbean islands; Gay & Lesbian Archives of the Pacific Northwest 2008a).

This review suggests that the status of sodomy laws varies widely throughout the world. In many nations, sexual acts between members of the same sex are legal. In a few nations, this status does not mean that gay men and lesbians are entirely free of persecution and prosecution, however. For example, Romania repealed its sodomy laws in 2001, but same-sex acts are still punishable by a five-year prison term if they tend to cause a "public scandal." Since law enforcement officers and courts have rather wide latitude in determining "public scandal," same-sex acts in Romania can hardly be said to be entirely legal. In Greece, same-sex acts have been legal since 1951, except in the case of male prostitution, which continues to be illegal. Sweden has eliminated all restrictions on same-sex acts, with the exception of all types of prostitution (Gay & Lesbian Archives of the Pacific Northwest 2008a; see specific laws for each country listed on this page).

Hate Crimes

Violent crimes based on a person's sexual orientation are common in many parts of the world and, according to the most recent data available, are on the increase. Few countries keep statistics on hate crimes based on sexual orientation (or, for that matter, on other criteria, such as race or ethnicity). Currently, the four nations that do so are Canada, Sweden, the United Kingdom, and the United States. In addition, the Netherlands and Norway have begun to monitor hate crimes based on sexual orientation, largely in response to an increase in the rate of such crimes.

In 2008, Canada released its first official report on hate crimes, showing that 892 such crimes had been reported in 2006. About 10 percent of that number were crimes based on sexual orientation, and about half of those were of a violent nature (Dauvergne, Scrim, and Brennan 2008; click on "Tables and Charts" for data). A report by Sweden's National Council for Crime Prevention, also released in 2008, found a total of just over 3,500 such crimes for the year 2007, about one-fifth (725) were classified as crimes based on sexual orientation (National Council for Crime Prevention 2008). In the United Kingdom, hate crimes based on sexual orientation are not counted separately. London's Metropolitan Police do keep such records, however, and have reported that about 1,200–1,300 such crimes have been reported in the last two years ([Metropolitan Police Authority] [n.d.]). (Data for hate crimes in the United States were reported in Chapter 1, page 40.)

In addition to governmental surveys, a number of nongovernmental organizations monitor hate crimes of all kinds, including those based on sexual orientation. In June 2008, for example, the English LGBT rights organization, Stonewall, released "Homophobic Hate Crime: The Gay British Crime Survey" (Dick 2008). Among the findings reported in that study were:

- One in five lesbians and gay men have been the victim of a hate crime within the past three years; one in eight were the victim of a hate crime within the preceding year.
- Seven of 10 victims of hate crimes did not report them to anyone, including law enforcement officials, friends, neighbors, or family.
- About 15 percent of the hate crimes against gay men and lesbians involved physical assaults.
- The rate of physical assaults against gay men and lesbians who are also people of color was about twice that for white gay men and lesbians (Dick 2008, 5).

In Germany, the gay rights organization Maneo conducted a survey in 2008 in which 40.6 percent of gay male respondents said they had experienced hate crimes based on their sexual orientation. That number was an increase over the 2006 rate of 35.5 percent. Such crimes included any action that is illegal under German law, ranging from verbal comments to serious physical assaults. Even in Berlin, widely regarded as one of the most tolerant cities in the world, 43 percent of all gay men reported being victims of hate crimes (Moore 2008).

One reason for the increase in hate crimes throughout most of Europe appears to be the increasing visibility of lesbians and gay men, especially at large public events such as gay pride marches. In its report on anti-gay hate crimes throughout the world in 2007, the nongovernmental organization Human Rights First described violence at gay pride parades—sometimes ignored by or even abetted by local police—in Bulgaria, the Czech Republic, Hungary, Moldova, Russia, and Slovenia (Human Rights First 2008a; Human Rights First 2008b).

A handful of nations around the world have hate crime laws that include sexual orientation. Those nations and the dates in which the laws were enacted are listed in Table 3.1. The wording of these laws is quite similar. In Iceland, for example, the law reads that "Anyone who does by means of ridicule,

TABLE 3.1
International Hate Crime Laws

Nation	Hate Crime Law Enacted
Andorra	2005
Australia[a]	—
Belgium	2003
Canada	2004
Croatia	2003
Denmark	1987
Estonia	2006
Finland	1995
France	2004
Germany	2005
Hungary	2004
Iceland	1996
Ireland	1989
Lithuania	2003
Luxembourg	1997
Netherlands	1993
New Zealand	2002
Norway	1981
Spain	1996
Sweden	2003
United Kingdom[b]	2005
United States[a]	—
Uruguay	2003

Source: Daniel Ottosson, "LGBT World Legal Wrap up Survey," 2006, http://typo3.lsvd.de/fileadmin/pics/Dokume
nte/Homosexualitaet/World_legal_wrap_up_survey_November2006.pdf, accessed November 8, 2008.
[a]Hate crime laws exist in some states, but there is no federal law.
[b]Law applies in England and Wales. Scotland has no such law. A hate crimes law was adopted in Northern Ireland in 2004.

calumniation, insult, threat or otherwise assault a person or group of persons on account of their nationality, colour, race, religion or sexual inclination shall be subject to fines or imprisonment for up to 2 years" [internal citations omitted]. (Article 233a 1940, as amended)

The relevant Canadian statute is found in section 718.2 of the Canadian Criminal Code. It says that, in imposing sentence, a court shall take into consideration the principle that:

> a sentence should be increased or reduced to account for any relevant aggravating or mitigating circumstances relating to the offence or the offender, and, without

limiting the generality of the foregoing, [based on] (i) evidence that the offence was motivated by bias, prejudice or hate based on race, national or ethnic origin, language, colour, religion, sex, age, mental or physical disability, sexual orientation, or any other similar factor. (Canadian Legal Information Institute 2008)

In the Spanish penal code, aggravating circumstances that can be taken into account during sentencing include, "commission of a crime for racist, antisemitic, or other types of discrimination referring to ideology, religion, or creed of the victim, ethnicity, race, or national origin to which he belongs, his sex or sexual orientation, or disease or handicap from which he suffers" (Judicial News 2008).

Concerns about hate crimes perpetrated on gay men and lesbians have now become an issue of regional interest also. In 2006, the European Parliament adopted a resolution on homophobia in Europe. That resolution contained 15 sections condemning violence based on sexual orientation, one of which called on member states to "ensure that LGBT people are protected from homophobic hate speech and violence and ensure that same-sex partners enjoy the same respect, dignity and protection as the rest of society" (European Parliament 2006; for a review of the status of hate crime legislation in Europe based on sexual orientation and gender identity, see De Schutter 2008). In 2008, the Organization of American States (OAS) made a breakthrough when it adopted a resolution that, for the first time in its history, included the words *sexual orientation* and *gender identity*. That resolution expressed concern "about acts of violence and related human rights violations committed against individuals because of their sexual orientation and gender identity." It also called for a discussion over issues of human rights, sexual orientation, and gender identity at the next general assembly of the OAS, and the development of specific programs through which the sense of this resolution could be carried out (Organization of the American States 2008).

Discrimination Based on Sexual Orientation

Concerns about discrimination against an individual on the basis of his or her sexual orientation vary widely throughout the world. In regions and nations where homosexual behavior is considered to be immoral, as one might expect, this issue simply never arises. In other parts of the world, however, efforts have been underway for at least a decade to pass legislation and take other actions that would elimination discrimination based on sexual orientation (and, more recently, on gender identity). For example, the Charter of Fundamental Rights of the European Union, adopted in 2000 states quite simply that "Any discrimination based on any ground such as sex, race, colour, ethnic or social origin, genetic features, language, religion or belief, political or any other opinion, membership of a national minority, property, birth, disability, age or sexual orientation shall be prohibited" ("Charter of Fundamental Rights of the European Union" 2000).

This philosophy of offering support for nondiscrimination based on sexual orientation has been expressed within the European Union in a number of ways. One of the most important steps occurred with the adoption of the Treaty of Amsterdam in October 1997. That treaty made a number of fundamental changes in the Treaty of the European Union, which established that body in 1992. One change included in the Treaty of Amsterdam was extension of human rights concerns beyond nationality and sex, as expressed in the original treaty, to racial or ethnic origin, religion or belief, disability, age, and sexual orientation. In an effort to put the principle of nondiscrimination based on these characteristics into practice, the European Union issued a new directive in 2000, called the Employment Equality Directive (2000/78/EC). This directive called on member states to develop legislation and programs that would prohibit discrimination in employment and training (but not other fields) based on religion or belief, disability, age, and sexual orientation (De Schutter 2008, 5).

In another step forward in 2007, the European Union established the European Union Agency for Fundamental Rights, charged with the responsibility of providing assistance and expertise to member states and other entities in accomplishing the goals set out in the Employment Equality Directive and other relevant documents (European Union Agency for Fundamental Rights 2008). One of the agency's first steps was to commission a pair of reports on "homophobia and discrimination based on sexual orientation in the Member States of the European Union" (De Schutter 2008, 5). The first of those reports, "Homophobia and Discrimination on Grounds of Sexual Orientation in the EU

Member States Part I—Legal Analysis," is perhaps the best single overview of the status of discrimination within the European Union states based on sexual orientation in a variety of areas, including employment, housing, freedom of movement, asylum protection, family reunification, freedom of assembly, criminal law (hate crimes), and transgender issues.

According to that report, seven states (Cyprus, Denmark, Greece, Italy, Latvia, Malta, and Portugal) have adopted nondiscrimination laws relating to sexual orientation only in the area of employment, as required by the Employment Equality Directive. The remaining 20 states all have laws that go beyond employment (DeSchutter 2008, 25–32). For example, Belgian law extends nondiscrimination for lesbians and gay men to "the provision of goods, facilities and services; social security and social benefits; employment in both the private and public sector; membership of or involvement in an employer's organisation or trade unions; official documents or (police) records; and access to and participation in economic, social, cultural or political activities accessible to the public." The law in Bulgaria is even more extensive. Since it applies explicitly to "the exercise of any legal right," it goes as far as any nondiscrimination law can (DeSchutter 2008, 25). Other national laws prohibit discrimination in a variety of fields, such as civil law transactions (Germany), health care (Spain), organizations and organizing (the Netherlands), and education (a number of states). In addition, at the time the report was being written, three members states— Finland, Latvia, and Sweden—were revising their statutes in such a way that nondiscrimination coverage was expected to be extended to more fields for lesbians and gay men.

The report on homophobia and discrimination ended with seven conclusions. It indicated, first, that member states were moving satisfactorily in the direction of satisfying the requirements of the Employment Equality Directive, although a few nations had not yet created specific agencies for ensuring that legislation was actually being carried out in practice. Three conclusions dealt with a problem of special significance in Europe, the movement of same-sex couples and their families across national borders. Although some progress had been made in ensuring that there were no barriers for such couples, some work remained to be done. Two other conclusions focused on the need for hate crime laws for the protection of gay men and lesbians and transgendered persons. A final conclusion called for greater research on the status of discriminatory practices in member states (DeSchutter 2008, 148–154).

One interesting new phenomenon has been the move by a few nations to include a ban on discrimination based on sexual orientation within their national constitutions. As of early 2009, five nations—Bolivia, Ecuador, Fiji, Portugal, and South Africa—had taken this step. The Bolivian constitutional amendment also includes a ban on discrimination based on gender identity, believed to be the first legislation of its kind in the world. In addition, the Supreme Court of Nepal ruled in December 2007 that discrimination based on sexual orientation violates the nation's interim constitution and directed the federal government to enact legislation that would specifically outlaw any such discrimination in the country (Amnesty International 2008). (The Nepal court decision also included the classes of gender identity [transgendered persons] and third gender, or "intersex" persons.)

The South African constitution, as an example, enshrines its protection for gay and lesbian rights in its bill of rights (Chapter 2), Section 9, Paragraph 3, which says:

> The state may not unfairly discriminate directly or indirectly against anyone on one or more grounds, including race, gender, sex, pregnancy, marital status, ethnic or social origin, colour, sexual orientation, age, disability, religion, conscience, belief, culture, language and birth. (South African Government Information 2008)

The constitution of Fiji has a similar provision. It states in its bill of rights (Chapter 4), Section 38:

> A person must not be unfairly discriminated against, directly or indirectly, on the ground of his or her:
> (a) actual or supposed personal characteristics of circumstances, including race, ethnic origin, colour, place of origin, gender, sexual orientation, birth, primary language, economic status, age or disability.... (International Constitutional Law 2008)

In the Nepal case, the Supreme Court based its decision on an analysis of Section 12 of the nation's new interim constitution, adopted in 2007. Paragraph 1 of that section says simply that "Every person shall have the right to live with dignity, and no law shall be made which provides for capital punishment" (Interim Constitution of Nepal 2007). The justices claimed in their ruling that their decision on this issue was influenced by the many international statements that had been made on the rights of all people, pointing in particular to Articles 2, 16, and 17 of the International Covenant on Civil and Political Rights (Equal Rights Trust 2008).

The International Covenant on Civil and Political Rights (ICCPR) was one of the first important statements on the civil rights of humans in nations throughout the world. It was adopted by the United Nations on December 16, 1966, and entered into force on March 23, 1976, after 35 nations had ratified the treaty. Given the early date of the treaty, it is not surprising that sexual orientation and gender identity are not specifically mentioned in the document. However, the sections on which the Nepalese Supreme Court (and other national courts) based its decision, in part, read as follows:

1. Each State Party to the present Covenant undertakes to respect and to ensure to all individuals within its territory and subject to its jurisdiction the rights recognized in the present Covenant, without distinction of any kind, such as race, colour, sex, language, religion, political or other opinion, national or social origin, property, birth or other status.
2. Where not already provided for by existing legislative or other measures, each State Party to the present Covenant undertakes to take the necessary steps, in accordance with its constitutional processes and with the provisions of the present Covenant, to adopt such laws or other measures as may be necessary to give effect to the rights recognized in the present Covenant (Office of the High Commissioner for Human Rights [n.d.], Article 2).

This principle is reiterated later in the document in somewhat different language: "Everyone shall have the right to recognition everywhere as a person before the law" (Office of the High Commissioner for Human Rights [n.d.], Article 16).

The International Covenant on Civil and Political Rights is only one of many international pronouncements dealing with discrimination on the basis of sexual orientation (and, in some cases, gender identity). Probably the oldest of these statements is the original charter of the United Nations, adopted on June 26, 1945. Like the ICCPR, this document does not mention sexual orientation specifically, although it does seem to make clear that the purpose of the relevant sections of the charter is to speak out against discrimination against humans on any basis whatsoever. Article I, Section 3, for example, says that one purpose of the United Nations is to

> achieve international co-operation in solving international problems of an economic, social, cultural, or humanitarian character, and in promoting and encouraging respect for human rights and for fundamental freedoms for all without distinction as to race, sex, language, or religion. (Charter of the United Nations. 1945, Article 1, Section 3)

Over the years, international treaties have begun to include more explicitly sexual orientation and, in some cases, gender identity, among the categories of individuals against whom discriminatory acts should be prohibited. For example, the Committee on Economic, Social and Cultural Rights of the United Nations released a report in 2000 on "Substantive Issues Arising in the Implementation of the International Covenant on Economic, Social and Cultural Rights" (E/C.12/2000/4). Section 18 of that report refers to this issue and

> proscribes any discrimination in access to health care and underlying determinants of health, as well as to means and entitlements for their procurement, on the grounds of race, colour, sex, language, religion, political or other opinion, national or social origin, property, birth, physical or mental disability, health status (including HIV/AIDS), sexual orientation and civil, political, social or other status, which has the intention or effect of nullifying or impairing the equal enjoyment or exercise of the right to health. (Committee on Economic, Social and Cultural Rights 2000)

Interestingly enough, some international groups appear to be implicitly expanding references to "sex" or "gender" in existing documents to include sexual orientation and, occasionally, gender identity (Decaux 2004). This change has resulted in the gradual inclusion of lesbians and gay men in nondiscrimination laws and regulations in an ever-expanding number of countries around the world.

Lesbians and Gay Men in the Military

The debate as to whether or not gay men and lesbians should be allowed to serve in the U.S. military has engendered an ongoing discussion as to how policies and practices in other nations of the world can provide information and guidance on the issue in the United States. In 1993, for example, Senator John W. Warner (R-Va.) asked the U.S. General Accounting Office (GAO; now the Government Accountability Office) to conduct a study to discover how other nations around the world dealt with the issue of having gay men and lesbians serve in their armed forces. In its survey of 25 nations, the GAO found that 11 countries had specific policies and regulations that prohibited gay men and lesbians from serving in the military, 11 had policies or regulations that specifically allowed gay men and lesbians to serve, and three had no specific policy or regulations one way or the other. Policies varied significantly among nations. Some countries—Belgium, France, and Israel, for example—simply allowed lesbians and gay men to serve, without any specific civil or military laws or regulations. Other countries—Chile, Greece, and Romania, for example—prohibited lesbians and gay men from serving on the basis of specific civil or military laws or regulations that banned their participation. Still other nations had a variety of policies that fit into neither of these categories. For example, Germany allowed any gay man or lesbian conscripted into service to join the armed forces, but excluded gay or lesbian volunteers from service. The Japanese military handled issues of homosexuality on a case-by-case basis (United States General Accounting Office 1993, Table 1, 5).

In the decade following the GAO report, a number of nations changed their policies to allow homosexuals to serve in the military or to broaden existing policies. As of early 2009, those nations included Austria, the Bahamas, Czech Republic, Estonia, Finland, Germany, Ireland, Lithuania, Netherlands, Norway, Slovenia, South Africa, Sweden, and Switzerland (Palm Center 2008). At that point, a number of nations still had policies prohibiting gay men and lesbians from serving in their armed services, including Argentina, Belarus, Brazil, Croatia, Greece, Hungary, Luxembourg, Peru, Poland, Portugal, Turkey, and Venezuela, and, perhaps of greatest significance, China, Russia, and the United States (Palm Center 2008).

The forces that cause nations to change their policies on gays in the military vary considerably. In some cases, a government simply decides that its earlier stance on the issue is incorrect and adopts new laws, policies, or regulations that allow (or, in a small number of cases, prohibit) gay men and lesbians from serving in the armed forces. Such was the case in the Netherlands, for example, which banned gay men and lesbians from the military until 1974. At that point, the Association of Dutch Homosexuals was able to convince the minister of defense that lesbians and gay men could serve in the Dutch army without causing harm to national security, and the government changed its policies (Konigsberg 1992, 10).

In other cases, governments may be forced to change their policies as the result of court cases. In Canada, for example, the nation's policy of prohibiting lesbians and gay men from serving in the armed forces was challenged in 1992 by Air Force Lieutenant Michelle Douglas on the grounds that the policy discriminated against her and was, therefore, unconstitutional under the Canadian Constitution. Before the case came to trial, the Canadian military decided to change its policy, and Douglas's case became moot (Bindman 2008).

The United Kingdom faced a similar situation in 1999 when the European Court of Human Rights ruled in two separate cases that the British government's policy prohibiting gay men and lesbians from serving in the armed forces violated provisions of the Convention for the Protection of Human Rights and Fundamental Freedoms (European Court of Human Rights 1999). In response to these two cases, the British government changed its policy in 2000 and began allowing lesbians and gay men to serve in all branches of its armed services (Goldhaber 2007, 44–45).

The experiences of nations around the world that allow lesbians and gay men to serve in the military are potentially instructive for lawmakers in the United States who are still confronted with that issue. Many lawmakers have expressed concern that allowing gay men and lesbians to serve in the U.S. military would have any number of dire consequences, including loss of unit morale, diminished fighting capacity, dependence of a unit on unqualified fighting personnel (i.e., gay men and lesbians), increased risks to non-gays of being approached sexually by gay men and lesbians, more attacks on lesbians and gay men, greater threat to national security because of fears of exposure by gay men and lesbians, and a general deterioration of the military's ability to carry out its missions (International Debate Education Association 2000).

Data about these concerns are available from two sources: anecdotal comments from individuals who have served in integrated units (units that include openly gay men and women) and scientific research. The first type of evidence is always somewhat suspect because one never knows if an individual's comment represents a majority view or a single person's opinion on a topic. However, most reports appear to suggest that few or none of the concerns expressed herein arise in integrated military units. In an overview of integrated military units in a number of nations, one reporter found that having gay men and lesbians as members of their fighting force was essentially a nonissue. According to a lieutenant in the Danish army, for example, the presence of lesbians and gay men in his unit is "not something you think about.... Homosexuality, we know it's legal and it's not an issue" (Konigsberg 1992, 10). A long-time member of the Dutch army expressed his view of the issue as follows: "Suppose you're on the beach in a skimpy bathing suit. The guy next to you might be gay. Does that harm your morale? Is that dangerous?" (Konigsberg 1992, 10).

Scientific surveys provide more valid and reliable data on the effects of having gay men and lesbians serving in a military unit. In 2000, researchers at the University of California conducted a study on the effects of lifting the ban on lesbians and gay men in the Canadian military in 1992. The major conclusions of that study were:

- Abolishing the ban on gays in the armed services has had no measurable effect on military performance.
- Self-identified gay men and lesbians who had served in the Canadian military since the ban had been lifted reported good working relationships with their peers with no damage to unit morale and cohesion.
- Sexual harassment against women in the military dropped 46 percent after the ban was lifted, although

some portion of this change could be explained by other factors.

- In a survey conducted in 1985, more than 60 percent of 6,500 male military personnel said that they would refuse to shower, undress, or sleep in a room with a man whom they knew to be gay. After the ban, there has been no increase in disciplinary, performance, recruitment, sexual misconduct, or resignation problems that one might associate with negative views expressed in the earlier survey.

- Of 905 cases of assault recorded in the Canadian military forces between 1992 and 1995, none could be attributed to gay bashing or any other issue related to sexual orientation (Belkin and McNichol 2000a, 2).

The authors of the report concluded their study by saying that:

The success of these steps has been borne out by all of the available evidence. An examination of all of the studies conducted in the year after the removal of the ban revealed not a single reported case of resignation, harassment, or violence because of the change in policy. Follow—up with the officials in charge of sexual harassment, sexual misconduct, and human rights complaints have reported few if any incidents related to sexual orientation. Sexual and personal harassment rates have actually decreased between 1992 and 1998, and a conflict management official has declared that he knows of no recently filed cases related to sexual orientation. CF [Canadian Forces] officials, military scholars, involved non—governmental and political leaders, and gay soldiers have all concurred that the removal of the ban has had, to their knowledge, no perceivable negative effect on the military. The issue of gay and lesbian soldiers in the Canadian Forces has all but disappeared from public and internal military debates. (Belkin and McNichol 2000b, 10)

Two other studies on the effects of integrating lesbians and gay men into fighting forces have been conducted. In one, focused on the elimination of the ban on gays in the military in Israel in 1993, the conclusions were essentially the same as those for the study of the Canadian military (Belkin and Levitt 2001, 541–565). In the second study, dealing with the integration of the Australian armed forces in 1992, the conclusions were also largely the same as those for the Canadian and Israeli studies. The authors of the study found that less than 5 percent of all complaints received by the Australian Defence Forces (ADF) involved sexual harassment, and that, at the time of the study, the only remaining issue about gays serving in the ADF concerned the extending of benefits to partners of gay men and lesbians serving in the military (Belkin and McNichol 2000b, 3).

Both anecdotal and research evidence, then, suggest that lifting the ban on lesbians and gay men in the armed forces does not necessarily lead to a collection of problems for those individuals, for fellow soldiers, or for the military itself, at least in those nations where that action has taken place. How policymakers in other nations, such as the United States, interpret and utilize that information is yet to be seen.

Same-Sex Adoption and Marriage

Patterns in the way nations treat same-sex adoption and same-sex marriage are very similar to those for other gay- and lesbian-related issues. Western European nations in general have moved forward in recognition of one or both of these rights, such that they have become a part of the legal structure of many countries. A few other non-Western countries around the world—Israel is one example—have taken similar steps. But, generally speaking, recognition of same-sex family rights is largely unheard of outside the Western world. As with other civil rights issues for lesbians and gay men, nations that regard homosexuality as immoral and sinful (which includes virtually the whole Islamic world) do not consider that gay men and lesbians have any rights in this matter any more than they do for issues of discrimination, hate crimes, and service in the military.

Same-Sex Adoption

The status of same-sex adoptions in the United States, as discussed in Chapter 2, is often ambiguous and uncertain.

Perhaps because efforts on the part of lesbians and gay men to legally adopt children are a relatively new phenomenon, the law has not yet had a chance to catch up with the disparate issues involved in such cases. That statement also applies to many nations around the world, especially those in Western Europe where a number of nations have now acknowledged the legitimacy of same-sex adoptions in one way or another.

As in the United States, one form of same-sex adoption involves the adoption by one member of a same-sex couple of a child. In a second form, a same-sex couple as a unit can adopt a child, as is the case with traditional adoptions by heterosexual couples. In a third form of adoption, one partner of a same-sex couple may adopt the biological child of his or her partner. Various countries, almost all of them in Western Europe, have adopted differing policies on same-sex adoption. Andorra, Iceland, Netherlands, South Africa, Spain, Sweden, the United Kingdom, and some parts of Australia and Canada permit same-sex couples to adopt children jointly. Meanwhile, Denmark, Germany, Israel, Norway, and some parts of Australia and Canada allow same-sex couples to adopt each other's children (Ottoson 2006, 5).

Policies on same-sex adoption sometimes arise as a result of legislative action and sometimes in response to court decisions. For example, the Icelandic Parliament unanimously approved new legislation in June 2006 granting to same-sex couples the right to adopt children (ILGA Europe 2006). (Included in the bills passed on this date was one that also granted to same-sex couples all of the rights enjoyed by married heterosexual couples.) At about the same time, the Belgian Parliament was voting on new legislation to permit same-sex couples to adopt. The lower house of Parliament passed the relevant bill in December 2005 by a vote of 77 to 62, and the upper house also approved the measure in April 2006 by a vote of 34 to 33, with two abstentions (BBC News 2006a).

The issue of same-sex adoption was apparently resolved in France not by legislative action, but as the result of a court decision. The relevant case arose when one member of a lesbian couple had a child through artificial insemination and attempted to register her partner as a parent of the child. A local court in Angers ruled that the partner had no rights with regard to the child and dismissed the case. That decision was overturned by the court of appeals, a ruling that was later confirmed by the nation's highest judicial court, the Cour de Cassation. The court ruled in 2006 that the French civil code does not forbid a single mother from sharing her parental rights "with the woman with whom she lives in a stable and continuous union, as long as the circumstances demand it and as long as the move conforms to the child's best interest" (CBS News 2006).

The status of laws on same-sex adoption in Western Europe may have become moot in January 2008 when the European Court of Human Rights ruled that laws banning adoption by same-sex couples violated Articles 8 and 14 of the European Convention on Human Rights (ECHR). The case involved an effort on the part of one member of a lesbian couple, "E.B." for purposes of the case, who wished to list her partner's name as co-parent of E.B.'s biological child. The local French authority refused that request, and E.B. appealed her case to the European Court of Human Rights. On January 22, 2008, the court ruled against the French government and in favor of E.B., saying that the government's action had violated the equal protection provisions of Articles 8 and 14 (Case of E. B. v. France [Application No. 43546/02] 2008). In principle, the court's ruling requires all signatories of the ECHR (all of the major nations of Europe) to abide by the court's decision and to make such adjustments as are necessary to bring national laws into harmony with that ruling. Within the foreseeable future, then, it may be that all or most of the nations in Europe will legally acknowledge some form of same-sex adoption procedure.

Granting rights of adoption to same-sex couples, under any circumstances whatsoever, is virtually unheard of anywhere outside of Europe. One exception is Israel. In February 2008, Attorney General Meni Mazuz announced that the Israeli government would no longer prohibit the adoption of a child by same-sex couples. He said that this decision was driven not only by the legitimate desire to provide same-sex couples with equal rights under Israeli law, but also to provide stable homes for foster children in the nation looking to be adopted (Zino 2008).

In three nations, same-sex adoption policies differ from state to state or province to province within the country: Australia, Canada, and the United States. In Canada, some form of same-sex adoption is permitted in every province except for

Alberta and in two territories, Nunavut and Northwest Territories. Its status in the Yukon is ambiguous, resulting from a 1998 decision of the legislative assembly making all territorial laws "gender neutral" (Hurley 2007).

In Australia, only two states, the Australian Capital Territory and Western Australia, permit same-sex adoption. All five other states have been considering changes in the status of same-sex adoption but, as of early 2009, none has made a change in state law. The state that has moved furthest on this issue appears to be Victoria. In March 2007, the Victorian Law Reform Commission issued a comprehensive report on assisted reproductive technology and adoption. Among the commission's many recommendations were some that dealt with same-sex adoption. It suggested, for example, that:

> The same-sex partner of the parent of a child should be able to apply to adopt the child in accordance with the same criteria that apply to opposite-sex partners.
> The Act [dealing with adoption] should otherwise be amended to recognise that some people to whom the Act applies will be married or in heterosexual de facto relationships, some will be in same-sex relationships and others will not have partners.
>
> The Adoption Act 1984 should be amended to allow the County Court to make adoption orders in favour of same-sex couples. (Victorian Law Reform Commission 2007)

In October 1997, the Dutch Parliament adopted legislation allowing same-sex couples to adopt children. Scarcely a decade later, all nations in the European Union appear poised to adopt a similar policy, although it may take some time for the necessary legislative actions to take place. Outside of Europe, there has also been some progress in allowing gay men and lesbians to adopt children, either domestically or internationally, but not on the scale of the European model. Most nations of the world, including the United States, still have no federal legislation permitting same-sex adoption, and few states within a nation have moved in this direction. It remains to be seen whether European nations are setting a trend in the field of adoption, or whether their actions will remain idiosyncratic on an international scale.

Same-Sex Marriage

The status of same-sex marriage worldwide mirrors to some extent the status of that institution within the United States. Just as various states in the Union have taken a variety of positions on allowing gay men and lesbians to participate in a civil marriage (called by that name), so various countries around the world have decided to allow same-sex marriages; to permit some other form of affiliation similar to (and in some cases, identical to) a civil marriage, but without that name; or to prohibit any form of legal affiliation between two men or two women.

In January 1998, the Dutch Parliament adopted a bill creating a category known as a *registered partnership*, generally similar to a marriage, but available to both same-sex and opposite-sex couples. That act was the first time that any nation granted to same-sex couples legal rights similar or identical to those available to opposite-sex couples. As the Parliament was debating the registered partnership bill, a special commission created by the legislature in 1995 was studying the possibility of extending traditional civil marriages to same-sex couples. That commission concluded its work in 2000 and recommended that this action be taken. A bill permitting same-sex marriage was introduced into the Parliament and passed in the same year. On midnight, April 1, 2001, the date on which the new law became effective, four same-sex couples were married at Amsterdam's city hall (Wikipedia 2008). About 2,400 same-sex couples were married in the first year following adoption of the law. That number has since declined to slightly more than about 1,000 same-sex marriages annually since then (Lozano—Bielat and Masci 2007).

Since the Dutch decision in 2000, five other nations have passed similar legislation, opening traditional civil marriages to same-sex couples. Those nations are Belgium (2003), Canada (2005), Norway (2009), South Africa (2006), and Spain (2005). As is the case with same-sex adoption, some national legislatures have had almost no choice in adopting such laws because national judiciaries have ruled that prohibition of same-sex marriages violates provisions of the federal constitution. In Canada, for example, by 2004 such rulings had been handed down by nine provincial and territorial supreme courts and by the Supreme Court of Canada (Globeandmail.com 2007). A similar history led to same-sex marriage legislation in South Africa. In December 2005, the Constitutional Court of South Africa ruled in *Minister of Home Affairs v. Fourie* that denying same-sex couples the right to marry was a violation of the national constitution. It gave the federal legislature one year to adjust marriage laws so as to allow any two persons, of the same or opposite sex, to be legally married. In 2006, the government adopted such a law (BBC News 2006b).

Among the nations that have approved same-sex marriages should also be listed the Coquille tribe in Oregon. In August 2008, the tribe announced that it would sanction a marriage between two women. Although the state of Oregon had earlier passed a law limiting marriage to one man and one woman, that law does not apply to the Coquille who, under U.S. law, are a separate and distinct nation. The tribal action followed a public meeting at which two members spoke against the decision, and 12 spoke in favor (Graves 2008).

Most countries that have decided to legalize same-sex relationships have chosen to adopt a marriage-like entity that has all or most of the rights of a civil marriage, but which does not carry the name *marriage*. These entities are known in various countries as civil unions, domestic partnerships, registered partnerships, or, in France only, a civil pact of solidarity (*pacte civil de solidarité*). These terms are sometimes used interchangeably and may or may not provide all of the rights associated with a civil marriage. The term *domestic partnership* is used almost exclusively in the United States, although some states also call such arrangements *civil unions*.

Denmark was the first nation in the world (1989) to offer such an arrangement, which was called a registered partnership. Registered partners in Denmark have all of the same rights as married couples, with four exceptions:

- They may not adopt children as a couple, except that one partner can adopt the biological child of his or her partner;
- They may not have joint custody of a child, except by adoption;
- They do not benefit from laws that make specific references to the genders of a married couple; and

- Provisions of international treaties do not apply to registered partners unless all signatories to a treaty specifically allow such applications (ILGA Europe 2008; this Web site also contains legal documents relating to all same-sex relationships for countries in which they exist).

An example of legislation creating civil unions is New Zealand's Civil Union Act of 2004, adopted by the legislature on December 9, 2004, by a vote of 65 to 55. That bill legalized an entity called a civil union between any two individuals of the same or opposite sex. It granted all civil rights to the members of that union except for laws that specifically referred to the genders of members of a couple. The law also allowed people to convert their marriages into civil unions and their civil unions into marriages, if certain conditions are met. The legislature then followed up this action in March 2005 by passing the Relationships (Statutory References) Bill, which removed gender references from a very large range of bills. In effect, then, civil unions in New Zealand are legally almost indistinguishable from civil marriages (New Zealand Legislation: Acts 2007).

Some registered partnership/civil union provisions fall considerably short of offering benefits equivalent to those of a civil marriage. In June 2005, for example, Slovenia adopted a registered partnership law that gave couples very limited rights. These rights included the right to own property jointly, the right of one member of the couple to provide medical care for the other member, and limited rights of inheritance. In response to objections about the limited scope of this law, the legislature enacted a second version of the act, to take effect in July 2006, that expanded property rights and added rights of inheritance. The law included some additional restrictions, however, such as limiting the civil union ceremony to the couple entering the relationship and the registrar (Outspoken 2008).

The only nation in the western hemisphere to adopt some form of legalized same-sex relationship is Uruguay. The Uruguayan senate adopted a bill permitting same- and opposite-sex civil unions in February 2007, followed by the congress in November of the same year. It was signed into law by President Tabare Vazquez on December 27 and went into effect on January 1, 2008 (Pink News 2007). Civil unions are available to same-sex or opposite-sex couples who have lived together for a minimum of five years. The law is somewhat narrow, however, in that it provides for equal rights with those of married couples only in the areas of inheritance, pensions, and child custody.

As is the case with same-sex adoption, same-sex marriage, civil unions, domestic partnerships, and registered partnerships are sometimes recognized by states or provinces within a country. As an example, the Brazilian state of Rio Grande do Sol passed legislation establishing civil unions in June 2006. That action came about largely as the result of a court decision earlier in the year by a panel of judges acting on a suit filed by a professor at the University in Rio Grande do Sul who was seeking partner benefits. The court had ruled that "Notwithstanding the ethical, philosophic, anthropological and religious discussion, the fact is that homosexual relations exist and, therefore, in the name of judicial security, deserve to be regulated" (Rohter 2004; also see Decker 2008).

Same-sex relationships have been legalized in two other states in Latin America, Argentina and Mexico. In Argentina, the Autonomous City of Buenos Aires (in 2002), the province of Rio Negro (2003), and the city of Villa Carlos Paz (2007) have all approved civil unions for same-sex and opposite-sex couples who have lived together for a minimum of two years (Mundoandino.com [n.d.]). The rights granted by these civil unions are very restricted, limited primarily to shared health and insurance benefits and rights of inheritance. Given the very strong opposition of the Roman Catholic Church throughout Latin America, however, even this modest gain is impressive.

In November 2006, the Mexico City legislature (*Asamblea Legislativa Distrito Federal*; ALDF) voted 43 to 17 (with five abstentions) to permit same-sex and opposite-sex couples to register in civil unions. Civil union status provides for some inheritance and pension rights as well as access to some social benefits provided by the government (Mex Files 2006). Two months later, the northern state of Coahuila passed a similar, but somewhat more comprehensive, civil union bill by a vote of 20 to 13. This decision was somewhat surprising in that Coahuila is a largely rural and ranching state not known for liberal policies (Reuters 2007).

The possibility of having same-sex unions in some nations raises issues for other countries in which such unions are not allowed. What would happen, for example, if a same-sex couple married in the Netherlands and then moved to France? Would France have to recognize the marriage that had been performed in the Netherlands? For opposite-sex couples, this problem has not been much of an issue. A person married in country A is also normally recognized as being married in country B (and county C, and country D, and so on). The comparable situation in the United States is covered by the Full Faith and Credit Clause of the U.S. Constitution (Article IV, Section 1). Not surprisingly, most countries have not yet taken a stand as to whether or not they will recognize same-sex marriage, civil unions, domestic partnerships, or registered partnerships approved in another nation. A few exceptions exist. The island country of Aruba was confronted with this issue in 2003 when a lesbian couple sued the government in an attempt for one member of the couple to obtain health benefits for her partner. The government was strongly opposed to this request, and the case worked its way up through the local courts in Aruba before being heard by the Supreme Court of the Netherlands. That court ruled that, as a member of the Kingdom of the Netherlands, Aruba was required to recognize all Dutch laws, including laws dealing with same-sex couples. By the time that decision was made, the lesbian couple, hounded by attacks in Aruba, had moved to the Netherlands and the case was moot. The court's decision means, however, that Aruba is required to recognize same-sex marriages performed in the Netherlands, although the chance of such marriages occurring in Aruba itself are very remote ("Same-Sex Marriage in the Caribbean" 2007).

Israel has also been confronted with this issue and forced to take a stand on same-sex unions. As one of the most progressive nations in the Middle East, Israel has a long record of extending benefits enjoyed by married heterosexual couples to gay men and lesbians. It has, however, never approved same-sex marriage, civil union, or other types of relationships. The reason is that all marriages in Israel are religious events, and the opposition of all religious groups to same-sex unions abrogates the possibility of such unions. Nonetheless, over the years, the Israeli government has extended a number of traditional marriage-related benefits to same-sex couples, including spousal benefits, survivor benefits for civil service employees, pension rights, the right of a partner to serve as guardian of a partner's children, and residency rights to a foreign partner of an Israeli citizen.

The question of a same-sex union came before the courts in 2006 when a gay male couple who had been married in Canada attempted to register their marriage upon their return to Israel. When the Israeli government refused to recognize their marriage, the couple sued. That case worked its way to the Supreme Court, which, in November 2006, ordered the government to recognize the marriage. By its action, the court obligated the Israeli government to recognize same-sex unions performed anywhere in the world. Although an important symbolic breakthrough for gay men and lesbians in Israel, the action probably had relatively little practical significance because same-sex couples in Israel had already been granted so many rights and benefits under the category of "common-law marriage" (Einhorn 2008, 222–235; Associated Press 2006).

The Future of Gay and Lesbian Rights Worldwide

The events summarized in this chapter might suggest that there is a rosy future for the expansion of civil rights for lesbians and gay men throughout the world. Certainly the nations of Europe have moved quickly over the past decade in enacting hate crime legislation, assimilating gay men and lesbians into the military, adopting nondiscrimination legislation, and creating the possibility of same-sex unions for lesbians and gay men.

Outside Europe, with a handful of exception, progress in these areas has been slow. In areas where religious influences are strong, as throughout most of the Middle East and Asia, it is difficult to imagine when and under what circumstances equal rights will be extended to gay men and lesbians. But in many parts of the world, governments are struggling with a problem that they probably could never have imagined a generation ago. Such is the case in South America, where a number of nations have at least begun to discuss the possibility of extending equal rights to gay men and lesbians and, in some cases, to have legislation to this effect discussed in national bodies. In Colombia, for example, the legal status of gay men, lesbians, and same-sex couples has begun to change significantly since national sodomy laws were abolished in 1980. Over time, same-sex couples were included in health plans (1999);

the Constitutional Court abolished the ban on gay men and lesbians in the military (1999); the same court ruled that lesbians and gay men could not be fired as school teachers (1998), nor could students be removed from a school for being gay or lesbian (1998); and partners in a same-sex union were allowed inheritance and disability benefits (2000) (Home Office [United Kingdom] 2002). In 2007, the Constitutional Court also extended common-law marriage property and inheritance rights to same-sex couples. At the time of the court's ruling, the national legislature was considering a bill to create civil unions for same-sex couples in Colombia (BBC News 2007).

The issue in Colombia, as it is in many countries, is that the legislature and/or the courts may move on gay and lesbian rights issues at a rate different from that of the general public: sometimes faster, and sometimes slower. The full recognition of gay men and lesbians as equal citizens with access to all rights available in a nation probably will not be achieved until all of these forces achieve, if not unanimity, at least a consensus as to what is best for a nation and all of its citizens. In this regard, a review of the status of gay men and lesbians around the world is useful for Americans not only because it reveals the situation "out there," but also because it allows Americans to reassess their own views on important legal issues. As one law professor has recently observed, "international law is a useful tool in understanding and defining the rights and privileges that should exist in any free state" (Schindler 2008, 10).

References

Amnesty International. 2008. "Love, Hate and the Law: Decriminalizing Homosexuality." London: Amnesty International, 9. Also available online at: http://www.amnestyusa.org/document.php?id=ENG POL300032008#sdendnote10anc. Accessed November 9, 2008.

Article 233a [Iceland]. General Penal Code No. 19, February 12, 1940, as amended. Available online at: http://www.legislationline.org/documents/action/popup/id/6894. Accessed November 8, 2008.

Associated Press. 2006. "Israel's Supreme Court Approves Same-Sex Marriages Performed Abroad." http://www.iht.com/articles/ap/2006/11/21/africa/ME_GEN_Israel_Same_Sex_Marriages.php. Accessed November 12, 2008.

BBC News. 2006a. "Belgium Passes Gay Adoption Law." http://news.bbc.co.uk/2/hi/europe/4929604.stm. Accessed November 10, 2008.

BBC News. 2006b. "S Africa Approves Same-Sex Unions." http://news.bbc.co.uk/2/hi/africa/6147010.stm. Accessed November 11, 2008.

BBC News. 2007 "Rights for Colombia Gay Couples." http://news.bbc.co.uk/2/hi/americas/6341593.stm. Accessed November 12, 2008.

Belkin, Aaron, and Melissa Levitt. 2001 "Homosexuality and the Israel Defense Forces; Did Lifting the Gay Ban Undermine Military Performance?" *Armed Forces and Society* 27 (4): 541–565. Also available online at: http://www.filmforum.org/films/yossi/israelstudyafs.pdf. Accessed November 10, 2008.

Belkin, Aaron, and Jason McNichol. 2000a. "The Effects of Including Gay and Lesbian Soldiers in the Australian Defence Forces: Appraising the Evidence." Santa Barbara: University of California at Santa Barbara. Also available online at: http://palmcenter.org/files/active/0/Australia_Final_Report.pdf. Accessed November 10, 2008.

Belkin, Aaron, and Jason McNichol. 2000b. "Effects of the 1992 Lifting of Restrictions on Gay and Lesbian Service in the Canadian Forces: Appraising the Evidence." Santa Barbara: University of California at Santa Barbara. Also available online at: http://palmcenter.org/files/active/0/Canada5.pdf. Accessed November 10, 2008.

Bindman, Stephen. 2008. "Activist Finds Home at Justice." *Justice Canada*. 2(3). http://www.justice.gc.ca/eng/dept—min/pub/jc/vol2/no3/index.html. Accessed November 9, 2008.

Blasius, Mark. 1997. *We Are Everywhere: A Historical Sourcebook of Gay and Lesbian Politics*. London: Routledge.

Canadian Legal Information Institute. 2008. "Criminal Code. Part XXIII: Sentencing. Purpose and Principles of Sentencing." Also available online at: http://www.canlii.org/ca/sta/c—46/sec718.2.html. Accessed November 8, 2008.

Case of E. B. v. France (Application no. 43546/02). 2008. http://cmiskp.echr.coe.int/tkp197/view.asp?item=3&portal=hbkm&action=html&highlight=E.B.%20%7C%20v%20%7C%20France&sessionid=15703313&skin=hudoc-en. Accessed November 10, 2008.

CBS News. 2006. "France Broadens Gays' Parental Rights." http://www.cbsnews.com/stories/2006/02/25/ap/world/mainD8FVTSJO0.shtml. Accessed November 10, 2008.

"Charter of Fundamental Rights of the European Union." 2000. *Official Journal of the European Communities*. December 18, 2000, C/364 1-C/364–22. Available online at: http://www.europarl.europa.eu/charter/pdf/text_en.pdf. Accessed on November 8, 2008.

Charter of the United Nations. 1945. Available online at: http://www. un.org/aboutun/charter/. Accessed November 9, 2008.

Committee on Economic, Social and Cultural Rights. 2000. "Substantive Issues Arising in the Implementation of the International Covenant on Economic, Social and Cultural Rights." Available online at: http://www.unhchr.ch/tbs/doc.nsf/(symbol)/E.C.12.2000.4.En. Accessed November 9, 2008.

Dauvergne, Mia, Katie Scrim, and Shannon Brennan. 2008. "Hate Crime in Canada." http://www.statcan.ca/english/research/ 85F0033MIE/85F0033MIE2008017.htm. Accessed November 8, 2008.

De Schutter, Olivier. 2008. "Homophobia and Discrimination on Grounds of Sexual Orientation in the EU Member States. Part I—Legal Analysis. European Union. Agency for Fundamental Rights. http://fra. europa.eu/fra/material/pub/comparativestudy/FRA_hdgso_part1_en. pdf. Accessed November 8, 2008.

Decaux, Emmanuel. 2004. "Economic, Social and Cultural Rights: Study on Non-Discrimination as Enshrined in Article 2, Paragraph 2, of the International Covenant on Economic, Social and Cultural Rights." http://www.unhcr.org/refworld/publisher,UNSUBCOM, 4152c5104,0.html. Accessed November 9, 2008.

Decker, Julia C. 2008. "The Development of Homosexual Political Movements and the Creation of Civil Union Legislation in the United States, Argentina, and Brazil." http://ecommons.txstate.edu/cgi/viewcontent. cgi?article=1001&context=polstad. Accessed November 11, 2008.

Dick, Sam. 2008. "Homophobic Hate Crime: The Gay British Crime Survey." [n.p.; n.d.]. Also available online at: http://www.stonewall. org.uk/documents/homophobic_hate_crime__final_report.pdf. Accessed November 8, 2008.

Einhorn, Talia. 2008. "Same-Sex Family Unions in Israeli Law." *Utrecht Law Review*, 4 (2): 222–235.

Equal Rights Trust. 2008. "Nepal Prohibits Discrimination on Grounds of Sexual Orientation and Gender Identity," January 16. http://www. equalrightstrust.org/newsstory16012008/index.htm. Accessed November 9, 2008.

European Court of Human Rights. 1999. *Smith and Grady v. the United Kingdom*. http://hei.unige.ch/clapham/hrdoc/docs/echrsmithandgrady. htm. Accessed November 9, 2008; and *Lustig-Prean and Beckett v. The United Kingdom*. http://www.unhcr.org/refworld/publisher,ECHR,GBR, 3ae6b6151c,0.html. Accessed November 9, 2008.

European Parliament. 2006. "European Parliament Resolution on Homophobia in Europe." http://www.europarl.europa.eu/sides/

getDoc.do;jsessionid=8C0AE76E1E72A83F416EB34126103A69.
node1? language=EN&reference=P6-TA-2006-0018&type=TA. Accessed
November 8, 2008.

European Union Agency for Fundamental Rights (FRA). 2008. http://
fra.europa.eu/fra/index.php. Accessed November 8, 2008.

Gay & Lesbian Archives of the Pacific Northwest. 2008a. "Sodomy
Laws: Laws around the World." http://www.sodomylaws.org/.
Accessed November 7, 2008.

Gay & Lesbian Archives of the Pacific Northwest. 2008b. "Sodomy
Laws: Laws in the United States." http://www.sodomylaws.org/.
Accessed November 7, 2008.

Globeandmail.com. 2007. Timeline: Same-sex Marriage in Canada."
http://www.theglobeandmail.com/v5/content/features/timelines/
same_sex. Accessed November 11, 2008.

Goldhaber, Michael D. 2007. *A People's History of the European Court of
Human Rights.* New Brunswick, NJ: Rutgers University Press.

Graves, Bill. 2008. "Gay Marriage in Oregon? Tribe Says Yes." *The
Oregonian.* August 20. http://www.oregonlive.com/news/index.ssf/
2008/08/coquille_tribe_will_sanction_s.html. Accessed November 11,
2008.

Home Office [United Kingdom]. 2002. "Colombia Country Assessment." http://www.asylumlaw.org/docs/colombia/ind0402_colombia_ca.
pdf. Accessed November 12, 2008.

Human Rights First. 2008a. "2008 Hate Crime Survey: LGBT. Violence
Based on Sexual Orientation and Gender Identity Bias." http://www.
humanrightsfirst.org/discrimination/reports.aspx?s=lgbt&p=index.
Accessed November 8, 2008.

Human Rights First. 2008b. *Country Panorama: 2008 Hate Crime Survey.*
New York: Human Rights First. Available online at: http://www.
humanrightsfirst.org/pdf/fd/08/fd-080924-panorama-web.pdf. Accessed
November 8, 2008.

Hurley, Mary C. 2007. "Sexual Orientation and Legal Rights."
Parliamentary Information and Research Service. [Ottawa]: Library of
Parliament. Available online at: http://www.parl.gc.ca/information/
library/PRBpubs/921-e.pdf. Accessed November 10, 2008.

ILGA Europe. 2006. "Important Improvements in Gay and Lesbian
Rights in Iceland." http://www.ilga-europe.org/europe/guide/coun
try_by_country/iceland/important_improvements_in_gay_and_lesbian_
rights_in_iceland. Accessed November 10, 2008.

ILGA Europe. 2008. "Marriage and Partnership Rights for Same-Sex
Partners: Country-by-Country." http://www.ilga-europe.org/europe/

issues/marriage_and_partnership/marriage_and_partnership_rights_
for_same_sex_partners_country_by_country. Accessed November 11,
2008.

Interim Constitution of Nepal. 2007. http://www.worldstatesmen.org/
Nepal_Interim_Constitution2007.pdf. Accessed November 9, 2008.

International Constitutional Law. 2008. Fiji Constitution. http://www.
servat.unibe.ch/law/icl/fj00000.html. Accessed November 9, 2008.

International Debate Education Association. 2000. "Gays in the Military." http://www.idebate.org/debatabase/topic_details.php?topicID=
103. Accessed November 10, 2008.

Judicial News [Noticias Juridicas]. 2008. "Data Base of Legislation"
[Base de Datos de Legislación]. Available online at: http://noticias.
juridicas.com/base_datos/Penal/lo10-1995.l1t1.html#c4. Accessed
November 8, 2008. In the original: " *Cometer el delito por motivos racistas,
antisemitas u otra clase de discriminación referente a la ideología, religión o
creencias de la víctima, la etnia, raza o nación a la que pertenezca, su sexo u
orientación sexual, o la enfermedad o minusvalía que padezca.*"

Khaitan, Tarunabh. [n.d.] "Violence against Lesbians in India." http://
www.altlawforum.org/Resources/lexlib/document.2004-12-21.955569
6555. Accessed November 6, 2008.

Konigsberg, Eric. 1992. "Gays in Arms: Can Gays in the Military
Work? In Countries around the World, They Already Do." *Washington
Monthly* 24: 10–13.

Lozano-Bielat, Hope, and David Masci. 2007. "Same-Sex Marriage:
Redefining Marriage around the World." Pew Forum on Religion and
Public Life. http://pewforum.org/docs/?DocID=235. Accessed
November 11, 2008.

Merrick, Jeffrey, and Bryant T. Ragan Jr., eds. 1996. *Homosexuality in
Modern France.* New York: Oxford University Press.

Metropolitan Police Authority. [n.d.] "London Race Hate Crime
Forum: Annual Report 2006–2007," 26. Accessed November 8, 2008.

Mex Files. 2006. "Mexico City Passes (Gay) Civil Unions Law!" http://
mexfiles.wordpress.com/2006/11/09/mexico-city-passes-gay-civil-
unions-law-2. Accessed November 11, 2008.

Moore, Michael Scott. 2008. "Does Germany Have a Problem with Gay
Hate Crime?" Spiegel Online International. http://www.spiegel.de/
international/germany/0,1518,562638,00.html. Accessed November 8,
2008.

Mundoandino.com. [n.d.]. "Civil Union in Argentina." http://www.
mundoandino.com/Argentina/Civil-union-in-Argentina. Accessed
November 11, 2008.

National Council for Crime Prevention. 2008. "Reported Hate Crimes." http://www.bra.se/extra/pod/?action=pod_show&id=59& module_instance=11. Accessed November 8, 2008.

New Zealand Legislation: Acts. 2007. "Civil Union Act 2004." Available online at: http://www.legislation.govt.nz/act/public/2004/ 0102/latest/DLM323385.html. Accessed November 11, 2008.

Office of the High Commissioner for Human Rights. [n.d.] International Covenant on Civil and Political Rights. Also available online at: http://www.unhchr.ch/html/menu3/b/a_ccpr.htm. Accessed November 9, 2008.

Organization of the American States. 2008. "Human Rights, Sexual Orientation, and Gender Identity." Resolution AG/RES. 2435 (XXXVIII-O/08). http://www.oas.org/dil/AGRES_2435.doc. Accessed November 8, 2008.

Ottoson, Daniel. 2006. "LGBT World Legal Wrap Up Survey." Stockholm: International Lesbian and Gay Association, November 2006.

Outspoken. 2008. "Slovenia OKs Domestic Partnerships." http:// theweddingparty.org/phpBB2/viewtopic.php?t=1877. Accessed November 11, 2008.

Pallone, Nathaniel J. 1999. *Race, Ethnicity, Sexual Orientation, Violent Crime: The Realities and the Myths.* London: Taylor & Francis.

Palm Center. 2008. "Gays in the Military: Think Tank Conference in SF." http://palmcenter.org/node/430. Accessed November 9, 2008.

Pink News. 2007. "Uruguay Becomes Latest Country to Legalise Civil Unions." http://www.pinknews.co.uk/news/articles/2005-6379.html. Accessed November 11, 2008.

Reuters. 2007. "Mexican State near Texas Passes Gay Union Law." *Washington Post.* January 11. Available online at: http://www.washing tonpost.com/wp-dyn/content/article/2007/01/11/AR2007011102502. html. Accessed November 11, 2008.

Rohter, Larry. 2004. "World Briefing: Americas: Brazil: State to Allow Same-Sex Unions." March 6. Available online at: http://query. nytimes.com/gst/fullpage.html?res=9A0CE2D81E3FF935A35750 C0A9629C8B63. Accessed November 11, 2008.

"Same-Sex Marriage in the Caribbean." 2007. http://ithithome. blogspot.com/2007/04/gay-marriage-in-caribbean.html. Accessed November 12, 2008.

Schindler, Devin. 2008. "When Judges Make Foreign Policy." *New York Times Magazine.* October 12.

South African Government Information. 2008. Constitution of the Republic of South Africa, 1996. http://www.info.gov.za/documents/constitution/1996/96cons2.htm#9. Accessed November 9, 2008.

United States General Accounting Office. 1993. "Homosexuals in the Military: Policies and Practices of Foreign Countries." Washington, DC: General Accounting Office, June. Also available online at: http://dont.stanford.edu/regulations/GAO.pdf. Accessed November 9, 2008.

United States Holocaust Memorial Museum. 2008. Nazi Persecution of Homosexuals, 1933–1945. http://www.ushmm.org/museum/press/kits/details.php?content=nazi_persecution_of_homosexuals&page=02-background. Accessed November 7, 2008.

Victorian Law Reform Commission. 2007. "Assisted Reproductive Technology and Adoption: Final Report." Melbourne, Victoria: Victorian Government Printer. Available online at: http://www.lawreform.vic.gov.au/wps/wcm/connect/Law+Reform/resources/file/eb22b94ec21531a/ART%20WEB%20VERSION.pdf. Accessed November 10, 2008.

Wikipedia. 2008. "Same-Sex Marriage in the Netherlands." http://en.wikipedia.org/wiki/Same-sex_marriage_in_the_Netherlands. Accessed November 11, 2008.

Zino, Aviram. 2008. "Attorney General Rules Same Sex Couples Eligible to Adopt." http://www.ynet.co.il/english/articles/0,7340,L-3505079,00.html. Accessed November 10, 2008.

4

Chronology

This chapter lists a number of events relating to the gay and lesbian rights movement over the past century and a half. In most cases, those events are political or legal in nature, such as important court decisions and new legislative actions involving the rights of lesbians, gay men, bisexuals, and transgendered (LGBT) persons. Also included in the chronology, however, are some events that, while not strictly political or legal, give some of the flavor of the changing social climate surrounding the LGBT movement.

The number of events that could be included in this chapter is virtually endless. Nearly every day, somewhere in the world, a gay protest is made, opposition to LGBT rights is expressed, new laws are passed, old laws are rescinded, and specific events occur in the lives of individual lesbians and gay men that illustrate the issues surrounding the LGBT rights movement. This chronology is intended to give the reader a taste of this complex mix of events.

(Note that some dates may be ambiguous, since legal action may occur in one year, to take effect in a later year.)

1553   The first civil laws against homosexual acts among men are passed in England.

1566   A French interpreter is accused of being a sodomite and is murdered by the Spaniards. The event might be called the first hate crime against a gay man in the United States.

1610   The Virginia colony passes the first antisodomy law in the United States, requiring the death penalty for anyone convicted under the law. Women are not included in the law's provisions.

1641   The Massachusetts Bay Colony enacts a new penal code that includes sodomy as a capital crime. The definition of *sodomy* is taken directly from Leviticus 20:13. By the end of the century, nearly all colonies had adopted similar laws against sodomy, requiring the death penalty for those convicted of the crime.

1778   Baron Frederich von Steuben, one of the great military strategists of the 18th century, is dismissed from the U.S. military service for engaging in sodomy with Lieutenant Gotthold Frederick Enslin. Von Steuben had earlier been dismissed from the Prussian army for similar offenses, after which he volunteered to serve for the United States in the Revolutionary War. The event might be considered the first instance of the U.S. military's dismissal of a member of the armed forces for homosexual behavior.

1786   Pennsylvania adopts a number of fundamental legal reforms, removing the death penalty for crimes such as burglary, robbery, sodomy, and buggery (sexual intercourse with animals). By the end of the century, a number of other states had followed suit and reduced the penalty for sodomy to loss of property, assignment to servitude, or some other punishment.

1861   Civil laws against homosexual acts among men are abolished in England and Ireland.

1869   The Hungarian physician Karl Maria Kertbeny (who was born as Karl Maria Benkert) coins the word *homosexual*.

1885   The British Parliament recriminalizes all male homosexual acts in both public and private.

1896   Adolf Brand, German writer, anarchist, and gay rights activist, publishes the first edition of *Der Eigene* ("The Community of the Special"), the first periodical dealing with issues of homosexuality. The publication continues until 1931, when it was closed down by edict of Adolf Hitler.

1897   Magnus Hirschfeld, Max Spohr, and Erick Oberg found the *Wissenschaftlich-humanitäres Komitee* (Scientific-Humanitarian Committee) in Germany. The organization is the first association in the world to campaign for social and legal recognition of lesbians, gay men, and transgendered persons.

Havelock Ellis, English physician, social reformer, and sexologist, publishes *Sexual Inversion*, generally regarded as the first serious book to treat homosexual behavior as a normal variant of human behavior rather than as a crime, a disease, or a sin.

1908   Edward Carpenter, English poet, social activist, gay rights proponent, and philosopher, publishes *The Intermediate Sex*, arguably his most influential book on gay issues.

1919   Magnus Hirschfeld establishes the *Institut für Sexualwissenschaft* (Institute for Sex Research), the first organization in history to deal with a wide range of sexual topics—including homosexual behavior—from a scientific standpoint.

1921   Magnus Hirschfeld founds the *Weltliga für Sexualreform* (World League for Sexual Reform) to promote reform of attitudes and laws about sexual behavior. The league eventually reaches a maximum membership of 130,000 men and women worldwide.

1924   Bavarian immigrant Henry Gerber and a group of friends found the Society for Human Rights, the first gay rights group in the United States. The society survives only a brief time and is disbanded when the wife of one of its directors reports the group's existence to the police. The organization publishes the first magazine for gay men in the United States, *Friendship and Freedom*.

1929   The Reichstag removes Paragraph 175, the section criminalizing same-sex sexual acts, from the German Constitution. The law had first been adopted in 1871, and its repeal never took effect because of the rise of the Nazi party in Germany in the early 1930s. Instead, the Nazi-controlled parliament actually extended the provisions of Paragraph 175 in 1934 to include as criminal acts "a kiss, an embrace, even homosexual fantasies."

1933   Young students loyal to the Nazi party destroy Hirschfeld's Institute for Sex Research and burn his vast collection of artistic and literary works.

1948   Alfred Kinsey, researcher at Indiana University, publishes *Sexual Behavior in the Human Male*, considered by many authorities still the best available data on sexual attitudes, feelings, and behaviors in American men.

1951   Henry Hay, Bob Hull, and Chuck Rowland found the Mattachine Society in Los Angeles. The society is created to provide aid and comfort to gay men and lesbians and to educate the general public on gay issues.

1951–
1958   The *Cultuur-en-Ontspannings Centrum* (Culture and Recreation Center), based in Amsterdam, sponsors five International Conferences for Sexual Equality. The agendas of the conferences include extensive consideration of gay rights issues.

1952   The McCarran-Walters Act bans "sexual deviates" from immigrating to the United States, a policy that the Supreme Court says in 1967 applies to lesbians and gay men.

Loan Receipt --- Loan Date: 01/26/2018

Dutchess Community College
Francis U. and Mary F. Ritz Library
53 Pendell Road
Poughkeepsie, NY 12601-1595
(845)431-8639

Title: Gay and lesbian rights : a reference handbook / David E. Newton.

Barcode: 7012261

DUE DATE: 02/09/2018

Title: Same-sex marriage : a reference handbook / David E. Newton.

Barcode: 7040989

DUE DATE: 02/09/2018

Title: Gay parenting / Beth Rosenthal, book editor.

Barcode: 7019788

DUE DATE: 02/09/2018

Title: LGBTQ rights / Susan Henneberg, book editor.

Barcode: 7038704

DUE DATE: 02/09/2018

FINES are 10 cents per day/item. You are responsible for all items listed.

RENEWALS may be made in person, by phone, or in myDCC through the Ritz Catalog, on or before due date.

1953   The German government begins the re-arrest of gay concentration camp survivors as "repeat offenders" when they refuse to renounce their intention of continuing to take part in homosexual acts.

Alfred Kinsey publishes *Sexual Behavior in the Human Female*, a companion volume to his 1948 book dealing with male sexuality.

1955   Del Martin and Phyllis Lyon found the first U.S. lesbian organization, the Daughters of Bilitis. They also publish the organization's journal, *The Ladder*.

1961   Illinois becomes the first state to decriminalize homosexual acts between consenting adults in private.

1962   The United Kingdom's Committee on Homosexual Offences and Prostitution, popularly known as the Wolfenden Committee, recommends that homosexual acts between consenting adults in private no longer be a criminal offense. The committee had been created five years earlier to study the issues of homosexual behavior and prostitution and to make recommendations regarding national policy on these subjects.

1964   The Society for Individual Rights (SIR), a club of gay men and lesbians, organizes in San Francisco for social and political purposes.

1965   For the first time in American history, gay men and lesbians (seven of the former and three of the latter) picket for gay rights. The action takes place in front of the White House on the same day that 20,000 antiwar protestors gather at the Washington Monument.

1966   Gay men and lesbians create the North American Conference of Homophile Organizations (NACHO) to coordinate protests against antigay discrimination by the federal government.

1967   The American Civil Liberties Union reverses its earlier position and declares its opposition to state sodomy laws.

1967 (*cont.*)	The British government enacts the Sexual Offences Act, incorporating the recommendations made by the Wolfenden Committee 10 years earlier.
1968	Gay French students, led by David Cohn-Bendit, riot and take over the campus of the Sorbonne in Paris.
1969	The Canadian parliament decriminalizes homosexual acts between consenting adults in private.
	The Stonewall riots of June 27 and 28 in New York City mark the symbolic beginning of the gay rights movement in the United States. Triggered by a police raid on the Stonewall, a popular gay bar in Greenwich Village, the riots begin in and around the bar and soon spread throughout lower Manhattan.
	West Germany repeals its laws against homosexual acts between consenting males. No German laws have ever existed against lesbian sexual acts.
	The American Sociological Association announces its support for legislation protecting the civil rights of gays and other sexual minorities.
1970	Carl Wittman summarizes many of the goals of the early gay rights movement in his "Gay Manifesto."
	New York City's Gay Pride parade draws about 10,000 marchers. The parade was the first of its kind anywhere in the world.
	The Lutheran Church in the United States calls for the repeal of all state sodomy laws and for legislation that will prohibit discrimination against lesbians and gay men. The church does not then apply (not has it since) that policy to its own clergy, however.
1971	The president's National Commission on Reform of Federal Criminal Laws recommends the repeal of all state sodomy laws.

1972   Legislation to prohibit discrimination against lesbians and gay men is introduced for the first time in the New York City Council. The legislation fails. After being introduced every year for more than a decade, the nondiscrimination law is finally passed in 1986 by a vote of 21 to 14.

East Lansing, Michigan, becomes the first city in the United States to adopt a policy that prevents discrimination in city hiring based on sexual orientation.

The U.S. Supreme Court refuses to hear a case in which the county clerk in Hennepin County, Minnesota, refused to issue a marriage license to two men, Richard Baker and James McConnell. The Court ruled that the case posed no "substantial federal question."

Paramus (New Jersey) High School teacher John Gish is fired for accepting the presidency of the local gay activist alliance. Gish appeals the decision, and the case continues for eight years. Gish's firing is finally upheld by New Jersey State Education Commissioner Fred G. Burke, who calls the teacher's actions "conduct unbecoming to a teacher."

1973   Members of the American Bar Association adopt a resolution supporting the repeal of state laws regarding sexual acts between consenting adults. The bar makes no mention, however, of support for antidiscrimination legislation based on sexual orientation.

The governing board of the American Psychiatric Association drops homosexual behavior from its list of behavioral disorders. When some members disagree with the board's action, its decision is put to a vote of the general membership, which, in 1974, upholds the board's decision 58 percent to 42 percent.

1974   Elaine Nobel of Massachusetts becomes the first openly gay or lesbian person elected to a state legislature.

1974   The Massachusetts Supreme Court rules that state
(*cont.*)   laws dealing with "unnatural and lascivious acts" do
              not apply to private consensual adult behavior.

              A federal gay and lesbian civil rights bill is introduced
              into the U.S. House of Representatives by New York
              City representatives Bella Abzug and Edward Koch.
              The bill fails, but is reintroduced in every future ses-
              sion of Congress, finally receiving approval in both
              houses of Congress 34 years later.

1975   The U.S. Air Force discharges Sergeant Leonard Mat-
              lovich because of his homosexuality. Matlovich had
              consistently received superior ratings for his work,
              but his sexual orientation automatically required that
              he be discharged. Five years later, a federal judge or-
              dered the Air Force to allow Matlovich to reenlist, but
              it chose instead to offer him a financial settlement of
              $160,000, which he accepted.

              The American Association for the Advancement of
              Science adopts a resolution opposing discrimination
              of any kind against lesbians and gay men.

              Clela Rorex, county clerk in Boulder, Colorado, issues
              marriage licenses to six same-sex couples because she
              finds no state law against same-sex marriage. The
              state attorney general, J. D. MacFarlane, later rules
              that such licenses are illegal.

              The American Medical Association adopts a resolu-
              tion calling for the repeal of all state sodomy laws.

              The state of Pennsylvania bans discrimination against
              gay men and lesbians in state employment.

              The Arkansas state legislature votes to repeal state
              sodomy laws. Two years later, the legislature changes
              its mind and votes to reinstate those laws.

1976   The U.S. Supreme Court votes 6 to 3 to uphold the
              state of Virginia's sodomy laws.

1977   Harvey Milk is elected San Francisco's first openly gay city supervisor.

The Dade County (Florida) Commission adopts an ordinance prohibiting discrimination against gay men and lesbians. The ordinance is overturned in a general election six months later. In the same year, gay rights ordinances are also repealed in Wichita, Kansas; Eugene, Oregon; and St. Paul, Minnesota; a similar ordinance in Seattle, Washington, is upheld.

The state legislature of Oklahoma unanimously passes a law requiring the dismissal of gay and lesbian school teachers and prohibiting the favorable mention of homosexual behavior in schools. In 1985, the U.S. Supreme Court invalidates the law.

The U.S. State Department announces that it will no longer regard sexual orientation as a reason for denying employment. Each case will be dealt with on an individual basis.

Officers of the National Gay Task Force (now the National Gay and Lesbian Task Force) meet on two occasions with Midge Constanza, assistant to President Jimmy Carter, to discuss gay rights issues. The meetings are the first of their kind in history.

The Episcopal Church ordains its first openly lesbian priest, Ellen Marie Barrett.

The International Association of Chiefs of Police and the Fraternal Order of Police both adopt resolutions opposing the hiring of lesbian and gay police officers.

Quebec includes gay men and lesbians among those who are covered by the province's Charter of Human Rights.

Toronto police raid the offices of *The Body Politic*, Canada's best known gay newspaper and one of the most highly respected gay publications in the world. The paper is acquitted six years later of charges that it was using the mails "to distribute immoral, indecent, and scurrilous material."

1978   Supervisor Harvey Milk and Mayor George Moscone of San Francisco are shot to death in their city hall offices by Supervisor Dan White. White is eventually convicted of voluntary manslaughter and sentenced to serve seven years in prison. He is released after serving five years of the sentence and, in 1985, commits suicide.

California's Proposition 6 (the "Briggs Initiative") provides for the firing of all gay and lesbian teachers and all teachers who allude to homosexual behavior positively in the classroom. The initiative is eventually defeated, to some extent because of the strong objections from Governor Ronald Reagan.

New York City Mayor Ed Koch issues an executive order that forbids discrimination against gay men and lesbians in city government. Largely through the efforts of the Roman Catholic archdiocese, the order is eventually overturned in the courts.

The San Francisco Board of Supervisors adopts the city's first gay rights ordinance.

1979   Governor Jerry Brown (California) appoints the first openly gay judge in the United States, Stephen M. Lachs. Before Brown leaves office at the end of 1981, he appoints three more gays and lesbians to the state bench. Among these is Mary Morgan, the first openly lesbian judge in the country. She served on the municipal court in San Francisco.

The First National Gay and Lesbian Civil Rights March on Washington is held in the nation's capital. A crowd estimated at more than 100,000 attends.

The first openly lesbian and gay officers are sworn in by the San Francisco Police Department.

1980   In Providence, Rhode Island, gay teenager Aaron Fricke sues his high school to allow him to bring a male date to the senior prom. He wins his suit and is accompanied by Paul Guilbert to the school dance. Fricke later writes of these events in a popular book, *Reflections of a Rock Lobster*.

The platform committee of the Democratic Party accepts a plank supporting federal gay rights legislation. The party eventually adopts the plank at its national convention. At the same convention, Mel Boozer, a gay black man, is nominated to become the party's candidate for the vice presidency under President Jimmy Carter. Minnesota senator Walter Mondale is selected for the position instead.

Georgetown University, run by Jesuits of the Roman Catholic Church, expels its gay student group from campus, forbidding it to use any university facilities. The student group takes the university to court and wins its case eight years later.

1981   The Council of Europe adopts a resolution supporting gay rights legislation in member nations. Three years later, the European Parliament adopts a similar resolution, 114 to 45.

A New York housing court judge approves the eviction of a lesbian couple from the apartment they have shared for two-and-one-half years because "to hold otherwise, this or any other court would lend itself to the ultimate destruction of the family unit, the foundation of society."

The Virginia Supreme Court rules that a lesbian mother cannot be deprived of visitation rights with her 11-year-old son. It states that "[w]e decline to hold that every lesbian mother or homosexual father is *per se* an unfit person."

Wisconsin becomes the first state to pass a law prohibiting discrimination against gay men and lesbians in employment, housing, and public accommodations.

1981 (*cont.*)	Congressman Roger Jepsen (R-Iowa) introduces a "Family Protection Act," the purpose of which is to "promote the virtues of family life." Included in the bill is a section that would withhold Social Security, welfare, and veteran's benefits from anyone who is homosexual or who suggests that homosexuality is an acceptable lifestyle. The bill does not pass, and Jepsen is later defeated for reelection when it is discovered that the "health spa" he belongs to is actually a house of prostitution. Legislation introduced by Democratic Georgia Congressman Larry McDonald dealing with similar issues is adopted, however. The McDonald Amendment prohibits the federal Legal Services Corporation from assisting in any case that "seeks to promote, defend, or protect homosexuality."
1982	A federal judge rules that the U.S. Immigration and Naturalization Service's policy of excluding gays from entering the United States is unconstitutional.
	The city of Philadelphia adds "sexual orientation" to its Fair Practices Code that prohibits discrimination in employment, housing, and public accommodations.
	By unanimous vote, 1,700 delegates to the national convention of the American Federation of State, County, and Municipal Employees adopt a resolution calling for federal, state, and local laws prohibiting discrimination against gay men and lesbians.
	The U.S. Olympic Committee sues a group of lesbians and gay men to prevent them from using the word *Olympic* in their planned "Gay Olympics." The name had previously been used for a number of other events without objection from the committee. In order to guarantee that the term *Olympics* not be used, the committee eventually obtains a lien on the home of former Olympic champion Tom Wardell, who is dying of AIDS-related illness at the time.

San Francisco mayor Dianne Feinstein vetoes a bill passed by the city's Board of Supervisors granting economic benefits to unmarried "domestic partners" of gay and non-gay citizens. A week later, the Parliament of Quebec passes nearly identical legislation for lesbians and gay men in the province.

1983   Linda Conway, a West Virginia kindergarten teacher, is fired from her job because her superiors think she looks like a lesbian, in spite of Conway's insistence that she is not a lesbian. Three years later, the state supreme court confirms the school board's right to dismiss Conway because of her appearance.

The California Compensation Appeals Board awards $25,000 in survivor benefits to a man whose partner of 27 years had committed suicide. The decision appears to have been the first of its kind in the United States.

1984   The Norwegian Supreme Court upholds the conviction of television evangelist Hans Bratterud for calling for the dismissal of gay men and lesbians from their jobs. Norway's antidiscrimination law includes a provision banning "statements of an aggravated insulting nature ... [against] ... homosexual tendencies, way of life or orientation."

For the first time, a gay civil rights bill passes both houses of the California legislature, but Republican governor George Deukmejian refuses to sign the bill, claiming that there is no evidence the bill is needed.

1985   The city of Berkeley, California, votes to extend to gay and lesbian employees the same benefits available to non-gay employees. The action is the first of its kind in the United States.

Manchester, England, elects the first openly lesbian mayor in British history, 44-year-old Margaret Roff.

1985 (*cont.*)	The Massachusetts House of Representatives votes to prohibit gay men and lesbians from acting as foster parents.

An official of the U.S. Immigration and Naturalization Service rules that "a bona fide marital relationship cannot exist between two faggots." An appeal on this ruling results in a federal court decision that one of the two men involved, a native Australian, must be deported to his native country. The two men had been in a monogamous relationship and living in the United States for more than 10 years.

1986	Pope John Paul II issues a papal letter declaring that homosexuality is "intrinsically disordered" and calling for all Catholics to oppose civil rights legislation for lesbians and gay men.

New Zealand repeals its laws prohibiting homosexual acts between consenting adults.

The province of Ontario passes a gay rights law.

The Supreme Court of Nevada, the only state with legalized prostitution, upholds the state's sodomy law.

For the first time in its history, the *New York Times* allows its writer to use the word *gay* in referring to homosexuality.

1988	The European Court of Human Rights orders Ireland to withdraw its penalty of life imprisonment for homosexual acts.

Utah's Republican senator Orrin Hatch calls the Democratic Party "the party of homosexuals."

In the November general election, Oregon voters repeal an executive order previously issued by governor Neil Goldschmidt prohibiting discrimination in employment against gay men and lesbians.

The U.S. Congress orders the District of Columbia to revoke its gay rights ordinance or lose all funding.

Commissioner of professional baseball Bart Giamatti fires National League umpire Dave Pallone, apparently because he is gay.

The state of Israel legalizes homosexual acts between consenting adults.

1989   The San Francisco Board of Supervisors passes domestic partnership legislation granting recognition to gay and lesbian relationships.

Denmark legalizes same-sex marriages.

More than 10 years after the issue first arose, the House of Delegates of the American Bar Association votes to support federal legislation prohibiting discrimination against lesbians and gay men. The tally shows that about a third of all lawyers still opposes the concept.

A New York housing court judge rules that a gay male couple can be considered a "family" for purposes of housing rules. The decision comes after the death of one man raises questions as to whether his partner of more than ten years can remain in the rent-controlled apartment.

Lesbians and gay men in Poland form the nation's first gay rights group, Lambda, with chapters in Warsaw, Gdansk, and Wroclaw.

1990   Officials at the Polk County (Florida) jail announce that they will no longer require gay prisoners to wear pink bracelets, reputedly originally instituted to reduce the spread of HIV/AIDS.

Congress votes to end the nation's immigration policy banning immigrants on the basis of their sexual orientation.

1990
(*cont.*)
A new group of gay men and lesbians, Queer Nation, is formed. The name is chosen as an act of defiance against antigay violence and discrimination. The organization soon had chapters in many American cities, although most remained active for no more than a few years.

1991
A superior court judge in Los Angeles rules that the Boy Scouts of America may legally prohibit an Eagle Scout from becoming a scoutmaster because of his sexual orientation. (Also see 2000.)

An Ohio appellate court rules that the state's domestic violence laws apply to lesbian and gay couples, broadening the state's existing definition of "spousal relationships."

Amnesty International decides for the first time in its history to include gay men and lesbians in its campaign to free individuals imprisoned worldwide because of political crimes.

Sherry Harris becomes the first black lesbian in the United States to win a major election when she is elected to a city council seat in Settle by a margin of 66 percent to 34 percent.

Lotus Development Corporation, of Cambridge, Massachusetts, announces that it will offer health benefits to gay and lesbian "spousal equivalents" of its employees.

1992
Amendment 2, prohibiting gay rights legislation in Colorado, is adopted. Comparable legislation in Oregon, Proposition 9, is defeated. The U.S. Supreme Court eventually rules in 1996 that Amendment 2 is unconstitutional because it deprives gay men and lesbians of certain constitutionally guaranteed civil rights. The city of Springfield, Oregon, becomes the first municipality in the nation to adopt an ordinance specifically forbidding the city from promoting, encouraging, or facilitating homosexuality.

The New York City Commission on Human Rights finds that Delta Airlines routinely asks prospective employees "embarrassing, inappropriate, and shocking" questions about their sexual orientation, HIV status, marital status, birth control practices, and abortion history.

Estonia becomes the third former Soviet republic to abolish its sodomy laws.

New Jersey becomes the fifth state to pass a gay rights bill.

1993   The Hawaii Supreme Court reverses a lower court decision against same-sex marriage, ruling that the state must prove a "compelling public interest" in banning such marriages.

The administration of President Bill Clinton agrees to a new military policy—called "Don't Ask, Don't Tell"—on the inclusion of gay men and lesbians in the nation's armed forces.

The Tenth Circuit Court of Appeals rules that school officials in Kansas may legally refuse to hire a teacher whom they suspect of being gay. In fact, the teacher-applicant is not gay, but the court's ruling allows the school district to refuse to employ him anyway.

San Francisco supervisor Roberta Achtenberg is confirmed by the U.S. Senate by a vote of 58 to 31 as assistant secretary for fair housing and equal opportunity in the U.S. Department of Housing and Urban Affairs. She is the first openly lesbian person to be nominated for such a high federal post. She is confirmed in spite of objections by opponents such as Senator Jesse Helms (R-N.C.), who refers to Achtenberg as "that damn lesbian."

Ireland overturns its 132-year-old ban on homosexual acts between consenting adults.

1993 (*cont.*)	National discount chain Target Stores settles a class action suit by agreeing to pay $2 million for requiring job applications to undergo psychological testing that includes "deeply personal" questions dealing with sexual interests, values, and religious beliefs.

The Wisconsin Supreme Court rules that landlords may refuse to rent to unrelated people who want to share housing because to do so would be "inconsistent with the public policy of this state which seeks to promote the stability of marriage and family."

Minnesota becomes the seventh state to pass a gay rights bill prohibiting discrimination in employment, housing, education, and public accommodation.

Henrico County (Virginia) circuit judge Buford Parsons, Jr., denies custody of 2-year-old Tyler Bottoms to his mother, Sharon Bottoms, because she is a lesbian. He rules that Virginia's sodomy law makes Bottoms a criminal and, therefore, unfit to be a mother. Bottom's mother, to whom custody of the child is awarded, tells the court that she fears the boy would grow up unable to distinguish between men and women.

Russia repeals its sodomy laws.

1994 The U.S. Immigration and Naturalization Service (INS) grants political asylum to a gay Mexican citizen who claims that his life would be in jeopardy if he were to return to Mexico. The decision appears to be the first instance in which the INS has recognized sexual orientation as a valid claim for asylum under the Refuge Act of 1980.

The British parliament lowers the age of consent for homosexual acts from 21 to 18. The age of consent for heterosexual acts is 16.

The Brazilian newspaper *Folha de São Paulo* reports that, on average, one antigay killing occurs every four days in the nation.

The European Parliament votes 159 to 96 to recommend that gay and lesbian couples be allowed to marry and to adopt children.

Massachusetts becomes the first state to outlaw discrimination against gay and lesbian students in public schools.

1995   Rhode Island becomes the ninth state to pass a gay rights bill.

The Rhode Island Supreme Court upholds the state's antisodomy law.

Utah governor Mike Leavitt (R) signs into law the first state ban on same-sex marriage. The law stipulates that the state does not have to recognize out-of-state marriages that violate state public policy.

Zimbabwe president Robert Mugabe says homosexuals are "lower than dogs and pigs."

President Bill Clinton signs an executive order ending the policy of denying security clearance to gay men and lesbians.

Penny Culliton, a teacher in New Ipswich, New Hampshire, is fired for listing as voluntary reading two gay-themed books, *Maurice*, by E. M. Forster, and *The Education of Harriet Hatfield*, by May Sarton.

1996   South Africa becomes the first nation in the world to prohibit discrimination on the basis of sexual orientation as part of its national constitution.

The U.S. Congress passes and President Bill Clinton signs into law the Defense of Marriage Act (DOMA) prohibiting the federal government from recognizing any same-sex marriage that may have been concluded legally in any state and allowing any state to refuse recognition of any same-sex marriage concluded in any other state.

1996   Iceland establishes a domestic-partnership relationship
(*cont.*) known as a registered partnership for same-sex couples.

Romania and Macedonia decriminalize same-sex relationships between consenting adults.

In the case of *Nabozny v. Podlesny* heard before the 7th Circuit Court of Appeals, a jury awards Jamie Nabozny $962,000 because administrators at his Wisconsin high school failed to protect him from antigay harassment. The case is important because of the precedence it establishes in similar cases of antigay harassment in schools throughout the nation.

1997   The People's Republic of China and Ecuador decriminalize sodomy.

Fiji becomes the second nation in the world to prohibit antigay discrimination in its constitution.

Legislatures in Maine and New Hampshire pass laws prohibiting discrimination against gays and lesbians in housing, employment, and public accommodations. The Maine law is overturned in a referendum vote in 1998; it is adopted again by the legislature in 2000 and overturned again in a referendum held in the same year.

A New Zealand court of appeals rules against same-sex marriage in the country.

A constitutional review committee in Florida votes 6 to 2 not to add sexual orientation to categories protected by the state constitution.

1998   In one of the most famous hate crimes of modern time, college student Matthew Shepard is murdered near Laramie, Wyoming.

South Africa's Constitutional Court invalidates the country's sodomy law.

Winnipeg, Manitoba, elects Glen Murray the first openly gay mayor of a major North American city.

Homosexual acts between consenting adults are decriminalized in Bosnia and Herzegovina, Chile, Cyprus, Kazakhstan, Kyrgyzstan, and Tajikistan.

In response to demands by religious activists, the Cayman Islands prohibits a gay cruise ship from docking in the islands.

The Maryland Supreme Court rules that a parent's sexual orientation does not restrict access to his or her children.

Voters in Hawaii approve a constitutional amendment allowing the state legislature to reserve the right of marriage to opposite-sex couples only.

1999   The state of Nevada bans discrimination on the basis of sexual orientation in the private sector.

The French National Assembly grants to unmarried couples of the same or opposite sex all of the same rights available to married heterosexual couples.

The city of San Jose, California, bans discrimination in the private sector based on sexual orientation.

Canada's Supreme Court rules that same-sex couples are entitled to all of the same rights available to married heterosexual couples. That decision is the first step on the road to approval of same-sex marriage in Canada, which occurs in 2005.

The government of Ontario makes widespread changes in its laws, providing same-sex couples with essentially all of the same rights and privileges as those enjoyed by married heterosexual couples.

The Queer Youth Alliance (now the Queer Youth Network) is founded in Great Britain as the world's first gay rights organization for gay and lesbian youth.

1999
(*cont.*)
The state of California passes three gay rights bills, one providing for a domestic partnership registry, one outlawing harassment of gay youth in schools, and one banning discrimination in housing, employment, and public accommodation.

After the U.S. Senate had refused for two years to act on President Bill Clinton's nomination of James Hormel, a gay man, as ambassador to Luxembourg, Clinton gave Hormel a recess appointment, making him the first openly gay ambassador in U.S. history.

2000
The ban on gay men and lesbians serving in the armed forces of the United Kingdom is abolished.

The Scottish Parliament repeals Section 28 of the Local Government Act of 1988, banning local authorities from "promoting homosexuality." It is the first unit of the United Kingdom to do so.

Azerbaijan, Gabon, and Georgia decriminalize homosexual acts between consenting adults.

California voters approve Proposition 22, prohibiting the state from recognizing same-sex marriages, no matter where they have been performed.

Vermont becomes the first state to permit same-sex civil unions, similar to marriages in many respects.

2001
The Netherlands legalizes same-sex marriage, with all rights and privileges identical to those of heterosexual marriage. The nation is the first country in the world to do so.

The state of Arizona repeals its sodomy law.

Bans on discrimination based on sexual orientation are enacted in the states of Indiana, Maryland, and Rhode Island, and the city of Fort Wayne, Indiana.

A law permitting civil unions goes into effect in Germany.

Eight couples in British Columbia sue the province, claiming that limiting marriage to opposite-sex couples is unconstitutional.

Seven gay and lesbian couples in Massachusetts apply for marriage licenses and are denied. They begin the process of suing the state.

In one of the most famous events of its kind, police officers and members of the Egyptian State Security Intelligence raid the *Queen Boat* while it is moored on the Nile in Cairo's Zamalek district. The arrest of 55 men and boys brings forth strong condemnation from gay rights supporters around the world, but has no effect on Egypt's policies on homosexuality.

Judge Charles R. Simpson III, chief judge of the U.S. District Court for the Western District of Kentucky, rules that the Kentucky Baptist Homes for Children is justified in firing Alicia Pedreira from her job as a therapist for being a lesbian. He says that the law protects religious freedom, not personal lifestyle choices.

President George W. Bush appoints, and the U.S. Senate confirms, Michael Guest as ambassador to Romania, the first openly gay man to be approved by the Senate. At Guest's swearing-in ceremony, Secretary of State Colin Powell publicly acknowledges Guest's domestic partner of six years, Alex Nevarez.

2002   On January 1, Saudi Arabia beheads three men found guilty of "engaging in the extreme obscenity and ugly acts of homosexuality."

The states of Alaska and New York ban discrimination based on sexual orientation.

Sweden legalizes adoption by same-sex couples.

2002
(*cont.*)
Residents of the canton of Zurich, Switzerland, vote 63 percent to 37 percent to give all the same civil rights to same-sex couples as are available to married heterosexual couples.

Buenos Aires, Argentina, becomes the first Latin American city to legalize same-sex unions.

The government of Jamaica rejects a recommendation by parliament to decriminalize homosexuality. Caribbean nations at the time, and even today, remain among the most intolerant of same-sex behavior of any region on Earth.

2003
Same-sex marriage becomes legal in Belgium.

Rep. Marilyn Musgrave (R-Colo.) introduces the Federal Marriage Amendment in the U.S. House of Representatives. The bill has 108 cosponsors.

In its decision in *Lawrence v. Texas*, the United States Supreme Court declares all state sodomy laws to be unconstitutional.

California becomes the first state to ban discrimination on the basis of gender identity.

The Massachusetts Supreme Court rules that bans on same-sex marriage violate the state constitution.

Wal-Mart adds "sexual orientation" to its corporate nondiscrimination policy.

Ted Nebbling, a member of the British Columbia Legislative Assembly, marries his partner of 32 years, Jan Holmberg, in what is thought to be the first same-sex marriage of a sitting cabinet minister. Nebbling is removed from the cabinet on the following day, an act his party calls "a coincidence."

2004
Tasmania becomes the first Australian state to recognize same-sex civil unions.

Gov. Bob Taft (R-Ohio) signs the state's Defense of Marriage Act, which denies recognition of same-sex marriages, civil unions, or domestic partner agreements performed in other states; prohibits same-sex marriage within the state; and forbids the awarding of state benefits to gay and lesbian couples.

On February 12, Mayor Gavin Newsom, of San Francisco, directs the city clerk to begin issuing marriage licenses to same-sex couples. A week later, Governor Arnold Schwarzenegger (R-Calif.) directs the state attorney general to take such action as necessary to revoke these licenses, saying that same-sex marriage is "an imminent risk to civil order." A month later, the state supreme court votes to void more than 4,000 marriages held in San Francisco.

Cape Verde and Marshall Islands legalize homosexuality.

Portugal becomes the fourth county in the world to add protection on the basis of sexual orientation to the nation's constitution.

The Brazilian state of Rio Grande do Sul approves same-sex civil unions.

New Zealand passes legislation establishing same-sex civil unions.

Massachusetts becomes the first state to permit same-sex marriage.

Australia adopts legislation defining marriage as an act between one man and one woman.

Voters in 11 U.S. states adopt amendments to state constitutions banning same-sex marriages and, in most cases, civil unions and domestic partnerships as well.

2005 New Zealand becomes the first country in the world to outlaw hate crimes and discrimination on the basis of gender identity.

2005
(*cont.*)

Latvia and Uganda amend their constitutions to prohibit same-sex marriages.

Andorra, Canada, and Spain legalize same-sex marriage.

The Supreme Court of South Africa rules that bans on same-sex marriage are unconstitutional.

At its annual convention, the American Psychiatric Association votes to support government-recognized same-sex marriages.

After two earlier failed attempts, the Maine Human Rights Act is amended to ban discrimination based on sexual orientation. A vote to overturn that decision loses in a November election.

Connecticut approves same-sex civil unions.

2006

The Czech Republic and Slovenia approve registered partnerships, very similar to marriages, for same-sex couples.

Mexico's Distrito Federal (Federal District), in which Mexico City is located, approves civil unions.

Illinois and Washington State add sexual orientation to their state nondiscrimination laws.

Missouri legalizes homosexual acts between consenting adults.

Republican governor Ernie Fletcher of Kentucky rescinds a 2003 executive order banning discrimination on the basis of sexual orientation.

The First Eastern European Pride is held in Zagreb, Croatia, with attendees from Albania, Bosnia and Herzegovina, Bulgaria, Kosovo, Latvia, Lithuania, Macedonia, Montenegro, Poland, Romania, Serbia, Slovakia, and Slovenia.

Voters in seven U.S. states—Colorado, Idaho, South Carolina, South Dakota, Tennessee, Virginia, and Wisconsin—vote to ban same-sex marriage. Arizona voters reject a similar proposal.

2007   The Mexican state of Coahuila legalizes same-sex marriages.

A group of human rights experts, including judges, academics, a former UN High Commissioner for Human Rights, and representatives of nongovernmental organizations meet in Yogyakarta, Indonesia, to adopt a statement of principles on the application of international human rights law to sexual orientation and gender identity.

Six states—Colorado, Iowa, Kansas, Michigan, Ohio, Oregon, and Vermont—ban discrimination in employment, housing, and public accommodation on the basis of sexual orientation and, in some cases, gender identity. In most cases, the action occurs as the result of an executive order by the state governor.

Uruguay becomes the first South American country to adopt a civil unions law.

Hungary approves registered partnerships.

2008   A civil unions law in New Hampshire and a domestic partnership law in Oregon go into effect.

Nicaragua decriminalizes same-sex acts between consenting adults.

The California Supreme Court rules that state laws banning same-sex marriage are unconstitutional. The state begins to perform same-sex marriages in June. In November, citizens adopt a referendum proposition changing the state's constitution to limit marriage to heterosexual couples, invalidating the court's earlier decision.

2008
(*cont.*)

A United Nations resolution condemning violence, discrimination, stigmatization, and prejudice based on sexual orientation and gender identity is introduced into the General Assembly. Sixty six nations sign the resolution, and 57 do not. Support comes primarily from the Americas and Europe, while opposition comes mostly from African and Asian nations. The United States signs the resolution in March 2009, after Barack Obama becomes president.

2009

Norway's same-sex marriage laws and Hungary's registered partnership law go into effect on January 1.

A Northern Cyprus law legalizing male homosexuality goes into effect on January 1.

Civil partnership laws in Austria and Ireland go into effect on December 1.

More than a dozen gay men in Iraq are murdered because of their sexual orientation by members of their tribes, usually after denunciation by their own families.

The Iowa Supreme Court rules that limiting marriage to opposite sex couples is a violation of the state's constitution, and same-sex marriage becomes legal in the state.

The Vermont legislature overrides a veto by Republican governor Jim Douglas of a bill allowing same-sex couples to marry in the state. Vermont becomes the fourth state, after Massachusetts, Connecticut, and Iowa, to allow same-sex marriage, and the first state to do so by legislative action.

Nine gay men in Senegal are sentenced to jail terms of eight years each for "unnatural acts." The case reflects a growing opposition to homosexual acts across much of the African continent.

Maine and New Hampshire legislatures approve same-sex marriage for their states, with governors John Baldacci (Maine) and John Lynch (New Hampshire) both signing the relevant acts. At this point, only Rhode Island remains among New England states with not having approved same-sex marriages.

Uruguay becomes the first Latin American country to permit adoption of children by same-sex couples.

5

Biographical Sketches

This chapter contains biographical sketches of some of the leading figures in the gay and lesbian rights movement, as well as some individuals involved in the campaign against gay and lesbian rights. Given the large number of men and women who have been involved in this campaign, the chapter should be seen primarily as an introductory to some of the best-known pioneers and workers in the field.

Tammy Baldwin (1962–)

Tammy Baldwin is the first woman from Wisconsin and the first openly gay person in the nation to have been elected to the U.S. House of Representatives. In addition to concerns for the needs of her own constituents in Wisconsin's Second Congressional District, Baldwin is a strong advocate for health care reform, preservation of Social Security and Medicare/Medicaid programs, and programs in support of those with disabilities.

Baldwin was born in Madison, Wisconsin, on February 11, 1962. She was raised by her mother and her maternal grandparents. She graduated from Madison West High School in 1980 as class valedictorian. Baldwin continued her studies at Smith College, from which she received her bachelor's degree in 1984, and at the University of Wisconsin Law School, where she earned her JD degree in 1989. Even before completing her education, Baldwin had become politically active. She was elected to the Dane County Board of Supervisors in 1986, a post she held until 1994. She also served in the Wisconsin House of

Representatives from 1993 to 1999. In 1998, she ran for the U.S. House of Representatives and was elected by a margin of 53% to 47%. She has been reelected five times since, most recently in 2008 by a margin of 69% to 31%.

Elizabeth M. Birch (1959–)

Elizabeth Birch served as president and executive director of the Human Rights Campaign (HRC) from 1995 to 2005. During that time, she was also head of the HRC Foundation, the organization's educational arm; founded HRC's WorkNet, a resource center for workplace advocacy for lesbian and gay concerns, and HRC's FamilyNet, a virtual online resource for gay, lesbian, bisexual, and transgendered families; launched HRC's National Coming Out Day Program; and created the Lesbian Health Project. She has authored a number of AIDS antidiscrimination policies that became law in California and is founder of AIDS Legal Services of northern California.

Birch was born in September 1956 in Dayton, Ohio, to a Canadian Air Force officer stationed in the United States and his wife. She left home while still a teenager to join the cast of Up With People (an organization dedicated to developing leaders with a global perspective). She entered the University of Hawaii at Manoa in 1979, where she earned a BA in political science and oceanography in 1983. Birch then continued her studies at the Santa Clara University School of Law, which awarded her a JD degree in 1985. She also returned to the University of Hawaii at Manoa from 2000 to 2004 to work on (and eventually earn) a PhD in humanities.

From 1985 to 1989, Birch was partner in the San Francisco law firm of McCutchen, Doyle, Brown, & Enersen (now Bingham McCutchen), where she specialized in high technology, intellectual property, securities, and antitrust issues. She then became general counsel at the Claris Corporation, a wholly owned subsidiary of Apple Computer. She left Claris in June 1989 to become director of litigation, worldwide and human resources at Apple, a post she held until being appointed president and executive director at HRC. After leaving HRC in January 2005, Birch established her own consulting firm, Birch and Company, where she now works.

In recognition of her accomplishments, Birch was awarded an honorary doctorate of humane letters by the University of Hawaii in 2002 and the Hubert Humphrey Award of the Leadership Conference on Civil Rights in the same year. The latter award is the highest award for advocacy on behalf of lesbian, gay, bisexual, and transgender and HIV/AIDS communities in the United States.

Howard Juniah Brown (1924–1975)

Brown served as the city of New York's first health services administrator in the administration of Mayor John Lindsay. In that position, he was in charge of coordinating programs of the Departments of Health and Hospitals, the Community Health Board, and the Office of the Chief Medical Examiner. He held that post slightly more than a year before resigning in December 1967, afraid that his being a gay man would soon become public knowledge. He then went on to become director of community medicine at Fordham University and, later, professor at New York University's School of Public Administration and its School of Medicine. In October 1973, after years of leading a double life, Brown announced at a meeting of 600 physicians that he was gay. At that moment, as he points out in his autobiography, *Familiar Faces, Hidden Lives*, he became "the most prominent self-confessed homosexual in America."

Howard Juniah Brown was born April 15, 1924, in Peoria, Illinois. His father's occupation as a civil engineer forced the family to move frequently. He remembers having his first homosexual feelings when he was about 18, but made no attempt to act on them. He was sure, he said, that "I must be the only homosexual in northern Ohio" (Brown 1976, 32). It took him five years to discover he was very much wrong on this point.

Brown entered Hiram College on a prelaw scholarship, but decided in his senior year to switch to medicine because he believed that a law career would be too risky, given his sexual orientation. He was accepted by Cleveland's Western Reserve Medical College in 1943, but was drafted before he could enroll. After serving in the army for a year, he was discharged and began his medical training at Western Reserve. After earning his medical degree, Brown moved to Detroit to do his residency. He worked at Jennings Memorial Hospital and the UAW-CIO Clinic until 1954, when he moved to New York City. There he took a job as director of professional services for the Health Insurance Plan of Greater New York. He held that position until 1961, when he was appointed head of the Gouverneur Ambulatory Care Unit on New York City's Lower East Side.

The notoriety that Brown received after his "coming out" announcement encouraged him to become active in a variety of gay and lesbian causes. In October 1973, he was one of the founding members of the National Gay Task Force (now the National Gay and Lesbian Task Force). One of his major activities at the Task Force was an effort to convince the American Psychiatric Association to change its classification of homosexuality as a mental disorder, an effort that was eventually successful. After suffering from coronary problems for many years, Brown died of a heart attack on February 1, 1975. An alternative health care clinic founded in Chicago in 1974 was later named in his honor, the Howard Brown Memorial Clinic. Today, the Brown Clinic is widely recognized as one of the nation's leading centers for gay, lesbian, bisexual, and transgendered health care problems.

Charlotte Bunch (1944–)

Charlotte Bunch is widely regarded as one of the most important and articulate theorists of the gay and lesbian movement, particularly with regard to feminism. She has written and lectured extensively on feminist theory and its relationship to lesbianism. She has authored, coauthored, edited, and coedited a dozen books and more than 250 scholarly papers and popular articles on feminist theory and related topics.

Bunch was born in West Jefferson, North Carolina, on October 13, 1944, but she grew up in Artesia, New Mexico. After graduating from Artesia High School in 1962, she returned to North Carolina for her college education, earning her BA degree in history and political science from Duke University in 1966. Strongly influenced by the turmoil surrounding the Vietnam War in progress at the time, Bunch decided to make political activism a career.

In 1967, Bunch married Jim Weeks, a man who shared many of her interests in political activism. Over the next four years, however, the two grew apart, and in 1971, Bunch came out as a lesbian. She later wrote that this decision was "not a reaction against my husband but a response to the power of sexual self-discovery" (Bunch 1987, 102). She rapidly became involved in the young lesbian-feminist movement and was one of the founding members of the Furies collective, a group committed to the development of a lesbian-feminist political analysis, culture, and movement.

From her days at Duke to the present, Bunch's life has been a whirlwind of political activity. Following her work in the civil rights and antiwar movements, she has been involved at one time or another in the National Organization for Women, the University Christian Movement, the National Council of Churches Conference on Church and Society, the National Gay and Lesbian Task Force, the President's National Advisory Committee for Women, the National Women's Program of the American Friends Service Committee, the New York City Commission on the Status of Women, the Organizing Committee for the Decade for Human Rights Education, and the National Council for Research on Women.

In 1989, Bunch founded the Center for Women's Global Leadership at Douglass College, Rutgers University, of which she remains the executive director. She also holds an appointment as distinguished professor in the Women's and Gender Studies Department at Rutgers University. In 2007, she was awarded an honorary doctor of laws degree by the University of Connecticut.

John D'Emilio (1948–)

John D'Emilio is one of the preeminent historians of the gay and lesbian rights movement. He is the author of six major books on the subject, including *Sexual Politics, Sexual Communities: The Making of a Homosexual Minority in the United States, 1940–1970* (University of Chicago Press, 1983); *Intimate Matters: A History of Sexuality in America* (with Estelle B. Freeman; Harper and Row, 1988); *Making Trouble: Essays on Gay History, Politics, and the University* (Routledge, 1992); *Creating Change:*

Sexuality, Public Policy and Civil Rights (St. Martin's Press, 2000; with William Turner and Urvashi Vaid); *The World Turned: Essays on Gay History, Politics, and Culture* (Duke University Press, 2002); and *Lost Prophet: Bayard Rustin and the Quest for Peace and Justice in America* (The Free Press, 2003).

D'Emilio was born in New York City on September 21, 1948. He attended Columbia University, from which he received his BA in 1970, his MA in 1972, and his PhD in 1982, all in history. He then accepted an appointment at the University of North Carolina at Greensboro, where he served as assistant professor (1983–1988), associate professor (1988–1992), and professor (1992–1998). From 1988 to 1993, he was also director of graduate studies. In 1995, D'Emilio was named founding director of the National Gay and Lesbian Task Force Policy Institute, generally regarded as the movement's primary "think tank" on ways of advancing equality for gay men and lesbians. In 1999, he was named Professor of History and Gender and Women's Studies at the University of Illinois at Chicago, a post he continues to hold.

In addition to his books, D'Emilio has written a number of articles, book chapters, and policy papers dealing with the history and philosophy of the lesbian and gay rights movement, including "The Military and Lesbians during the McCarthy Years" (1984), "The Homosexual Menace: The Politics of Sexuality in Cold War America" (1989), "Power at the Polls: The Gay/Lesbian/Bisexual Vote" (1996); "Cycles of Change, Questions of Strategy: The Gay and Lesbian Movement after Fifty Years" (2000); and "Placing Gay in the Sixties" (2001). Among the more than 30 awards received by D'Emilio are nominee for the 1983 Pulitzer Prize in history; Best Book Award of the Task Force on Gay Liberation of the American Library Association (1984); David R. Kessler Lecturer, Center for Lesbian and Gay Studies, City University of New York (1999); Editor's Choice, Best Book Award, Lambda Literary Foundation (2003); American Library Association, Stonewall Award, Best Gay and Lesbian Nonfiction Book (2004); a "Chicagoan of the Year" award (*Chicago Tribune*; 2004); Brudner Prize, Yale University, for lifetime contribution to the development of lesbian and gay studies (2005); and induction to the City of Chicago Gay and Lesbian Hall of Fame (2005).

Martin Bauml Duberman (1930–)

Duberman is a highly respected historian and gay rights activist. He has taught at Yale, Princeton, and the City University of New York (CUNY), where he was distinguished professor of history from 1971 to the present day, a post he now holds as emeritus distinguished professor. Duberman has written more than 20 books on a variety of historical topics, specializing in the struggles of minority groups, including blacks and gay men and lesbians. He was a founding member of the National Gay Task Force, the Gay Academic Union, and the Center for Lesbian and Gay Studies at CUNY.

Martin Duberman was born in New York City on August 6, 1930, the son of Joseph M. Duberman and the former Josephine Bauml. He earned his BA at Yale in 1952, and then an MA in 1953 and a PhD in history at Harvard in 1957. Duberman reports that he was sexually attracted to other men as far back as he can remember, but did not act on this feelings until his freshman year at Yale. He then entered a long period during which he tried to understand and deal with his homosexual feelings, an experience he has eloquently recounted in his 1991 book *Cures: A Gay Man's Odyssey*.

Duberman has held a series of increasingly prestigious academic appointments: instructor at Yale; Morse Fellow, bicentennial preceptor, and assistant professor of history at Princeton; and associate professor, professor, and distinguished professor at the Lehman Graduate Center at CUNY. In addition, he has been a prolific author, biographer, and playwright. His books on gay-related themes have included *Hidden from History: Reclaiming the Gay and Lesbian Past* (1989), coedited with Martha Vicinus and George Chauncey Jr., an anthology on gay and lesbian history; *About Time: Exploring the Gay Past* (1986), a collection of his essays on the young gay and lesbian movement; *Stonewall* (1994), Duberman's own account of the early years of the gay liberation movement; and *Midlife Queer: Autobiography of a Decade* (1996), a memoir dealing with the gay and lesbian movement during the 1970s. Duberman's most recent book, *The Worlds of Lincoln Kirstein*, was one of two finalists for the 2007 Pulitzer Prize. His play *In White America* won the Drama Desk Award for Best Off-Broadway Production in 1963.

Steve Endean (1949–1993)

Steve Endean has been called "one of the most important GLBTQ activists of the post-Stonewall era" (Endean, Steve (1949–1993) 2008). He was instrumental in passage of a gay rights bill by the state of Minnesota legislature in 1993. In 1978, he founded the Gay Rights National Lobby, for which he became executive director. And in 1982, Endean founded the Human Rights Campaign, currently one of the two largest gay and lesbian political organizations (along with the National Gay and Lesbian Task Force) in the United States.

Endean was born in Davenport, Iowa, on August 6, 1949. He moved to Minneapolis in 1968 in order to study political science at the University of Minnesota. He received his bachelor's degree in that field in 1972. He had always hoped to pursue a career in politics, but abandoned those plans when he became convinced that that course of action was not available to an openly gay man in the 1970s. Instead, he decided to work in gay politics while supporting himself in a variety of jobs, such as tending bar and working as a coat check boy and a (poorly paid) lobbyist for gay and lesbian causes. In 1971, Endean founded the Minnesota Committee for Gay Rights (later the Gay Rights Legislative Committee), the first of many gay and lesbian rights organizations he established or helped to found. After a flurry of activity in Washington in the 1970s and early 1980s, Endean was diagnosed with AIDS in 1985, forcing his semiretirement from active involvement in gay and lesbian politics. He completed his memoir, *Bringing Lesbian and Gay Rights into the Mainstream* (Haworth Press, 2006), shortly before his death of HIV-related complications in Washington, D.C., on August 4, 1993.

Barbara Gittings (1932–2007)

Gittings was a pioneer activist in the young lesbian and gay rights movement of the 1950s. She founded the New York City chapter of the Daughters of Bilitis in 1958 and served as editor of the organization's magazine, *The Ladder*, from 1958 to 1966. During the 1950s and 1960s, Gittings was visible at virtually every public protest on the behalf of gay and lesbian rights.

Although not a librarian herself, she found herself at home in the gay and lesbian caucus of the American Library Association founded in 1970. She was particularly interested in developing positive images of lesbians and gay men in literature available to the general public. In 1972, she was a leader in the effort to have the American Psychiatric Association remove homosexuality from its list of mental disorders, an effort that was eventually successful.

Barbara Gittings was born in Vienna, Austria, on July 31, 1932. Her father was a member of the diplomatic service, stationed in Austria at the time. Upon returning to the United States, she attended high school in North Carolina and Maryland. After graduation, she entered Northwestern University to study drama. Her experience at Northwestern was a disaster as she discovered her erotic interest in other women. She became so engrossed in attempting to learn more about homosexuality, spending endless hours at the library, that she eventually dropped out of college and moved to Philadelphia, where she continued to look for additional information—especially positive information—about homosexuality.

During a visit to California in 1956, Gittings met Del Martin and Phyllis Lyon, founders of the Daughters of Bilitis (DOB). Martin and Lyon convinced Gittings to return to New York to form a local chapter of DOB. For many years, she supported herself in a variety of jobs, including 10 years as a mimeograph operator for an architectural firm, while devoting her real energies to the gay and lesbian movement. In addition to her local efforts, Gittings was also involved in national organizations, such as the East Coast Homophile Organization (ECHO) and the North American Conference of Homophile Organizations (NACHO).

Gittings met her partner, Kay Tobin Lahusen, in 1961, and they lived together until Gittings's death on February 18, 2007. In her later years, she continued her activist efforts, working to get the American Association of Retired Persons to provide health insurance to same-sex couples at the same price as for opposite-sex couples. The American Library Association has named its award for the best gay or lesbian novel of the year for her, and the Gay and Lesbian Alliance against Defamation has established the Barbara Gittings Award to honor organizations and individuals that develop positive media images of gay men and lesbians.

Henry (Harry) Hay (1912–2002)

Along with Bob Hull, Dale Jennings, and Chuck Rowland, Hay founded the International Bachelors Fraternal Order for Peace and Social Dignity in 1950. The organization, one of the first gay political action groups in the United States, was soon renamed the Mattachine Society. With a strong background in the Communist Party, Hay envisioned a person's sexual orientation as not strictly a personal characteristic, but an indication of one's membership in a "cultural minority" that had to be organized in order to achieve a variety of social and political goals. Hay, Hull, Jennings, and Rowland remained in the Mattachine Society for only about three years. They then resigned because the organization regarded their membership in the Communist Party as deleterious to the survival and success of the Mattachine group. In the late 1970s, Hay was one of the founders of the Racial Faeries, a group of gay men who reject efforts to assimilate gays and lesbians into the dominant heterosexual society and emphasize the feminine aspect of a man's personality.

Hay was born in Worthing, Sussex, England, on April 7, 1912, to Henry (known as Harry) Hay and the former Margaret Neall. The Hays were American citizens living in England at the time. They returned to the United States in 1917, where Hay eventually graduated from Los Angeles High School in 1929. He then enrolled at Stanford University, planning to major in dramatics. A year later, tired of hiding his sexual orientation, he announced to his friends that he was gay. Hay later reported that many friends decided to avoid further contact with him, but his closest friends responded with a casual, "Okay, what else is new?"

By 1933, Hay had decided that acting was unlikely to provide him with a decent living, so he decided to become active in guerrilla theater productions staged in connection with strikes and other types of worker demonstrations. He later told writer John D'Emilio that the experience was "just something tremendous ... You couldn't have been a part of that and not have your life completely changed (D'Emilio 1983, 59). In fact, that is just what happened. Hay spent the next 15 years working for the Communist Party, first as a union organizer, then in various cultural projects. To appease the party's strong antihomosexual position, Hay married another party member, Anita Platky, and lived a heterosexual life for 15 years. The Hays had two daughters, Hannah and Kate.

That phase of Hay's life came to an end in 1948. During a "beer bust" at the University of Southern California, a group of Hay's friends—all gay—began to banter about the idea of a "Bachelors for Wallace" political organization that would support the presidential candidacy of Henry Wallace on the Progressive Party ticket. Gradually, it occurred to Hay that it would be helpful for gay men to organize themselves formally, if for no other reason than to defend themselves and combat the rising tide of virulent antihomosexualism of Senator Joseph McCarthy. Out of that realization came the establishment of the Mattachine Society.

After leaving the Mattachine Society, Hay became interested in the nascent Native American movement and participated in a variety of workshops, protests, and other political activities. He was also involved in a variety of gay political organizations and activities throughout his life. In the 1970s, Hay and his domestic partner of 39 years, John Burnside, moved to New Mexico, where he operated a trading post on the San Juan Pueblo Indian reservation. He and Burnside then returned to Los Angeles and, eventually, to San Francisco, where he died of lung cancer on October 24, 2002.

Magnus Hirschfeld (1868–1935)

Hirschfeld was a physician, sex researcher, and early advocate for the rights of gay men and lesbians. In 1897, he and two friends, Max Spohr and Erich Oberg, founded the *Wissenschaftlich-humanitäres Komitee* (Scientific-Humanitarian Committee) in Berlin. The purpose of the organization was to work for social recognition of gay men, lesbians, and transgendered persons and against their persecution by the government and its agencies. It was the leading voice for gay and lesbian rights in Germany until it was suppressed by the Nazi Party in 1933. Hirschfeld seemed possessed of limitless energy, devoting every moment of his life to writing, speaking, and organizing for the rights of lesbians, gay men, and transgendered persons. In 1913, he was one of the founders of the Medical Society for

Sexual Science and Eugenics. Five years later he established the Magnus Hirschfeld Foundation for Sex Research and then, a year later, the Institute for Sexual Science.

Hirschfeld was born in Kolberg, Germany, on May 14, 1868, the son of the esteemed Jewish physician Herman Hirschfeld. After graduating from the *Domgymnasium* in Kolberg in 1887, he studied philosophy and philology at the University of Breslau and then medicine in Berlin, Heidelberg, Munich, and Strasbourg. In 1892, he received his doctoral degree from the University of Berlin. In the early 1890s, Hirschfeld set out on the first of what was to become numerous foreign travels. His initial goal was the 1893 Chicago World's Fair, after which he traveled across the United States and then on to Asia, Africa, and Europe. In 1895, he established a medical practice in Charlottenburg, where he remained until 1909. He then transferred his practice to Berlin, where he specialized in problems of the nervous system and in human sexuality.

A gay man himself, Hirschfeld believed that sexual orientation was a "deep, inner-constituted natural instinct," not a conscious choice that one makes (Adam 1987, 231). Gay men and lesbians cannot, therefore, be accused of being ill or sinful, Hirschfeld wrote. The goal of the medical profession, he went on, should be to help lesbians and gay men adjust to their condition, not to try to change that condition.

An important focus of Hirschfeld's work was the attempt to have Paragraph 175 of the German constitution, outlawing same-sex acts, revoked. After three decades of struggle, that objective was obtained when the Reichstag removed homosexual acts from the nation's penal code in 1929. But it was a pyrrhic victory for Hirschfeld and his allies. The Nazi Party was already on the rise in German politics and it strongly opposed those who were engaged in homosexual acts, as it opposed other groups such as Jews, gypsies, and non-Aryans. By 1932, Hirschfeld found it necessary to flee first to Switzerland and later to France to escape Nazi oppression. He spent the last few years of his life in France and died in Nice on May 15, 1935. He left behind his domestic partner of many years, Kurt Giese, who committed suicide in Prague in 1936.

The accomplishments of the Scientific-Humanitarian Committee were rapidly obliterated in the early years of National Socialism. The climatic event in that purge occurred on May 6, 1933, when hundreds of students from a nearby Nazi school for physical education attacked Hirschfeld's Institute for Sexual Science, sacked its contents, and burned the building. About 12,000 books and 35,000 photographs, most of them irreplaceable, were destroyed.

Franklin Kameny (1925–)

Kameny has been described by a historian of gay and lesbian rights as "[o]ne of the most significant figures" in the American gay rights movement (Bullough 2002, 207). Trained as an astronomer, Kameny became active in the gay and lesbian rights movement when he was fired from his job with the Army Map Service (now the Defense Mapping Agency) in January 1958 for being gay. He has spent the rest of his life working for gay and lesbian rights, largely in response to this action. Throughout his career, he has taken a strong, confrontational approach in an effort to obtain equal rights for gay men and lesbians. In 1965, for example, he and Jack Nichols organized the first picket line around the White House in pushing for gay and lesbian rights. He is also credited with having created the slogan "Gay is good" in 1968. In 1971, Kameny became the first openly gay man to run for national public office when he ran for the post of nonvoting delegate to the U.S. House of Representatives from the District of Columbia.

Kameny was born in New York City on May 21, 1925. His parents were Polish and Austro-Hungarian Jews. He taught himself to read by the age of four, and two years later had decided that he wanted to become an astronomer. He entered Queens College at the age of 15, but his education was interrupted by World War II. At the war's conclusion, he returned to Queens and earned his BS in physics in 1948. He then continued his education at Harvard College, from which he received his master's degree in astronomy in 1949 and his PhD in astronomy in 1956. After a year of teaching at Georgetown University, Kameny took a position with the Army Map Service. He served in that position for only a brief period of time before being fired for being gay. Not given to yielding on matters of principle, Kameny then began a long series of court battles to regain his job. His fundamental premise throughout this fight was that his employer (the U.S. government) had no right to inquire into his personal life unless it interfered with his work, a claim the government never made. No organization, including the American Civil Liberties Union, was willing to support Kameny's position, and when his case finally reached the Supreme Court, he had to write his own brief. The court declined in March 1961 to hear Kameny's case, and he decided that his life thenceforward would have a new direction—he was going to become a gay activist.

One of his first acts was to organize (with Nichols) a Washington chapter of New York City's Mattachine Society. Kameny began to put into practice his attitudes about the gay rights issue. It was necessary not for gays to change and adapt to an oppressive society, he argued, but to help educate the non-gay world and help them to recognize the legitimacy of the gay rights cause. He outlined his position in an article he wrote for *The Ladder* in 1965 when he said, "We ARE right; those who oppose us are both morally and factually wrong.... We must DEMAND our rights boldly, not beg cringingly for mere privileges, and not be satisfied with the crumbs tossed to us" (Blasius and Phelan 1997, 335).

In 2002, the Harvard Gay and Lesbian Caucus gave its lifetime Achievement Award to Kameny for his contributions to the gay and lesbian rights movement.

Larry Kramer (1935–)

Larry Kramer is an author, playwright, and activist for gay and lesbian rights. He is perhaps best known as the founder of the AIDS Coalition to Unleash Power (ACT-UP), an organization formed to confront governmental agencies and private corporations for a more aggressive approach to the health problems resulting from the HIV/AIDS epidemic. He has also written a number of powerful works dealing with the epidemic and with the social and political issues faced by lesbians and gay men in the United States.

Kramer was born in Bridgeport, Connecticut, on June 25, 1935. After graduating from high school in Maryland, Kramer matriculated at Yale University in 1953. Like many young gay men of the time, Kramer struggled with his sexual identity, often wondering if he were the only person with homosexual feelings in the world. At Yale, he had his first long-term relationship with a man, his German professor, which ended when the professor returned to Europe. Kramer received his bachelor's degree in English in 1957.

Kramer's first job after graduation was with Columbia Pictures, where he worked as a teletype operator, an assistant story editor, and a production executive. He then moved to United Artists as assistant to the president of the company. In 1969, he wrote the screenplay for and produced Ken Russell's film *Women in Love*, for which he received an Academy Award nomination. In 1978, Kramer published his first novel, *Faggots*, a satire on the promiscuous life of gay men at the time. Although it received some critical acclaim, the novel was roundly criticized by most gay men for presenting such a strongly negative portrayal of gay society.

The rising HIV/AIDS epidemic of the early 1980s transformed Kramer's life and work. Upon learning of the rapid spread of the disease and the extent to which it was being ignored by government agencies, Kramer began to write and speak about the need for gay men themselves to push more strongly for assistance from health agencies. In 1982, he became a member of New York City's Gay Men's Health Crisis (GMHC), an organization created to support people with HIV/AIDS and to work for research on and treatments for the disease. When he felt that GMHC was moving too slowly to deal with the problem of HIV/AIDS, he moved on to form ACT-UP.

Kramer also used his authorial skills to battle the disease and the government's inertia in dealing with it. In 1985, he produced *The Normal Heart*, a play dealing with HIV/AIDS-related issues. The play is one of the most powerful statements about the epidemic that has ever been written and is sometimes credited with bringing the urgency of the disease before the gay and non-gay public as no other work of art has ever done. The play is still the longest-running production ever at New York's Public Theater. It has been produced more than 600 times over the past two decades.

Phyllis Lyon (1924–)

Lyon's name is inextricably linked with that of Del Martin, her domestic partner of 56 years. Lyon and Martin founded the Daughters of Bilitis in 1955, the first political and social organization in the United States designed specifically for lesbians. Throughout their lives, Lyon and Martin were involved in a number of gay, lesbian, and feminist organizations, including the Council of Religion and Homosexuality, whose goal it was to encourage religious leaders to include gay men and lesbians in church activities, and the Alice B. Toklas Memorial Democratic Club, the first gay and lesbian political organization in San Francisco, and still one of the most influential such groups in the city.

Phyllis Lyon was born in Tulsa, Oklahoma, on November 10, 1924. She grew up in Seattle, southern California, and San Francisco, graduating from Sacramento High School in 1943. She then attended the University of California at Berkeley, from which she received her BA in journalism in 1946. Like many women of her day, Lyon felt that her life would eventually have to center on a man. As she told historian John D'Emilio, "If you were a woman, you had to have a man. There was no other way" (D'Emilio 1983, 102). By the 1950s, however, she learned otherwise. After a stint as a general reporter for the *Chico Enterprise-Record*, Lyon moved to Seattle to work on a trade magazine. There she met Del Martin and fell in love. In 2004, they were the first same-sex couple to be married in San Francisco after Mayor Gavin Newsom issued an order permitting same-sex marriage licenses in the city. Four years later, after the California Supreme Court ruled that same-sex marriages were legal in the state, the couple was married a second time.

In 1972, Lyon and Martin coauthored *Lesbian/Woman*, a book that discussed lesbian lives in a strongly positive tone, an approach that was virtually unknown at the time. *Publisher's Weekly* called the book one of the 20 most important women's books of its generation. In the last three decades, Lyon has been especially interested in the topic of human sexuality in general and, in 1970s, cofounded the Institute for Advanced Study of Human Sexuality in San Francisco, from which she received her EdD in 1976. She also served on the San Francisco Human Rights Commission for more than a decade, acting as chairperson for two of those years.

Del Martin (1921–2008)

With her long-time domestic partner, Phyllis Lyon, Martin was deeply involved in the gay and lesbian political rights movement for more than half a century. In 1955, Martin and Lyon founded the Daughters of Bilitis, the first organization created to push for political rights of lesbians in the United States. A year later, they also founded and edited the nation's first lesbian periodical, *The Ladder*. The two women were also involved in creating the Council on Religion and the Homosexual in 1964 and San Francisco's Alice B. Toklas Memorial Democratic Club in 1972.

Martin was born Dorothy L. Taliaferro in San Francisco on May 5, 1921. Early in life, she became better known as Del. She attended George Washington High School in San Francisco before matriculating at the University of California at Berkeley. She later transferred to San Francisco State College (now San Francisco State University), where she met her future husband, James Martin. She then left San Francisco State, gave birth to a daughter, Kendra, and moved with her family to the suburbs. Before long, she realized that her longstanding attraction to women made her marriage impossible, and she was divorced from Martin (although she did keep her husband's surname).

In 1950, Martin moved to Seattle to take a job with a publisher of construction trade information. There she met Lyon, who was working with the same company. They made a commitment to each other in 1952 and, in 1955, moved to San Francisco. There they bought a house where they continued to live for more than 50 years.

In addition to her political activities, Martin wrote two important books, *Lesbian/Woman* (with Lyon) and *Battered Wives*, a book that became critical in the development of a national movement against domestic violence. Martin and Lyon were married twice, the first time in 2004, and again in 2008. She died in San Francisco on August 27, 2008, as the result of complications arising from a broken arm that exacerbated her already poor health.

Leonard Matlovich (1943–1988)

Leonard Matlovitch may well have been the best-known American gay man in the early 1970s. His picture appeared on the cover of *Time* magazine on September 8, 1975, with the caption: ''I Am a Homosexual: The Gay Drive for Acceptance.'' Matlovich was featured in the story because, in spite of a spotless personnel record, he had been discharged from the U.S. Air Force for being gay. After his discharge, he devoted most of his life to activities related to gay and lesbian rights issues.

Matlovich was born in Savannah, Georgia, on July 6, 1943, to a career Air Force sergeant. He grew up on air bases in the United States and England as, according to his own account, an ultraconservative, flag-waving racist grounded in a very traditional Roman Catholic house. After graduating from high school in England in 1962, Matlovich immediately joined the Air Force at least partly, he later said, because he had long been aware of his homosexual feelings and felt that he had to prove that he was a real man. He immediately volunteered to serve in the Vietnam conflict, eventually serving three tours of duty there. When he returned to the United States, he had been awarded a Bronze Star, a Purple Heart, and an Air Force Meritorious Service Medal for his service in Vietnam.

After the war, Matlovich was assigned to a new kind of duty as a race-relations instructor at Virginia's Langley Air Force Base. At the time, Matlovich was still a virgin, very much uncertain and considerably appalled about his own sexuality. Only after exposure to gay bars in Florida, where he was later stationed, did he realize that he was hardly the only gay man in the world, and that others like him that he met were decent, successful members of society. As a result of this experience, he decided to inform his military superiors of his sexual orientation, which he did in a letter written in March 1975. Although Matlovich had a spotless military record including a number of commendations for his work, the U.S. Air Force began proceedings to release him with a general discharge. (A general discharge ranks below an honorable discharge, but above a dishonorable discharge, permitting the recipient to receive some, but not all, military benefits after leaving the service.)

Matlovich refused to passively accept the Air Force's decision and began a long battle to gain reinstatement to the military services. After four years, the Air Force offered Matlovich a cash payment of $160,000, a promotion, and an honorable discharge. By that point, Matlovich no longer wanted to return to the Air Force, and he accepted the settlement. In the remaining years of his life, Matlovich was popular as a speaker on issues of gays and lesbians in the military and on AIDS, which he had contracted. He ran unsuccessfully in 1978 for a seat on the San Francisco Board of Supervisors. Matlovich died in San Francisco on June 23, 1988, of complications of AIDS. The epitaph he selected for his tombstone reads: "When I was in the military, they gave me a medal for killing two men, and a discharge for loving one."

Harvey Milk (1930–1978)

Harvey Milk is arguably the most famous gay politician of the 20th century. In 1975, he was elected to the San Francisco Board of Supervisors, the first openly gay man to be elected to a major office in any American city. He served in that position for only three years before being assassinated by former supervisor Dan White on November 27, 1978.

Milk was born in New York City on May 22, 1930, to William Milk, who worked in his family's dry goods store, and the former Minerva (Minnie) Karns, a stenographer before her marriage. Harvey attended Bayshore High School, where he was a member of the basketball, football, track, and wrestling teams. Like many other gay men and lesbians, Milk was aware of his attraction to members of his own sex, but worked hard to keep these feelings separate from his school activities.

In 1947, Milk entered the New York State College for Teachers at Albany (now the University at Albany), where he majored in mathematics. Three months after receiving his bachelor's degree in 1951, Milk enlisted in the U.S. Navy. He eventually rose to the rank of chief petty officer before returning to civilian life. He then worked as an actuarial statistician at the Great American Insurance Company in New York City until 1963 and then became a researcher at the Wall Street investment firm of Bache & Company. After transferring to Bache's Dallas office for a brief period, Milk resigned from the company and followed his domestic partner of the time to San Francisco.

Milk rapidly became enchanted with the exciting politics of his new home town and abandoned his traditional Republican conservatism for its brash Democratic liberalism. He opened a camera shop on Castro Street, an area with a rapidly growing gay and lesbian population, and the shop soon became better known as the social and political center of the neighborhood than as a source of photographic supplies. Before long, Milk had earned the nickname "The Mayor of Castro Street," also the title of a biography of Milk written by Randy Shilts in

1988. He also began having citywide political aspirations and in 1973 announced that he was a candidate for the city's board of supervisors.

Few political observers gave him much chance of being elected. The old-line gay Democratic club had already chosen its candidate for the board and regarded Milk as an upstart who should best be ignored. As expected, Milk was not elected although he did receive 17,000 votes, finishing a respectable tenth among 32 candidates. In his second try at office in 1975, Milk gained 30 percent of the vote in a slate of 16 candidates, earning him a seat on the board. His tenure ended three years later when White, a former fire fighter and city supervisor, killed both Milk and Mayor George Mascone. White was later convicted of manslaughter, rather than murder, and given a seven-year prison sentence. He was given the lighter sentence because his defense team had convinced the court that White was mentally disturbed at the time of the killing because he had been eating too much junk food (an argument later known as the "Twinkie defense").

Milk's memory is honored today in a number of ways, including the Harvey Milk Gay and Lesbian Democratic Club, the Harvey Milk Memorial Plaza, the Harvey Milk Memorial Community Center, and the Harvey Milk Branch of the San Francisco Public Library, all in San Francisco. His life was memorialized in the 2008 motion picture *Milk*, directed by Gus Van Sant, and starring Sean Penn, Emile Hirsch, and Josh Brolin.

Troy Perry (1940–)

Troy Perry founded the first Christian church in the United States with a special mission to lesbians and gay men. The church's first service was held in Perry's living room in Los Angeles on October 16, 1968, and attracted 12 people. The church, now known as the Metropolitan Community Church, currently has 43,000 members and adherents in almost 300 congregations in 22 countries.

Perry was born in Tallahassee, Florida, on July 27, 1940, the oldest of five boys born to Troy Perry and Edith Allen, whom Perry later described as "the biggest bootleggers in Northern Florida" (Tobin and Wicker 1975, 14). Although his parents were not particularly religious, Perry decided at an early age that he wanted to become a minister. His early upbringing occurred within the Baptist and Pentecostal Churches, and he soon adopted the strict moral code imposed by the latter denomination. He did not attend movies, dance, or play cards or games involving dice. He claims that he and his dates always knelt and prayed before they went out together, asking to have the strength to avoid temptations.

Although his first homosexual experience was at the age of nine, Perry convinced himself that he was not "that way." He decided that his constant homosexual fantasies were just "different" from what other boys experienced. He had no reservations or doubts, then, when he married a pastor's daughter in 1958 at the age of 18. Two sons resulted from that marriage, which ended in divorce five years later.

In the meanwhile, Perry attended the Midwest Bible College and the Moody Bible Institute in Chicago. In 1962, he was ordained a minister in the Church of God and became a pastor at a small church in Santa Ana, California. He found it increasingly difficult to reconcile his homosexual feelings with his denomination's teachings and his church responsibilities, however, and in 1964, he left the church and took a job with Sears Roebuck.

After a stint in the Army, a failed relationship with another man, and an attempted suicide, Perry made a momentous decision—he would start a church with a special mission to the gay and lesbian community. Of the 12 attendees at the first meeting of that church, Perry later said, "Nine were my friends who came to console me and to laugh, and three came as a result of the ad [which he had placed in the gay magazine *The Advocate*]" (Tobin and Wicker 1975, 19–20). This inauspicious beginning gave no hint whatsoever of the spectacular success the Metropolitan Community Church was later to experience.

Perry later wrote about his own life in the book *The Lord Is My Shepherd and He Knows I'm Gay* (Nash Publishing, 1972) and its sequel, *Don't Be Afraid Any More* (St. Martin's Press, 1990). Perry was the first openly gay person to serve on the Los Angeles County Commission on Human Relations. He has been honored with the Humanitarian Awards of the Lesbian and Gay Rights Chapter of the American Civil Liberties Union and of the Gay Press Association. He holds honorary doctorates from Boston's Episcopal Divinity School, Samaritan College of Los Angeles, and Sierra University in Santa Monica, California.

Karl Heinrich Ulrichs (1825–1895)

Karl Ulrichs is sometimes regarded as the first person in modern European history to publicly acknowledge his attraction to other men. Over a period of more than a decade, he wrote extensively about the nature of homosexuality and worked continuously to educate the general public on the subject and to have the laws dealing with same-sex acts in Germany abolished. Ulrich's first effort in this area was a 12-volume work published under the pseudonym Numa Numantius in 1864. He then wrote another dozen books in the next six years, all published under his own name. In 1867, he tried to bring the issue of civil rights for gay men and lesbians to the attention of the Congress of German Jurists, but he was shouted down and prevented from speaking on the subject.

Ulrichs was born in Hannover, Germany, on August 28, 1825. He studied law and theology at Göttingen University in 1846 and history at Berlin University from 1846 to 1848. After completing his studies, Ulrichs was given a position as a lawyer in the Hannoverian government. Four years later he was promoted, but two years after that he was dismissed from his position because of his sexual activities with other men.

In his many books, Ulrichs developed many fundamental ideas about homosexuality and civil rights for gay men and lesbians. He suggested the notion that homosexuals constituted a third sex, intermediary between male and female, that he called *uranian*. Since homosexuality was an inborn, natural condition, he argued, society could not call the condition sinful, perverted, or depraved.

Many of Ulrichs's ideas, primitive as they were, are reflected in ideas still to be found in the modern gay and lesbian rights movement. For example, a common theme in the movement today is that sexual orientation is an inborn, genetic trait, similar to skin color or sex, and that, as such, it is unreasonable to discriminate against people with a homosexual orientation.

Ulrichs's spurt of creative energy during the 1860s apparently exhausted him. He left Germany for Italy in 1870, where he lived in Naples and then, for the last 12 years of his life in Aquila, where he died on July 14, 1895. Ulrichs had virtually no impact on mainstream social or political thought in Germany. However, many of his ideas were eventually incorporated into medical thought on the subject of homosexuality. He is remembered today in an annual award presented by the International Lesbian and Gay Law Association, the Karl Heinrich Ulrichs Award.

Urvashi Vaid (1958–)

Urvashi Vaid has served as media director and executive director of the National Gay and Lesbian Task Force (NGLTF) and as director of the organization's Policy Institute, the nation's primary think tank for gay and lesbian issues.

Vaid was born in New Delhi, India, on October 8, 1958. In 1966, she moved with her family to Potsdam, New York, and became politically involved at an early age. Among her first activities was participation in a number of protests against the Vietnam War at the age of 11. A bright and eager student, Vaid graduated from high school in three years and entered Vassar College, from which she received her bachelor's degree in English in 1979. It was at Vassar that Vaid first met a group of out lesbians, confirming her own long-held feelings that she was more attracted to women than to men.

After leaving Vassar, Vaid enrolled at Northeastern University in Boston, from which she received her law degree in 1983. At Northeastern she focused on legal issues faced by gay men, lesbians, and women in general. She was also cofounder of the Boston Lesbian/Gay Political Alliance. Her first job after leaving Northeastern was as a staff attorney for the American Civil Liberty Union's National Prisons Project (ACLU-NPP) in Washington, D.C. In 1984, she initiated the ACLU-NPP's program for prisoners who had contracted the human immunodeficiency virus (HIV).

In 1986, Vaid was appointed director of public information at NGLTF, where she also served on the organization's board of directors. In 1989, she was promoted to executive director at NGLTF, a post she held until 1992. She then left the organization for a period of five years during which she worked on her book, *Virtual Equality: The Mainstreaming of Gay and Lesbian*

Liberation (Anchor Books, 1996). In the book, Vaid reviews the history of the gay and lesbian rights movement in the United States, analyzes the movement's shift toward conservatism, and discusses the options facing the movement in coming years.

In 1997, Vaid returned to the Task Force as executive director of its Policy Institute. During her four years in that position, she coedited (with John D'Emilio and Bill Turner) an anthology on the history of gay, lesbian, bisexual, and transgender public policy issues entitled *Creating Change: Public Policy, Sexuality and Civil Rights* (St. Martin's Press, 2000). In 2001, Vaid left NGLTF again to take a position as deputy director of the Governance and Civil Society Unit of the Ford Foundation, where she remained until 2005. She then accepted an appointment as executive director of the Arcus Foundation, headquartered in Kalamazoo, Michigan. Arcus is a grant-making organization whose mission is to "achieve social justice that is inclusive of sexual orientation, gender identity and race, and to ensure conservation and respect of the great apes" (Arcus Foundation, 2008).

Bruce Voeller (1934–1994)

Bruce Voeller was a biochemist who spent most of his adult life working for the advancement of gay and lesbian causes. He was among the founders of New York City's Gay Activist Alliance (GAA) in 1971, serving as the group's president for two years. Along with Martin Duberman, Ron Gold, Barbara Gittings, Frank Kameny, Dr. Howard Brown, and Nathalie Rockhill, he then broke with GAA to establish the National Gay Task Force (now the National Gay and Lesbian Task Force) in 1973, an organization of which he was executive director until 1978. He then left the Task Force to establish (along with Karen DeCrow and Aryeh Neier) the Mariposa Foundation, an organization committed to improving the understanding of the medical profession and the clergy of issues related to human sexuality, especially those of concern to lesbians and gay men.

Voeller was born in Minneapolis, Minnesota, on May 12, 1934. He attended high school in Roseburg, Oregon, where he graduated in 1952. He then entered Reed College. He claimed to have experienced homosexual feelings as early as junior high school, but both his minister at the time and, later, a counselor at Reed assured him that he was not gay because he did not display typical characteristics of gay men, such as effeminacy and dislike of sports.

After graduating from Reed with a BA in biology in 1956, Voeller began graduate study in biology at the Rockefeller Institute in New York City, from which he received his PhD in 1961. He then became research associate (1961–1962), assistant professor (1962–1966), and associate professor (1966–1972) at Rockefeller. During the same period, he held posts as adjunct professor at Hunter College and Visiting Field Professor of Biology for Harvard University in Mexico.

Voeller's life seemed to be moving along a traditional and predictable academic and personal pathway. In addition to his promotions and growing list of publications, he had met and married Kytja Scott in graduate school and become the father of three children. By 1971, however, Voeller could no longer ignore his strong homosexual feelings. He decided to leave academic life and his marriage in order to devote himself full time to the young and growing gay and lesbian liberation movement. At the Mariposa Foundation, he is probably best remembered for his research on the reliability of various brands of condoms and on the safety and effectiveness of the (then) recently approved female condom. He remained active in a variety of gay and lesbian organizations until his death in Topanga, California, on February 13, 1994, as the result of complications from AIDS. He left behind his life partner of 15 years, Richard Lucik.

Tom Waddell (1937–1987)

Tom Waddell founded the Gay Games in the early 1980s. He originally hoped to stage a "Gay Olympics" in which all men and women, of whatever nationality, race, age, or sexual orientation would be welcome. When the U.S. Olympic Committee (USOC) heard of Waddell's plans, however, they filed suit against Waddell, claiming that the USOC had exclusive use of the term *Olympic* in the United States. Under the title of Gay Games, however, the event envisioned by Waddell was carried out in San Francisco in August 1982. More than 1,300 male and female athletes from 12 countries participated in the event. At the most recent reenactment of the event, Gay Games VII in Chicago in 2006, more than 11,000 athletes from more than 70 countries took part in 30 different events.

Waddell was born Tom Flubacher on November 1, 1937, in Paterson, New Jersey, the second of three sons born to Elmer and Marion Flubacher. At an early age, he befriended Gene Waddell, an acrobat, and his wife, Hazel, a dancer. He became so close to the Waddells that in college he changed his last name to theirs. After graduating from high school, Waddell matriculated at Springfield College in Massachusetts, where he originally planned to major in physical education, but eventually changed to a premedical curriculum. At Springfield he also competed in gymnastics and football before deciding to concentrate on the decathlon.

Upon graduation from Springfield in 1959, Waddell entered the New Jersey College of Medicine (now the University of Medicine and Dentistry of New Jersey), from which he earned his medical degree in 1962. After completing his internship, Waddell was drafted into the Army in 1966, where he became a preventative-medicine officer and paratrooper. In 1968, the Army assigned Waddell to a new assignment: training for the 1968 Olympic Games as a competitor in the decathlon. He eventually finished sixth among 33 competitors at the Mexico City games.

After being discharged from the Army, Waddell completed residencies at Georgetown University and Montefiore Hospital in the Bronx, New York. He then applied for and was given a graduate fellowship at Stanford University in 1970. Over the next decade, Waddell divided his time between the gay community in San Francisco, to which he had moved, and a variety of medical opportunities made available to him because of his expertise in infectious diseases. For example, he served as personal physician to a Saudi Arabian prince and a Saudi Arabian businessman, and worked as team physician for the Saudi team at the 1976 Montreal Olympics.

In 1986, Waddell was diagnosed with HIV. That diagnosis forced him to resign from his current post as chief physician at San Francisco's Central Emergency Facility and to focus on his own health. Unfortunately, he also had to deal for the last two years of his life with a lien placed on his home by the USOC in an attempt to recover $96,000 in legal fees it had spent in the court case against Waddell's plans for a Gay Olympics. Waddell died of complications from AIDS in San Francisco on July 11, 1987.

References

Adam, Barry D. 1987. *The Rise of a Gay and Lesbian Movement*. Boston: Twayne Publishers.

Arcus Foundation. 2008. http://www.arcusfoundation.org/pages_2/home.cfm. Accessed on November 1, 2008.

Blasius, Mark, and Shane Phelan. 1997. *We Are Everywhere: A Historical Sourcebook of Gay and Lesbian Politics*. New York: Routledge.

Brown, Howard. 1976. *Familiar Faces, Hidden Lives*. New York: Harcourt Brace Jovanovich.

Bullough, Vern L., ed. 2002. *Before Stonewall: Activists for Gay and Lesbian Rights in Historical Context*. New York: Haworth Press.

Bunch, Charlotte. 1987. *Passionate Politics: Feminist Theory in Action*. New York: St. Martin's Press.

D'Emilio, John. 1983. *Sexual Politics, Sexual Communities: The Making of a Homosexual Minority in the United States, 1940–1970*. Chicago: University of Chicago Press.

"Endean, Steve (1949–1993)." 2008. glbtq. An Encyclopedia of Gay, Lesbian, Bisexual, Transgender, and Queer Culture. http://www.glbtq.com/social-sciences/endean_s.html. Accessed on November 4, 2008.

Tobin, Kay, and Randy Wicker. 1975. *The Gay Crusaders*. New York: Arno Press.

6

Data and Documents

This chapter contains a number of important documents dealing with gay and lesbian rights issues, along with some data and statistics dealing with those issues. The documents and data are arranged according to type: policy statements, legislation, court cases, and data. In all of the following selections, omitted citations are indicated by an asterisk and ellipses (* . . .).

Policy Statements

Don't Ask, Don't Tell (1993)

As of early 2009, U.S. policy on the role of gay men and lesbians is controlled by H.R. 2401, the appropriations act for the Department of Defense for the fiscal year 1994 (also Public Law 103–160 [10 U.S.C. § 654]), adopted on October 6, 1993. The portion of that act dealing with gays and lesbians in the military is found in section 546, an extract of which is provided here.

> SEC. 546. POLICY CONCERNING HOMOSEXUALITY IN THE ARMED FORCES.
>
> (a) CODIFICATION.—(1) Chapter 37 of title 10, United States Code, is amended by adding at the end the following new section:
>
> **§ 654. Policy concerning homosexuality in the armed forces**

(a) FINDINGS.—Congress makes the following findings:

(1) Section 8 of article I of the Constitution of the United States commits exclusively to the Congress the powers to raise and support armies, provide and maintain a Navy, and make rules for the government and regulation of the land and naval forces.

(2) There is no constitutional right to serve in the armed forces.

(3) Pursuant to the powers conferred by section 8 of article I of the Constitution of the United States, it lies within the discretion of the Congress to establish qualifications for and conditions of service in the armed forces.

(4) The primary purpose of the armed forces is to prepare for and to prevail in combat should the need arise.

(5) The conduct of military operations requires members of the armed forces to make extraordinary sacrifices, including the ultimate sacrifice, in order to provide for the common defense.

(6) Success in combat requires military units that are characterized by high morale, good order and discipline, and unit cohesion.

(7) One of the most critical elements in combat capability is unit cohesion, that is, the bonds of trust among individual service members that make the combat effectiveness of a military unit greater than the sum of the combat effectiveness of the individual unit members.

(8) Military life is fundamentally different from civilian life in that—

(A) the extraordinary responsibilities of the armed forces, the unique conditions of military service, and the critical role of unit cohesion, require that the military community, while subject to civilian control, exist [sic] as a specialized society; and

(B) the military society is characterized by its own laws, rules, customs, and traditions, including numerous restrictions on personal behavior, that would not be acceptable in civilian society.

(9) The standards of conduct for members of the armed forces regulate a member's life for 24 hours

each day beginning at the moment the member enters military status and not ending until that person is discharged or otherwise separated from the armed forces.

(10) Those standards of conduct, including the Uniform Code of Military Justice, apply to a member of the armed forces at all times that the member has a military status, whether the member is on base or off base, and whether the member is on duty or off duty.

(11) The pervasive application of the standards of conduct is necessary because members of the armed forces must be ready at all times for worldwide deployment to a combat environment.

(12) The worldwide deployment of United States military forces, the international responsibilities of the United States, and the potential for involvement of the armed forces in actual combat routinely make it necessary for members of the armed forces involuntarily to accept living conditions and working conditions that are often spartan, primitive, and characterized by forced intimacy with little or no privacy.

(13) The prohibition against homosexual conduct is a longstanding element of military law that continues to be necessary in the unique circumstances of military service.

(14) The armed forces must maintain personnel policies that exclude persons whose presence in the armed forces would create an unacceptable risk to the armed forces' high standards of morale, good order and discipline, and unit cohesion that are the essence of military capability.

(15) The presence in the armed forces of persons who demonstrate a propensity or intent to engage in homosexual acts would create an unacceptable risk to the high standards of morale, good order and discipline, and unit cohesion that are the essence of military capability.

(b) POLICY.—A member of the armed forces shall be separated from the armed forces under regulations prescribed by the Secretary of Defense if one or more of the following findings is made and approved in accordance with procedures set forth in such regulations:

(1) That the member has engaged in, attempted to engage in, or solicited another to engage in a homosexual act or acts unless there are further findings, made and approved in accordance with procedures set forth in such regulations, that the member has demonstrated that—

(A) such conduct is a departure from the member's usual and customary behavior;

(B) such conduct, under all the circumstances, is unlikely to recur;

(C) such conduct was not accomplished by use of force, coercion, or intimidation;

(D) under the particular circumstances of the case, the member's continued presence in the armed forces is consistent with the interests of the armed forces in proper discipline, good order, and morale; and

(E) the member does not have a propensity or intent to engage in homosexual acts.

(2) That the member has stated that he or she is a homosexual or bisexual, or words to that effect, unless there is a further finding, made and approved in accordance with procedures set forth in the regulations, that the member has demonstrated that he or she is not a person who engages in, attempts to engage in, has a propensity to engage in, or intends to engage in homosexual acts.

(3) That the member has married or attempted to marry a person known to be of the same biological sex.

[Following sections deal with "housekeeping" issues, such as definitions of terms and publication of this policy. The section concludes with the following statement:]

(a) SENSE OF CONGRESS.—It is the sense of Congress that—

(1) the suspension of questioning concerning homosexuality as part of the processing of individuals for accession into the Armed Forces under the interim policy of January 29, 1993, should be continued, but the Secretary of Defense may reinstate that questioning with such questions or such revised questions as he considers appropriate if the Secretary determines that it is necessary to do so in order to effectuate the policy set forth in section 654 of title 10, United States Code, as added by subsection (a); and

(2) the Secretary of Defense should consider issuing guidance governing the circumstances under which members of the Armed Forces questioned about homosexuality for administrative purposes should be afforded warnings similar to the warnings under section 831(b) of title 10, United States Code (article 9 31(b) of the Uniform Code of Military Justice).

Source: 103rd Congress, 1st Session, H.R. 2401. [Washington, DC: Government Printing Office], October 6, 1993. Also available online at: http://frw ebgate.access.gpo.gov/cgi-bin/getdoc.cgi?dbname=103_cong_bills&docid =f:h2401eas.txt.pdf.

The Threat to Marriage from the Courts (2003)

By mid-2003, most observers seemed confident that the Massachusetts Supreme Judicial Court would rule that same-sex couples would have a constitutional right to marry in the state. Groups opposed to same-sex marriage began to discuss the impact of this decision on other states and on federal marriage policies. One of the strongest statements on this question was issued on July 29, 2003, by the Senate Republican Policy Committee. An extract of that statement is reprinted here. All footnotes and citations in the document are omitted.

The statement begins with a review of the case pending in Massachusetts, Goodridge v. Massachusetts Department of Public Health, and of recent U.S. Supreme Court decisions that appear to "override public opinion and force same-sex marriage on society." It warns that:

Gay marriage activists can be expected to pursue several court strategies:

- *Full Faith and Credit Challenges.* Same-sex couples will "marry" in Massachusetts and then file lawsuits in other States to force those States to recognize the Massachusetts marriage. They likely will argue that federal DOMA is unconstitutional as an overly broad interpretation of the Full Faith and Credit clause and as inconsistent with principles of equal protection and substantive due process.
- *Goodridge Copycat Cases.* Activists will file new cases similar to Goodridge in other States and demand recognition of same-sex marriage as a constitutional right under state law. The Massachusetts decision will serve as persuasive precedent for other courts interpreting parallel provisions in their state constitutions.

- *The Supreme Court Strategy.* Same-sex couples who have "married" in Massachusetts (or who have civil unions, as some do in Vermont) will apply for federal benefits such as federal employee health insurance, and under federal DOMA those requests will be denied. They may then sue in federal court and argue that the definition of marriage in DOMA (for federal purposes) is unconstitutional as a matter of federal equal protection and substantive due process. Such a case could end up in the Supreme Court.

    This proliferation of lawsuits could well produce additional victories for gay marriage advocates.

[The statement then reviews efforts by same-sex marriage advocates to "remake marriage through the courts" and a major response to that effort, the Defense of Marriage Act (DOMA) of 1996. It then discusses two recent court cases that it regards as crucial in the battle against same-sex marriage, the Goodridge case in Massachusetts and Lawrence v. Texas, decided by the U.S. Supreme Court in 2003. The statement next attempts to predict future steps by same-sex marriage advocates, and the kind of response that must be offered to these steps.]

The Next Wave of Lawsuits to Impose Same-Sex Marriage

Gay marriage activists have developed a coordinated, nationwide strategy to force legal recognition of same-sex marriage. The long-time leader of the Marriage Project at LAMBDA Legal, Evan Wolfson, has formed "Freedom to Marry," a legal advocacy firm solely devoted to spreading same-sex marriage throughout the nation, in large part through litigation. Joining that group's efforts are the Gay & Lesbian Advocate Defenders, the American Civil Liberties Union, LAMBDA Legal, the NOW Legal Defense and Education Fund, Human Rights Watch, and many other activist groups. In Massachusetts, the state bar association also filed a brief in support of the plaintiffs' claim. The gay marriage activists have a zealous leadership, a sincere belief in the justice of their cause, and more than adequate funding to continue to push their claims in the courts. They have a simple goal: the legitimization and constitutionalization of same-sex marriage, and no state or federal DOMA will dissuade them from this effort.

Strategy #1: Exporting Massachusetts Marriages and Challenging DOMA
As soon as the Goodridge decision is announced, some same-sex couples will marry in Massachusetts. When gay marriage advocates deem it appropriate strategically, one or more of those couples will seek recognition of a Massachusetts marriage in another State. Activists already have made clear that this will be their strategy. When these suits are filed, the activists will challenge as unconstitutional States' preexisting

right not to recognize other States' marriages under the "public policy" doctrine, federal DOMA, and the state DOMAs passed by 37 States.

The fate of the activists' constitutional challenges is uncertain. It is a well-established principle of law that a marriage valid in the jurisdiction where performed shall be valid in other States. However, it is equally well established that a jurisdiction may refuse to recognize a marriage from another State if doing so would conflict with a strong local public policy. In part to ensure that their States' "public policy" on marriage was clear, 37 States have enacted "state DOMAs" that define marriage as between a man and a woman. And the public policy doctrine does not depend on a clear statement of policy via state DOMAs; it is quite possible that every state court in a State without same-sex marriage would conclude that a strong public policy barred recognition of another State's same-sex marriage.

Congress was aware of the public policy doctrine when it enacted DOMA, but determined that the doctrine should be bolstered through federal legislation. This was because the Full Faith and Credit clause of the U.S. Constitution requires States to recognize the "public Acts, Records, and judicial Proceedings of every other State." Thus, to remove any doubt about the reach of the Full Faith and Credit clause and any possible conflict with the public policy doctrine, Congress enacted DOMA pursuant to its authority—also under the Full Faith and Credit clause—to "prescribe the Manner in which such Acts, Records and Proceedings shall be proved, and the Effect thereof." Section 2 of DOMA provides that States are not required to recognize "a relationship between persons of the same sex that is treated as a marriage" in another State "or a right or claim arising from such relationship."

As noted above, 37 States have also passed their own DOMAs. The reach of each DOMA varies, but all have the effect of establishing the "public policy" of each State. Four States—Alaska, Hawaii, Nebraska, and Nevada—have enacted state constitutional amendments that prevent recognition of same-sex marriages. The remaining States passed statutes that made clear the State's refusal to permit same-sex marriage in those States and the States' refusal to recognize those marriages (and in some cases, lesser "civil unions") from other States. No state supreme court has considered whether any of the statutory state DOMAs comply with the State's constitution, however. In other words, most of these state DOMAs survive solely at the whim of state supreme courts.

Defenders of traditional marriage and of DOMA have several arguments to respond to gay marriage advocates' lawsuits, but these arguments are not foolproof. Since same-sex marriage became a national issue in the mid-1990s, proponents and their allies in the legal academy have been working to devise ways to force States to recognize other States' same-sex marriages. One widely cited article in the

Yale Law Journal argues that the public policy doctrine is unconstitutional and States do not have the right to refuse to recognize another State's valid marriage. Others have argued that if the public policy exception is applied only to exclude same-sex marriages, then the Equal Protection clause may be implicated. Although most state DOMAs were passed for the express purpose of ensuring that the public policy of the State was made clear, those laws will face similar challenges. Finally, federal DOMA, often seen as a backup to the state protections, may be challenged either under the theory that Congress lacked the authority to limit the scope of the Full Faith and Credit clause, or that it violates the Equal Protection clause. The Equal Protection argument would be weak under current understandings of the Constitution because only Justice O'Connor adopted such an analysis in Lawrence. Whether courts will seek to expand that jurisprudence in light of Justice O'Connor's concurring opinion in Lawrence and the Supreme Court's earlier decision in Romer v. Evans remains to be seen.

It is difficult to predict the success of these challenges to federal DOMA, state DOMAs, and the public policy doctrine. Even the Clinton Justice Department opined that DOMA was constitutional. But through careful forum shopping, gay marriage activists can put these arguments before activist judges throughout the country. To rely solely on DOMA ultimately is to trust that all judges will uphold that law.

Strategy #2: Filing Copycat Suits and Reproducing *Goodridge*   Every state constitution contains the same basic constitutional protections found in the Massachusetts Constitution, including those provisions that the plaintiffs in Goodridge argue mandate a right to same-sex marriage. While other States' courts are not bound to follow Goodridge, it takes little imagination to recognize that some judges—especially those protected from the wrath of voters—could be tempted to use their power to invent a new constitutional right.

Gay marriage advocates have already filed such lawsuits in Arizona, Indiana, and New Jersey, and more cases can be expected after Goodridge is announced. It is impossible to predict how these other state courts will rule. Many can be expected to dismiss these lawsuits as frivolous, but the results are unlikely to be uniform. After all, it was the New Jersey Supreme Court that in 1999 wrote the expansive opinion mandating that the Boy Scouts accept homosexual Scout Leaders. For the 46 States that lack a state constitutional amendment barring same-sex marriage, the future of the marital institution currently resides in the state supreme courts, not in the legislatures. If the Goodridge case is decided as anticipated, the activists will have a "model case" upon which to rely in those other States' courts.

Strategy #3: Filing Federal Lawsuits Using the Lawrence Decision Gay
marriage advocates have yet another avenue to pursue. Homosexual
federal employees surely will include those who marry in Massachusetts
post-Goodrige. At some point, one of those employees will apply for
spousal benefits such as health insurance or pension benefits. Because
federal DOMA defines marriage as between a man and a woman for the
purposes of all federal laws and regulations, the benefit claim will be
denied. Thus, the same-sex "spouse" would have no rights as a
"spouse," even if Massachusetts or another State believed otherwise.
The federal employee and his or her partner will then sue in federal
court, arguing that the federal definition of marriage in DOMA is
unconstitutional as a matter of federal Equal Protection and Substantive
Due Process law. The plaintiffs also may argue that Congress lacks the
power to "regulate" the terms of marriage because marriage is conven-
tionally a State matter, citing the Supreme Court's recent federalism jurisprudence as support. Although federal courts should reject such
claims and uphold DOMA's definition of marriage for federal purposes,
it is well known that some federal jurisdictions are more activist than
others. Insofar as advocates will be able to pick their courts—for example, by filing suit in San Francisco subject to review by the famously-
liberal Ninth Circuit Court of Appeals—their prospects for success (even
if temporary) expand dramatically. Just as with the eventual challenges
to DOMA's Full Faith and Credit provision and the efforts to impose
same-sex marriage through state courts, judges hold the final power
absent any constitutional amendment. And in the case of any federal
court challenge such as the one contemplated here, the judges are
unelected, lifetime appointees. None of the political constraints that exist
with most state court judges will apply.

**The Willingness of the Courts to Take Pro-Same-Sex
Marriage Positions**
Despite public opposition to same-sex marriage, it is reasonable to
expect more than a few judges will accede to the gay marriage activists' court campaign. The legal profession itself is predisposed to support a remaking of marriage. The dissenting Justices in Lawrence
charged that the Supreme Court itself has become imbued with the
"law profession's anti-anti-homosexual culture," and argued that the
Court had dismissed mainstream values throughout the nation. Some
members of the Supreme Court increasingly rely upon European laws
and norms when crafting their opinions, as was apparent in the Lawrence decision. Although most state court judges do face the ballot in
some fashion, they still went to the same law schools where professors
treat the advancement of homosexual rights as the next logical step in
the civil rights movement. They and their young law clerks still read

the same legal scholarship that so overwhelmingly advocates recognition of same-sex marriage and labors to craft ways to convince those courts to invent the right thereto. To expect all judges to follow popular opinion and strictly to adhere to the Constitution is an act of faith.

Ultimately the Supreme Court will rule on same-sex marriage, but that may not occur until several States and even some federal courts have altered the institution and thousands of couples have gained legal status as a result. Nor should the Supreme Court's intervention be seen as a panacea. The Supreme Court itself has shown that it will show little regard for public opinion when it takes sides in cultural divisions that emerge in society. The Court persists in upholding abortion laws that 60 percent of the public wants tightened. In 2002, the Supreme Court held the execution of the mentally retarded was inconsistent with current "standards of decency" even though only 18 of the 38 capital punishment States had acted to ban the practice. And the Court recently approved the University of Michigan's racial preferences regime, despite the fact that 69 percent of those polled believe that every applicant should be admitted "solely" based on merit. These examples illustrate what should be obvious to any student of the Supreme Court: insofar as the Supreme Court considers public opinion at all, it considers that of the elites to the exclusion of all Americans collectively. And it is the elites who scorn traditional views on sexual orientation and who are most likely to favor same-sex marriage.

The Time to Act Is Now

When same-sex marriage is legalized in Massachusetts, thousands of homosexual couples from in and out of that Commonwealth will rush to marry. Any later attempts to "react" to the growth of same-sex marriage will then be construed as an effort to deprive those homosexual couples of their legal status. A constitutional amendment to ban same-sex marriage would be taking away a right that has been invented and granted by a court. It is imperative that Congress not allow the institution to spread before Congress acts; otherwise, homosexual couples will rely upon the court edicts and remake their lives accordingly. The legal complications that will ensue, as well as the risk that society will be less willing to confront the question itself when faced with the reality of thousands of same-sex marriages, argue strongly in favor of prompt action to confront this issue.

It is important also to recognize that same-sex marriages in Massachusetts inevitably will impact the legal and social life of other States. Homosexual couples that marry in Massachusetts would have all the benefits of married couples in that Commonwealth. Many will buy property in and out of the State, adopt and rear children, get divorced, incur child support and alimony obligations, and enmesh themselves in the same kinds of legal obligations that most traditionally married couples do. It is inevitable, though, that many of those homosexual couples will move out of Massachusetts and seek to enforce those legal obligations in other States' courts. For example, it is easy to anticipate issues relating to child support, alimony, and property division at the time of divorce spilling over into other States.

What will the other States' courts do when asked to adjudicate disputes grounded in Massachusetts same-sex marriages? A complex body of law known as "choice of law" has evolved to address these matters in the context of traditional marriages. Moreover, federal and state statutes have been enacted to regularize the treatment of these kinds of obligations across State lines. In the context of same-sex marriage, where 37 States have indicated their opposition to the institution, judges may refuse to apply these statutes. (Recall that federal DOMA defines "marriage" and "spouse" for purposes of all federal laws and regulations.) But no state court will be able to put its head in the sand for long because the practical legal and human problems will proliferate—problems of children in need of child support payments, of custody disputes for divorced homosexual couples, of homosexual former spouses being denied benefits rightfully theirs under Massachusetts law, and so forth. All the efforts to craft uniform solutions to matters of family law over the past half century could prove useless in the context of homosexual couples who have left Massachusetts. Nor is it a sufficient response to say that these couples should not leave that Commonwealth, because such a solution would threaten the right to travel among the States as recognized by the Supreme Court.

Given our integrated national economy and the mobility of the nation's citizenry, same-sex marriages in Massachusetts will end up affecting the laws and cultures of all other States. As the States struggle to react, the risk of Supreme Court intervention to create a uniform standard (or at the least to permit recognition of out-of-state homosexual unions) will only increase.

The Need for a Constitutional Response

The Massachusetts court is expected to break down traditional marriage—to redefine its most historic and natural characteristic and ask society simply to hope that the institution endures. If this is the ruling, it cannot help but remake the social infrastructure of an entire State. The question that Congress must ask is whether it is willing to allow the courts to redefine the marital institution based on conclusions of a few judges, or whether the people's strong preference to preserve traditional marriage should be respected and preserved.

Additional Statutes Will Not Be Enough to Stop the Courts   Constitutional amendments ought to be rare—employed only when no other

legislative response will do the job. However, no statutory solution appears to be available to address the current campaign through the courts. Congress already has passed DOMA, but as discussed above, its effectiveness in the face of strenuous challenges in the courts remains to be seen. Some have suggested that Congress pass a "Super DOMA"—a repeat of DOMA coupled with an effort to deprive the federal courts of jurisdiction to review it under article III, section 2 of the Constitution. But such a strategy would not prevent state courts from creating same-sex marriage, and litigants surely would challenge such a dramatic effort by Congress to deny litigants the chance to have their purported fundamental rights (be they due process, equal protection, or otherwise) reviewed in federal court. Similarly, some have suggested that Congress should deny States funds unless they protect marriage through a state DOMA. Such an option would also face constitutional challenges and would have the policy effect of harming many Americans in their greatest time of need. If Congress is to prevent the courts from undoing its work and, once and for all, ensure the preservation of traditional marriage, then it should begin to consider constitutional options.

Principles to Govern the Constitutional Response   Any effort to amend the Constitution should emphasize the following principles:

- Federal DOMA must be defended from the courts. DOMA ensures that (a) the traditional man-woman marriage standard governs for all federal law, and (b) States' right to deny recognition of other States' untraditional legal relationships remains intact. As discussed above, the Goodridge and Lawrence developments demonstrate that neither of these provisions is immune from constitutional challenge.
- The U.S. Constitution should not be construed to change the traditional definition of marriage. The premise of this paper is that most Americans believe, and it should be United States policy, that no court—from the U.S. Supreme Court down through all federal, state, and territorial courts—should have the power to change the traditional definition of marriage. Neither the original Constitution nor any of its amendments was adopted with such an intention.
- States should retain the right to grant some legal benefits to same-sex couples. The Constitution should not limit the ability of States, through their elected representatives or by popular will, to address the question of whether homosexual couples (as couples) should enjoy certain benefits, such as a right to file joint state tax returns, access to medical records, access to pension or other state employment benefits of homosexual partners, inheritance rights, or a variety of other civil benefits.

An Existing Proposal: The Federal Marriage Amendment There exists at present a vehicle to pursue the above principles, a constitutional amendment proposed in the House called the Federal Marriage Amendment ("FMA"). H.J. Res. 56 provides:

> Marriage in the United States shall consist only of the union of a man and a woman. Neither this constitution or the constitution of any state, nor state or federal law, shall be construed to require that marital status or the legal incidents thereof be conferred upon unmarried couples or groups.

This amendment would create a uniform national definition for "marriage" for purposes of federal and state law, and would prevent any state from creating same-sex marriage. However, the amendment is designed to preserve the ability of state legislatures to allocate civil benefits within each State. State courts (like Massachusetts) would not be able to create this new right. In addition, no court at any level would be able to rely upon a state or federal constitution to mandate recognition of another State's distribution of benefits (the "legal incidents of marriage") to nontraditional couples.

The Federal Marriage Amendment is the only proposed constitutional amendment presently pending before Congress to address the likely ramifications of the Goodridge and Lawrence decisions. The FMA has bipartisan support in the House, but it also has been criticized from both ends of the political spectrum. Some social conservative groups, such as the Concerned Women for America, oppose the FMA in part because it still permits state legislatures to create civil unions. In contrast, some legal scholars have questioned whether the text of the FMA would in fact permit civil unions. And some FMA opponents argue that questions relating to marriage should be left to the States altogether, with no federal role. The Senate should examine these and other questions about the details of this amendment in timely hearings in the Judiciary Committee.

Conclusion

The pace of the gay marriage activists' campaign through the nation's courts is uncertain, but it is not at all certain that DOMA or other legislation will stop determined activists and their judicial allies from pursuing this agenda—only a constitutional amendment can do that. The Senate should evaluate the Federal Marriage Amendment seriously and consider whether it, or any other constitutional amendment, is the appropriate response.

Source: "The Threat to Marriage from the Courts." Press release from the Senate Republican Policy Committee, Washington, D.C., July 29, 2003. Also available online at: http://rpc.senate.gov/releases/2003/jd072903.pdf.

Legislation

Federal Defense of Marriage Act (1996)

In September 1996, the U.S. Congress passed and President Bill Clinton signed the Federal Defense of Marriage Act, declaring that marriage was defined as a legal relationship between a man and a woman. The act was codified in two parts of the Federal Code, Chapter 1, Section 7, and Chapter 28, Section 1738C. Those sections are reprinted here.

> **TITLE 1. CHAPTER 1. §7. Definition of "marriage" and "spouse"**
> In determining the meaning of any Act of Congress, or of any ruling, regulation, or interpretation of the various administrative bureaus and agencies of the United States, the word "marriage" means only a legal union between one man and one woman as husband and wife, and the word "spouse" refers only to a person of the opposite sex who is a husband or a wife.

> **TITLE 28. PART V. CHAPTER 115. §1738C. Certain acts, records, and proceedings and the effect thereof**
> No State, territory, or possession of the United States, or Indian tribe, shall be required to give effect to any public act, record, or judicial proceeding of any other State, territory, possession, or tribe respecting a relationship between persons of the same sex that is treated as a marriage under the laws of such other State, territory, possession, or tribe, or a right or claim arising from such relationship.

Source: U.S. Code, Chapters 1 and 28.

Federal Marriage Amendment (2003)

In 2003, Representative Marilyn Musgrave (R-Colo.) introduced into the U.S. House of Representatives a proposed amendment to the U.S. Constitution dealing with the issue of same-sex marriage. The amendment, with a slight modification, has been reintroduced every year since then, except for 2007. (The modification consists of a deletion of the italicized phrase in the following document.) The most favorable action on the amendment thus far occurred in 2006, when the House voted 236 to 187 in favor of the amendment, although a cloture motion to force a vote on the amendment in the Senate failed 49 to 48. (A two-thirds vote is required in both houses for adoption of the amendment.)

Marriage in the United States shall consist only of the union of a man and a woman. Neither this Constitution or the constitution of any State, *nor state or federal law*, shall be construed to require that marital status or the legal incidents thereof be conferred upon unmarried couples or groups.

Source: Calendar No. 479. 110th Congress. 1st Session. H. R. 3685. Government Printing Office. Available online at: http://frwebgate.access.gpo.gov/cgi-bin/getdoc.cgi?dbname=110_cong_bills&docid=f:h3685pcs.txt.pdf.

Employment Nondiscrimination Act (2007)

In every Congress since 1974, bills have been introduced to prohibit discrimination against individuals on the basis of their sexual orientation. None of those bills passed either house of Congress until 2007, when HR was approved 235 to 184. The bill was then sent on to the Senate, which took no action on the bill over the following year. Although the bill failed to reach the desk of President George W. Bush (who promised to veto it), its passage by the House was a historic moment in the history of gay and lesbian rights legislation in the United States. Important portions of the bill are extracted here.

AN ACT
To prohibit employment discrimination on the basis of sexual orientation.

Be it enacted by the Senate and House of Representatives of the United States of America in Congress assembled,

SEC. 1. SHORT TITLE.
This Act may be cited as the "Employment Non-Discrimination Act of 2007."

SEC. 2. PURPOSES.
The purposes of this Act are—

(1) to provide a comprehensive Federal prohibition of employment discrimination on the basis of sexual orientation;
(2) to provide meaningful and effective remedies for employment discrimination on the basis of sexual orientation; and
(3) to invoke congressional powers, including the powers to enforce the 14th amendment to the Constitution, and to regulate interstate commerce and provide for the general welfare pursuant to section 8 of article I of the Constitution, in order to prohibit employment discrimination on the basis of sexual orientation.

[Section 3 defines important terms used in the bill.]

SEC. 4. EMPLOYMENT DISCRIMINATION PROHIBITED.

(a) EMPLOYER PRACTICES.—It shall be an unlawful employment practice for an employer—

    (1) to fail or refuse to hire or to discharge any individual, or otherwise discriminate against any individual with respect to the compensation, terms, conditions, or privileges of employment of the individual, because of such individual's actual or perceived sexual orientation; or

    (2) to limit, segregate, or classify the employees or applicants for employment of the employer in any way that would deprive or tend to deprive any individual of employment or otherwise adversely affect the status of the individual as an employee, because of such individual's actual or perceived sexual orientation.

(b) EMPLOYMENT AGENCY PRACTICES.—It shall be an unlawful employment practice for an employment agency to fail or refuse to refer for employment, or otherwise to discriminate against, any individual because of the actual or perceived sexual orientation of the individual or to classify or refer for employment any individual on the basis of the actual or perceived sexual orientation of the individual.

(c) LABOR ORGANIZATION PRACTICES.—It shall be an unlawful employment practice for a labor organization—

    (1) to exclude or to expel from its membership, or otherwise to discriminate against, any individual because of the actual or perceived sexual orientation of the individual;

    (2) to limit, segregate, or classify its membership or applicants for membership, or to classify or fail or refuse to refer for employment any individual, in any way that would deprive or tend to deprive any individual of employment, or would limit such employment or otherwise adversely affect the status of the individual as an employee or as an applicant for employment because of such individual's actual or perceived sexual orientation; or

    (3) to cause or attempt to cause an employer to discriminate against an individual in violation of this section.

(d) TRAINING PROGRAMS.—It shall be an unlawful employment practice for any employer, labor organization, or joint labor-management committee controlling apprenticeship or other training or retraining, including on-the job training programs, to discriminate against any individual because of the actual or perceived sexual orientation of the individual in admission to, or employment in, any program established to provide apprenticeship or other training.

(e)   ASSOCIATION.—An unlawful employment practice described in any of subsections (a) through (d) shall be considered to include an action described in that subsection, taken against an individual based on the actual or perceived sexual orientation of a person with whom the individual associates or has associated.

(f)   NO PREFERENTIAL TREATMENT OR QUOTAS.—Nothing in this Act shall be construed or interpreted to require or permit—

(1)   any covered entity to grant preferential treatment to any individual or to any group because of the actual or perceived sexual orientation of such individual or group on account of an imbalance which may exist with respect to the total number or percentage of persons of any actual or perceived sexual orientation employed by any employer, referred or classified for employment by any employment agency or labor organization, admitted to membership or classified by any labor organization, or admitted to, or employed in, any apprenticeship or other training program, in comparison with the total number or percentage of persons of such actual or perceived sexual orientation in any community, State, section, or other area, or in the available work force in any community, State, section, or other area; or

(2)   the adoption or implementation by a covered entity of a quota on the basis of actual or perceived sexual orientation.

(g)   DISPARATE IMPACT.—Only disparate treatment claims may be brought under this Act.

[Remaining portions of the bill deal primarily with "housekeeping" provisions, such as prohibition of retaliation against claimants under the act, exemption for religious organizations and members of the military services, collection of statistics, and enforcement of the act.]

Source: H.R. 3685, as provided by the Government Printing Office. Available online at: http://frwebgate.access.gpo.gov/cgi-bin/getdoc.cgi?dbname=110_cong_bills&docid=f:h3685pcs.txt.pdf.

Oregon Family Fairness Act (2007)

Almost all states in the United States currently have prohibitions against same-sex marriage in their state constitutions or in laws dealing with the issue. However, a number of states have adopted, or are considering, legislation that provides all the benefits and responsibilities of marriage without calling the relationship by that name. The most common alternative to same-sex marriage thus far has been a domestic partnership. The most recent state to adopt domestic partnership legislation, an extract of which is provided here, is Oregon. In the final versions of the bill, the term "civil union" was replaced by the term "domestic partnership."

House Bill 2007
SUMMARY

Establishes requirements and procedures for entering into *[civil union]* domestic partnership contract between individuals of same sex.

Provides that any privilege, immunity, right or benefit granted by law to individual who is or was married is granted to individual who is or was in *[civil union]* domestic partnership. Provides that any responsibility imposed by law on individual who is or was married is imposed on individual who is or was in *[civil union]* domestic partnership.

Provides that any privilege, immunity, right, benefit or responsibility granted or imposed by law to or on spouse with respect to child of either spouse is granted to or imposed on partner with respect to child of either partner.

A BILL FOR AN ACT

Relating to same-sex relationships; creating new provisions; and amending ORS 107.615, 192.842, 205.320, 409.300, 432.005, 432.235, 432.405 and 432.408.

Be It Enacted by the People of the State of Oregon:

SECTION 1. Sections 1 to 9 of this 2007 Act may be cited as the Oregon Family Fairness Act.

[Section 2 lists the findings of the state legislature that have led to this bill. Only the first of those findings is listed here.]

SECTION 2. The Legislative Assembly finds that:

(1) Section 20, Article I of the Oregon Constitution, has always enshrined the principle that all citizens of this state are to be provided with equal privileges and immunities under the laws of the State. In addition, as provided in ORS 659A.006, it has long been the public policy of this state that discrimination against any of the citizens of this state is a matter of state concern that threatens not only the rights and privileges of the state's inhabitants but menaces the institutions and foundation of a free democratic state. These fundamental principles are integral to Oregon's constitutional form of government, to its guarantees of political and civil rights and

to the continued vitality of political and civil society in this state.

[Section 3 provides definitions for important terms used in the bill.]
[Section 4 lists certain types of domestic partnerships that are prohibited.]
[Section 5 mandates the forms to be used in registering domestic partnerships.]
[Sections 6–8 state the requirements to be followed by individuals registering for a domestic partnership.]
[Section 9 provides a general overview of the rights and responsibilities associated with domestic partnerships, as extracted here.]

SECTION 9.

(1) Any privilege, immunity, right or benefit granted by statute, administrative or court rule, policy, common law or any other law to an individual because the individual is or was married, or because the individual is or was an in-law in a specified way to another individual, is granted on equivalent terms, substantive and procedural, to an individual because the individual is or was in a domestic partnership or because the individual is or was, based on a domestic partnership, related in a specified way to another individual because the individual is or was in a domestic partnership or because the individual is or was, based on a domestic partnership, related in a specified way to another individual.

(2) Any responsibility imposed by statute, administrative or court rule, policy, common law or any other law on an individual because the individual is or was married, or because the individual is or was an in-law in a specified way to another individual, is imposed on equivalent terms, substantive and procedural, on an individual because the individual is or was in a domestic partnership or because the individual is or was, based on a domestic partnership, related in a specified way to another individual.

(3) Any privilege, immunity, right, benefit or responsibility granted or imposed by statute, administrative or court rule, policy, common law or any other law to or on a spouse with respect to a child of either of the spouses is granted or imposed on equivalent terms, substantive and procedural, to or on a partner with respect to a child of either of the partners.

(4) Any privilege, immunity, right, benefit or responsibility granted or imposed by statute, administrative or court rule, policy, common law or any other law to or on a former or surviving spouse with respect to a child of either of the spouses is granted or imposed on equivalent terms, substantive and

procedural, to or on a former or surviving partner with respect to a child of either of the partners.

(5) Many of the laws of this state are intertwined with federal law, and the Legislative Assembly recognizes that it does not have the jurisdiction to control federal laws or the privileges, immunities, rights, benefits and responsibilities related to federal laws.

(6) Sections 1 to 9 of this 2007 Act do not require or permit the extension of any benefit under ORS chapter 238 or 238A, or under any other retirement, deferred compensation or other employee benefit plan, if the plan administrator reasonably concludes that the extension of benefits would conflict with a condition for tax qualification of the plan, or a condition for other favorable tax treatment of the plan, under the Internal Revenue Code or regulations adopted under the Internal Revenue Code.

(7) Sections 1 to 9 of this 2007 Act do not require the extension of any benefit under any employee benefit plan that is subject to federal regulation under the Employee Retirement Income Security Act of 1974.

(8) For purposes of administering Oregon tax laws, partners in a domestic partnership, surviving partners in a domestic partnership and the children of partners in a domestic partnership have the same privileges, immunities, rights, benefits and responsibilities as are granted to or imposed on spouses in a marriage, surviving spouses and their children.

[Remaining sections of the bill deal with "housekeeping" issues and with bringing this act into agreement with other relevant state laws.]

Source: 74th Oregon Legislative Assembly—2007 Regular Session. A-Engrossed. House Bill 2007. Available online at: http://www.leg.state.or.us/07reg/measpdf/hb2000.dir/hb2007.a.pdf.

Uniting American Families Act (2007)

Under U.S. immigration law, a man or woman may sponsor his or her wife or husband from a country other than the United States to live and work permanently in this country. Same-sex spouses do not have the same privilege. Even couples that have been legally married in the United States or some other country are not eligible to take advantage of the privileges offered by immigration law to heterosexual couples. In 2007, Senator Patrick Leahy (D-Vt.) sponsored legislation to revise immigration law so that it would apply to same-sex couples as well as to opposite-sex couples. The extract of Leahy's bill below shows how changes in definition and terminology in the original immigration laws would accomplish this objective.

Section 2 of the bill provides the fundamental changes required to make the necessary adjustments in existing immigration law:

SEC. 2. DEFINITIONS OF PERMANENT PARTNER AND PERMANENT PARTNERSHIP.

Section 101(a) (8 U.S.C. 1101(a)) is amended—

(1) in paragraph (15)(K)(ii), by inserting "or permanent partnership" after "marriage"; and

(2) by adding at the end the following:

"(52) The term 'permanent partner' means an individual 18 years of age or older who—

"(A) is in a committed, intimate relationship with another individual 18 years of age or older in which both individuals intend a lifelong commitment;

"(B) is financially interdependent with that other individual;

"(C) is not married to, or in a permanent partnership with, any individual other than that other individual;

"(D) is unable to contract with that other individual a marriage cognizable under this Act; and

"(E) is not a first, second, or third degree blood relation of that other individual.

"(53) The term 'permanent partnership' means the relationship that exists between 2 permanent partners."

SEC. 3. WORLDWIDE LEVEL OF IMMIGRATION.

Section 201(b)(2)(A)(i) (8 U.S.C. 1151(b)(2)(A)(i)) is amended—

(1) by "spouse" each place it appears and inserting "spouse or permanent partner";

(2) by striking "spouses" and inserting "spouse, permanent partner,";

(3) by inserting "(or, in the case of a permanent partnership, whose permanent partnership was not terminated)" after "was not legally separated from the citizen"; and

(4) by striking "remarries." and inserting "remarries or enters a permanent partnership with an other person."

SEC. 4. NUMERICAL LIMITATIONS ON INDIVIDUAL FOREIGN STATES.

(a) PER COUNTRY LEVELS.—Section 202(a)(4) (8 U.S.C. 1152(a)(4)) is amended—

(1) in the paragraph heading, by inserting ", PERMANENT PARTNERS," after "SPOUSES";

(2) in the heading of subparagraph (A), by inserting ", PERMANENT PARTNERS," after "SPOUSES"; and

(3) in the heading of subparagraph (C), by striking "AND DAUGHTERS" inserting "WITHOUT PERMANENT PARTNERS AND UNMARRIED DAUGHTERS WITHOUT PERMANENT PARTNERS."

(b) RULES FOR CHARGEABILITY.—Section 202(b)(2) (8 U.S.C. 1152(b)(2)) is amended—

(1) by striking "his spouse" and inserting "his or her spouse or permanent partner";

(2) by striking "such spouse" each place it appears and inserting "such spouse or permanent partner"; and

(3) by inserting "or permanent partners" after "husband and wife."

[Following sections make changes in the allocation of immigrant visas, procedures for granting immigrant status, admission of immigrants for emergency purposes, inadmissible aliens, conditional permanent resident status, and related issues.]

Source: 110th Congress, 1st Session. S. 1328. [Washington, DC: Government Printing Office, May 8, 2007.]

Matthew Shepard Act (2007)

A number of federal laws currently protect a person from attacks based on race, color, religion, or national origin (so-called "hate crimes"), when that person is engaged in a federally protected activity. Those laws date to 1969 (encoded as 18 U.S.C. § 245(b)(2)) and have been amended and updated a number of times. Gender, gender orientation, and gender identity (as well as disability) are not currently included in federal hate crime legislation. For a number of years, efforts have been made to amend federal hate crimes laws to include these categories. The most recent effort was an act introduced by Representative Barney Frank (D-Mass.) in 2007, H.R. 1592, summarized here. The act was officially entitled the Local Law Enforcement Hate Crimes Prevention Act of 2007 and was popularly known as the Matthew Shepard Act, in honor of the Wyoming student murdered in 1998 because of his sexual orientation. That act passed the House of Representatives and the Senate as an amendment to the 2008

Department of Defense authorization bill. Under threat of veto by President George W. Bush, that amendment was removed from the bill. As of late 2008, no further action has been taken on Frank's original bill or another version of it. Section 6 of the bill, reprinted below, contains new provisions for those who are to be covered by this bill and by existing federal legislation on hate crimes.

110th CONGRESS
1st Session
H. R. 1592
AN ACT

To provide Federal assistance to States, local jurisdictions, and Indian tribes to prosecute hate crimes, and for other purposes.

Be it enacted by the Senate and House of Representatives of the United States of America in Congress assembled,

SEC. 1. SHORT TITLE.

This Act may be cited as the 'Local Law Enforcement Hate Crimes Prevention Act of 2007.'

[Section 2 defines terms used in the bill.]

[Section 3 is the core of the bill, outlining the types of support that the bill provides for various governmental agencies in the campaign against hate crimes.]

[Section 4 describes the nature of grants to be awarded for the purposes of achieving the goals of this bill along with the mechanisms for awarding those grants.]

[Section 5 authorizes funds for carrying out provisions of this bill.]

SEC. 6. PROHIBITION OF CERTAIN HATE CRIME ACTS.

    (a) In General—Chapter 13 of title 18, United States Code, is amended by adding at the end the following:
Sec. 249. Hate crime acts

    (a) In General—

        (1) OFFENSES INVOLVING ACTUAL OR PERCEIVED RACE, COLOR, RELIGION, OR NATIONAL ORIGIN—Whoever, whether or not acting under color of law, willfully causes bodily injury to any person or, through the use of fire, a firearm, or an explosive or incendiary device, attempts to cause bodily injury to any person, because of the actual or perceived race, color, religion, or national origin of any person—

(A) shall be imprisoned not more than 10 years, fined in accordance with this title, or both; and

(B) shall be imprisoned for any term of years or for life, fined in accordance with this title, or both, if—

    (i) death results from the offense; or

    (ii) the offense includes kidnaping or an attempt to kidnap, aggravated sexual abuse or an attempt to commit aggravated sexual abuse, or an attempt to kill.

(2) OFFENSES INVOLVING ACTUAL OR PERCEIVED RELIGION, NATIONAL ORIGIN, GENDER, SEXUAL ORIENTATION, GENDER IDENTITY, OR DISABILITY—

(A) IN GENERAL—Whoever, whether or not acting under color of law, in any circumstance described in subparagraph (B), willfully causes bodily injury to any person or, through the use of fire, a firearm, or an explosive or incendiary device, attempts to cause bodily injury to any person, because of the actual or perceived religion, national origin, gender, sexual orientation, gender identity or disability of any person—

    (i) shall be imprisoned not more than 10 years, fined in accordance with this title, or both; and

    (ii) shall be imprisoned for any term of years or for life, fined in accordance with this title, or both, if—

        (I) death results from the offense; or

        (II) the offense includes kidnaping or an attempt to kidnap, aggravated sexual abuse or an attempt to commit aggravated sexual abuse, or an attempt to kill.

(B) CIRCUMSTANCES DESCRIBED—For purposes of subparagraph (A), the circumstances described in this subparagraph are that—

    (i) the conduct described in subparagraph (A) occurs during the course of, or as the result of, the travel of the defendant or the victim—

        (I) across a State line or national border; or

        (II) using a channel, facility, or instrumentality of interstate or foreign commerce;

    (ii) the defendant uses a channel, facility, or instrumentality of interstate or foreign commerce in connection with the conduct described in subparagraph (A);

(iii) in connection with the conduct described in subparagraph (A), the defendant employs a firearm, explosive or incendiary device, or other weapon that has traveled in interstate or foreign commerce; or

(iv) the conduct described in subparagraph (A)—

(I) interferes with commercial or other economic activity in which the victim is engaged at the time of the conduct; or

(II) otherwise affects interstate or foreign commerce.

[The remainder of this section deals with additional definitions and provisions for enforcing this section of the act.]

[Section 7 is a standard part of many bills, indicating that, should any one section be found to be unconstitutional, that decision does not affect the remaining portions of the act.]

[Section 8 notes that no provision of this act is to infringe on a person's right of free speech.]

Source: Government Printing Office. "H.R. 1592." Available online at: http://frwebgate.access.gpo.gov/cgi-bin/getdoc.cgi?dbname=110_cong_bills&docid=f:h1592eh.txt.pdf. Passed May 3, 2007.

Court Cases

Lawrence v. Texas 539 U.S. 558 (2003)

On March 26, 2003, the U.S. Supreme Court heard arguments in the case of John Geddes Lawrence and Tyron Garner, Petitioners versus the State of Texas, on appeal from a decision made by the U.S. Court of Appeals for the Fourteenth District of Texas. The case involved an arrest by officers of the Harris County (Houston) police department of two men engaged in sex in the home of one of the men. The question at hand was whether the Fourteenth Amendment of the U.S. Constitution provided same-sex couples with the same guarantee of privacy as it did for opposite-sex couples. In the case, the Court was also asked to overrule its previous, precedent-setting case of Bowers v. Hardwick *(478 U.S. 186; 1986). The court agreed with the plaintiffs in their decision and, at the same time, rejected its earlier ruling in* Bowers v. Hardwick. *Writing for the majority, Justice Kennedy began his decision by noting that:*

Liberty protects the person from unwarranted government intrusions into a dwelling or other private places. In our tradition the State is not omnipresent in the home. And there are other spheres of our lives and existence, outside the home, where the State should not be a dominant presence. Freedom extends beyond spatial bounds. Liberty presumes an autonomy of self that includes freedom of thought, belief, expression, and certain intimate conduct. The instant case involves liberty of the person both in its spatial and more transcendent dimensions.

[He then went on to explain the basis for the Court's decision. (Omitted sections are indicated in italics.)]

The question before the Court is the validity of a Texas statute making it a crime for two persons of the same sex to engage in certain intimate sexual conduct.

[Kennedy then reviews the facts in the case. He then states the fundamental issue facing the Court.]

We conclude the case should be resolved by determining whether the petitioners were free as adults to engage in the private conduct in the exercise of their liberty under the Due Process Clause of the Fourteenth Amendment to the Constitution. For this inquiry we deem it necessary to reconsider the Court's holding in Bowers.

[In Bowers v. Hardwick, *the U.S. Supreme Court had upheld the state of Georgia's laws criminalizing oral and anal sex between consenting adults. In its review of the Bowers case here, the Court summarizes its earlier thinking and points out the errors in the logic presented there.]*

The Court began its substantive discussion in Bowers as follows: "The issue presented is whether the Federal Constitution confers a fundamental right upon homosexuals to engage in sodomy and hence invalidates the laws of the many States that still make such conduct illegal and have done so for a very long time." * . . . That statement, we now conclude, discloses the Court's own failure to appreciate the extent of the liberty at stake. To say that the issue in Bowers was simply the right to engage in certain sexual conduct demeans the claim the individual put forward, just as it would demean a married couple were it to be said marriage is simply about the right to have sexual intercourse. The laws involved in Bowers and here are, to be sure, statutes that purport to do no more than prohibit a particular sexual act. Their penalties and purposes, though, have more far-reaching consequences, touching upon the most private human conduct, sexual behavior, and in the most private of places, the home. The statutes do seek to control a personal relationship that, whether or not entitled to formal recognition in the law, is within the liberty of persons to choose without being punished as criminals.

This, as a general rule, should counsel against attempts by the State, or a court, to define the meaning of the relationship or to set its boundaries absent injury to a person or abuse of an institution the law protects. It suffices for us to acknowledge that adults may choose to enter upon this relationship in the confines of their homes and their own private lives and still retain their dignity as free persons. When sexuality finds overt expression in intimate conduct with another person, the conduct can be but one element in a personal bond that is more enduring. The liberty protected by the Constitution allows homosexual persons the right to make this choice.

Having misapprehended the claim of liberty there presented to it, and thus stating the claim to be whether there is a fundamental right to engage in consensual sodomy, the Bowers Court said: "Proscriptions against that conduct have ancient roots." * . . . In academic writings, and in many of the scholarly amicus briefs filed to assist the Court in this case, there are fundamental criticisms of the historical premises relied upon by the majority and concurring opinions in Bowers. * . . . We need not enter this debate in the attempt to reach a definitive historical judgment, but the following considerations counsel against adopting the definitive conclusions upon which Bowers placed such reliance.

[The Court then reviews the history of legislation dealing with homosexual conduct in England and the United States. It concludes that:]

In summary, the historical grounds relied upon in Bowers are more complex than the majority opinion and the concurring opinion by Chief Justice Burger indicate. Their historical premises are not without doubt and, at the very least, are overstated.

[Kennedy then continues his historical analysis, expanding the range of sources beyond those presented in Bower. He finally concludes that:]

Equality of treatment and the due process right to demand respect for conduct protected by the substantive guarantee of liberty are linked in important respects, and a decision on the latter point advances both interests. If protected conduct is made criminal and the law which does so remains unexamined for its substantive validity, its stigma might remain even if it were not enforceable as drawn for equal protection reasons. When homosexual conduct is made criminal by the law of the State, that declaration in and of itself is an invitation to subject homosexual persons to discrimination both in the public and in the private spheres. The central holding of Bowers has been brought in question by this case, and it should be addressed. Its continuance as precedent demeans the lives of homosexual persons.

[Kennedy then states the Court's new view of private consensual sexual relationships between two adults.]

The rationale of Bowers does not withstand careful analysis. In his dissenting opinion in Bowers Justice Stevens came to these conclusions:

"Our prior cases make two propositions abundantly clear. First, the fact that the governing majority in a State has traditionally viewed a particular practice as immoral is not a sufficient reason for upholding a law prohibiting the practice; neither history nor tradition could save a law prohibiting miscegenation from constitutional attack. Second, individual decisions by married persons, concerning the intimacies of their physical relationship, even when not intended to produce offspring, are a form of "liberty" protected by the Due Process Clause of the Fourteenth Amendment. Moreover, this protection extends to intimate choices by unmarried as well as married persons." * . . .

Justice Stevens' analysis, in our view, should have been controlling in Bowers and should control here.

Bowers was not correct when it was decided, and it is not correct today. It ought not to remain binding precedent. Bowers v. Hardwick should be and now is overruled.

The present case does not involve minors. It does not involve persons who might be injured or coerced or who are situated in relationships where consent might not easily be refused. It does not involve public conduct or prostitution. It does not involve whether the government must give formal recognition to any relationship that homosexual persons seek to enter. The case does involve two adults who, with full and mutual consent from each other, engaged in sexual practices common to a homosexual lifestyle. The petitioners are entitled to respect for their private lives. The State cannot demean their existence or control their destiny by making their private sexual conduct a crime. Their right to liberty under the Due Process Clause gives them the full right to engage in their conduct without intervention of the government. "It is a promise of the Constitution that there is a realm of personal liberty which the government may not enter." * . . . The Texas statute furthers no legitimate state interest which can justify its intrusion into the personal and private life of the individual.

Had those who drew and ratified the Due Process Clauses of the Fifth Amendment or the Fourteenth Amendment known the components of liberty in its manifold possibilities, they might have been more specific. They did not presume to have this insight. They knew times can blind us to certain truths and later generations can see that laws once thought necessary and proper in fact serve only to oppress. As the Constitution endures, persons in every generation can invoke its principles in their own search for greater freedom.

The judgment of the Court of Appeals for the Texas Fourteenth District is reversed, and the case is remanded for further proceedings not inconsistent with this opinion.

It is so ordered.

Source: Lawrence v. Texas 539 U.S. 558 (2003). Available online at: http://www.law.cornell.edu/supct/html/02-102.ZO.html.

In re Marriage Cases: Opinion (2008)

One of the most important legal breakthroughs in the matter of same-sex marriages was the decision by the California Supreme Court in May 2008 that state bans on such marriages are unconstitutional. In a 121-page, four-to-three decision, Chief Justice Ronald M. George laid out the majority's reasoning for this opinion. All citations in the extract below are omitted.

In *Lockyer v. City and County of San Francisco* * . . . , this court concluded that public officials of the City and County of San Francisco acted unlawfully by issuing marriage licenses to same-sex couples in the absence of a judicial determination that the California statutes limiting marriage to a union between a man and a woman are unconstitutional. Our decision in *Lockyer* emphasized, however, that the substantive question of the constitutional validity of the California marriage statutes was not before this court in that proceeding, and that our decision was not intended to reflect any view on that issue. * . . . The present proceeding, involving the consolidated appeal of six cases that were litigated in the superior court and the Court of Appeal in the wake of this court's decision in *Lockyer*, squarely presents the substantive constitutional question that was not addressed in *Lockyer*.

In considering this question, we note at the outset that the constitutional issue before us differs in a significant respect from the constitutional issue that has been addressed by a number of other state supreme courts and intermediate appellate courts that recently have had occasion, in interpreting the applicable provisions of their respective state constitutions, to determine the validity of statutory provisions or common law rules limiting marriage to a union of a man and a woman. * . . . These courts, often by a one-vote margin * . . . , have ruled upon the validity of statutory schemes that contrast with that of California, which in recent years has enacted comprehensive domestic partnership legislation under which a same-sex

couple may enter into a legal relationship that affords the couple virtually all of the same substantive legal benefits and privileges, and
imposes upon the couple virtually all of the same legal obligations
and duties, that California law affords to and imposes upon a married couple. Past California cases explain that the constitutional validity of a challenged statute or statutes must be evaluated by taking
into consideration all of the relevant statutory provisions that bear
upon how the state treats the affected persons with regard to the
subject at issue. * . . . Accordingly, the legal issue we must resolve is
not whether it would be constitutionally permissible under the
California Constitution for the state to limit marriage only to
opposite-sex couples while denying same-sex couples any opportunity to enter into an official relationship with all or virtually all of
the same substantive attributes, but rather whether our state Constitution prohibits the state from establishing a statutory scheme in
which both opposite-sex and same-sex couples are granted the right
to enter into an officially recognized family relationship that affords
all of the significant legal rights and obligations traditionally associated under state law with the institution of marriage, but under
which the union of an opposite-sex couple is officially designated a
"marriage" whereas the union of a same-sex couple is officially designated a "domestic partnership." The question we must address is
whether, under these circumstances, the failure to designate the official relationship of same-sex couples as marriage violates the California Constitution. It also is important to understand at the outset
that our task in this proceeding is not to decide whether we believe,
as a matter of policy, that the officially recognized relationship of a
same-sex couple should be designated a marriage rather than a
domestic partnership (or some other term), but instead only to
determine whether the difference in the official names of the relationships violates the California Constitution. We are aware, of
course, that very strongly held differences of opinion exist on the
matter of policy, with those persons who support the inclusion of
same-sex unions within the definition of marriage maintaining that
it is unfair to same-sex couples and potentially detrimental to the fiscal interests of the state and its economic institutions to reserve the
designation of marriage solely for opposite-sex couples, and others
asserting that it is vitally important to preserve the long-standing
and traditional definition of marriage as a union between a man and
a woman, even as the state extends comparable rights and responsibilities to committed same-sex couples. Whatever our views as individuals with regard to this question as a matter of policy, we
recognize as judges and as a court our responsibility to limit our
consideration of the question to a determination of the constitutional
validity of the current legislative provisions.

As explained hereafter, the determination whether the current California statutory scheme relating to marriage and to registered domestic partnership is constitutionally valid implicates a number of distinct and significant issues under the California Constitution. First, we must determine the nature and scope of the "right to marry"—a right that past cases establish as one of the fundamental constitutional rights embodied in the California Constitution. Although, as an historical matter, civil marriage and the rights associated with it traditionally have been afforded only to opposite-sex couples, this court's landmark decision 60 years ago in *Perez v. Sharp* (1948) 32 Cal.2d 7114—which found that California's statutory provisions prohibiting interracial marriages were inconsistent with the fundamental constitutional right to marry, notwithstanding the circumstance that statutory prohibitions on interracial marriage had existed since the founding of the state—makes clear that history alone is not invariably an appropriate guide for determining the meaning and scope of this fundamental constitutional guarantee. The decision in *Perez*, although rendered by a deeply divided court, is a judicial opinion whose legitimacy and constitutional soundness are by now universally recognized.

As discussed below, upon review of the numerous California decisions that have examined the underlying bases and significance of the constitutional right to marry (and that illuminate why this right has been recognized as one of the basic, inalienable civil rights guaranteed to an individual by the California Constitution), we conclude that, under this state's Constitution, the constitutionally based right to marry properly must be understood to encompass the core set of basic substantive legal rights and attributes traditionally associated with marriage that are so integral to an individual's liberty and personal autonomy that they may not be eliminated or abrogated by the Legislature or by the electorate through the statutory initiative process. These core substantive rights include, most fundamentally, the opportunity of an individual to establish—with the person with whom the individual has chosen to share his or her life—an officially recognized and protected family possessing mutual rights and responsibilities and entitled to the same respect and dignity accorded a union traditionally designated as marriage. As past cases establish, the substantive right of two adults who share a loving relationship to join together to establish an officially recognized family of their own—and, if the couple chooses, to raise children within that family—constitutes a vitally important attribute of the fundamental interest in liberty and personal autonomy that the California Constitution secures to all persons for the benefit of both the individual and society.

Furthermore, in contrast to earlier times, our state now recognizes that an individual's capacity to establish a loving and long-term committed relationship with another person and responsibly to care for and raise children does not depend upon the individual's sexual orientation, and, more generally, that an individual's sexual orientation—like a person's race or gender—does not constitute a legitimate basis upon which to deny or withhold legal rights. We therefore conclude that in view of the substance and significance of the fundamental constitutional right to form a family relationship, the California Constitution properly must be interpreted to guarantee this basic civil right to all Californians, whether gay or heterosexual, and to same-sex couples as well as to opposite-sex couples.

In defending the constitutionality of the current statutory scheme, the Attorney General of California maintains that even if the constitutional right to marry under the California Constitution applies to same-sex couples as well as to opposite-sex couples, this right should not be understood as requiring the Legislature to designate a couple's official family relationship by the term "marriage," as opposed to some other nomenclature. The Attorney General, observing that fundamental constitutional rights generally are defined by substance rather than by form, reasons that so long as the state affords a couple all of the constitutionally protected substantive incidents of marriage, the state does not violate the couple's constitutional right to marry simply by assigning their official relationship a name other than marriage. Because the Attorney General maintains that California's current domestic partnership legislation affords same-sex couples all of the core substantive rights that plausibly may be guaranteed to an individual or couple as elements of the fundamental state constitutional right to marry, the Attorney General concludes that the current California statutory scheme relating to marriage and domestic partnership does not violate the fundamental constitutional right to marry embodied in the California Constitution.

We need not decide in this case whether the name "marriage" is invariably a core element of the state constitutional right to marry so that the state would violate a couple's constitutional right even if—perhaps in order to emphasize and clarify that this civil institution is distinct from the religious institution of marriage—the state were to assign a name other than marriage as the official designation of the formal family relationship for all couples. Under the current statutes, the state has not revised the name of the official family relationship for all couples, but rather has drawn a distinction between the name for the official family relationship of opposite-sex couples (marriage) and that for same-sex couples (domestic partnership). One of the core elements of the right to establish an officially recognized family that is embodied in the California constitutional right to marry is a couple's right to have their family relationship accorded dignity and respect equal to that accorded other officially recognized families, and assigning a different designation for the family relationship of same-sex couples while reserving the historic designation of "marriage" exclusively for opposite-sex couples poses at least a serious risk of denying the family relationship of same-sex couples such equal dignity and respect. We therefore conclude that although the provisions of the current domestic partnership legislation afford same-sex couples most of the substantive elements embodied in the constitutional right to marry, the current California statutes nonetheless must be viewed as potentially impinging upon a same-sex couple's constitutional right to marry under the California Constitution.

Furthermore, the circumstance that the current California statutes assign a different name for the official family relationship of same-sex couples as contrasted with the name for the official family relationship of opposite-sex couples raises constitutional concerns not only under the state constitutional right to marry, but also under the state constitutional equal protection clause. In analyzing the validity of this differential treatment under the latter clause, we first must determine which standard of review should be applied to the statutory classification here at issue. Although in most instances the deferential "rational basis" standard of review is applicable in determining whether different treatment accorded by a statutory provision violates the state equal protection clause, a more exacting and rigorous standard of review—"strict scrutiny"—is applied when the distinction drawn by a statute rests upon a so-called "suspect classification" or impinges upon a fundamental right. As we shall explain, although we do not agree with the claim advanced by the parties challenging the validity of the current statutory scheme that the applicable statutes properly should be viewed as an instance of discrimination on the basis of the suspect characteristic of sex or gender and should be subjected to strict scrutiny on that ground, we conclude that strict scrutiny nonetheless is applicable here because (1) the statutes in question properly must be understood as classifying or discriminating on the basis of sexual orientation, a characteristic that we conclude represents—like gender, race, and religion—a constitutionally suspect basis upon which to impose differential treatment, and (2) the differential treatment at issue impinges upon a same-sex couple's fundamental interest in having their family relationship accorded the same respect and dignity enjoyed by an opposite-sex couple.

Under the strict scrutiny standard, unlike the rational basis standard, in order to demonstrate the constitutional validity of a challenged statutory classification the state must establish (1) that the state interest intended to be served by the differential treatment not only is a constitutionally legitimate interest, but is a compelling state interest, and (2) that the differential treatment not only is reasonably related to but is necessary to serve that compelling state interest. Applying this standard to the statutory classification here at issue, we conclude that the purpose underlying differential treatment of opposite-sex and same-sex couples embodied in California's current marriage statutes—the interest in retaining the traditional and well-established definition of marriage—cannot properly be viewed as a compelling state interest for purposes of the equal protection clause, or as necessary to serve such an interest.

A number of factors lead us to this conclusion. First, the exclusion of same-sex couples from the designation of marriage clearly is not necessary in order to afford full protection to all of the rights and benefits that currently are enjoyed by married opposite-sex couples; permitting same-sex couples access to the designation of marriage will not deprive opposite-sex couples of any rights and will not alter the legal framework of the institution of marriage, because same-sex couples who choose to marry will be subject to the same obligations and duties that currently are imposed on married opposite-sex couples. Second, retaining the traditional definition of marriage and affording same-sex couples only a separate and differently named family relationship will, as a realistic matter, impose appreciable harm on same-sex couples and their children, because denying such couples access to the familiar and highly favored designation of marriage is likely to cast doubt on whether the official family relationship of same-sex couples enjoys dignity equal to that of opposite-sex couples. Third, because of the widespread disparagement that gay individuals historically have faced, it is all the more probable that excluding same-sex couples from the legal institution of marriage is likely to be viewed as reflecting an official view that their committed relationships are of lesser stature than the comparable relationships of opposite-sex couples. Finally, retaining the designation of marriage exclusively for opposite-sex couples and providing only a separate and distinct designation for same-sex couples may well have the effect of perpetuating a more general premise—now emphatically rejected by this state—that gay individuals and same-sex couples are in some respects "second-class citizens" who may, under the law, be treated differently from, and less favorably than, heterosexual individuals or opposite-sex couples. Under these circumstances, we cannot find that retention of the traditional definition of marriage constitutes a compelling state interest. Accordingly, we conclude that to the extent the current California statutory provisions limit marriage to opposite-sex couples, these statutes are unconstitutional.

Source: In re Marriage Cases (2008). 43 Cal.4th 757 [76 Cal.Rptr.3d 683, 183 P.3d 384]. Available online at: http://www.courtinfo.ca.gov/opinions/documents/S147999.PDF.

In re Marriage Cases: Dissent (2008)

In the previous case, In re Marriages, a dissenting opinion was offered by Associate Justice Marvin R. Baxter. His fundamental position is outlined in the extract below from his dissent.

The majority opinion reflects considerable research, thought, and effort on a significant and sensitive case, and I actually agree with several of the majority's conclusions. However, I cannot join the majority's holding that the California Constitution gives same-sex couples a right to marry. In reaching this decision, I believe, the majority violates the separation of powers, and thereby commits profound error.

Only one other American state recognizes the right the majority announces today. So far, Congress, and virtually every court to consider the issue, has rejected it. Nothing in our Constitution, express or implicit, compels the majority's startling conclusion that the age-old understanding of marriage—an understanding recently confirmed by an initiative law—is no longer valid. California statutes already recognize same-sex unions and grant them all the substantive legal rights this state can bestow. If there is to be a further sea change in the social and legal understanding of marriage itself, that evolution should occur by similar democratic means. The majority forecloses this ordinary democratic process, and, in doing so, oversteps its authority.

The majority's mode of analysis is particularly troubling. The majority relies heavily on the Legislature's adoption of progressive civil rights protections for gays and lesbians to find a constitutional right to same-sex marriage. In effect, the majority gives the Legislature indirectly power that body does not directly possess to amend the Constitution and repeal an initiative statute. I cannot subscribe to the majority's reasoning, or to its result.

[At this point, Baxter acknowledges the points on which he agrees with the majority opinion. He then goes on to say, however, that:]

However, I respectfully disagree with the remainder of the conclusions reached by the majority.

The question presented by this case is simple and stark. It comes down to this: Even though California's progressive laws, recently adopted through the democratic process, have pioneered the rights of same-sex partners to enter legal unions with all the substantive benefits of opposite-sex legal unions, do those laws nonetheless violate the California Constitution because at present, in deference to long and universal tradition, by a convincing popular vote, and in accord with express national policy * . . . , they reserve the label "marriage" for opposite-sex legal unions? I must conclude that the answer is no. The People, directly or through their elected representatives, have every right to adopt laws abrogating the historic understanding that civil marriage is between a man and a woman. The rapid growth in California of statutory protections for the rights of gays and lesbians, as individuals, as parents, and as committed partners, suggests a quickening evolution of community attitudes on these issues. Recent years have seen the development of an intense debate about same-sex marriage. Advocates of this cause have had real success in the marketplace of ideas, gaining attention and considerable public support. Left to its own devices, the ordinary democratic process might well produce, ere long, a consensus among most Californians that the term "marriage" should, in civil parlance, include the legal unions of same-sex partners.

But a bare majority of this court, not satisfied with the pace of democratic change, now abruptly forestalls that process and substitutes, by judicial fiat, its own social policy views for those expressed by the People themselves. Undeterred by the strong weight of state and federal law and authority, the majority invents a new constitutional right, immune from the ordinary process of legislative consideration. The majority finds that our Constitution suddenly demands no less than a permanent redefinition of marriage, regardless of the popular will.

In doing so, the majority holds, in effect, that the Legislature has done indirectly what the Constitution prohibits it from doing directly. Under article II, section 10, subdivision (c), that body cannot unilaterally repeal an initiative statute, such as Family Code section 308.5, unless the initiative measure itself so provides. Section 308.5 contains no such provision. Yet the majority suggests that, by enacting other statutes which do provide substantial rights to gays and lesbians—including domestic partnership rights which, under section 308.5, the Legislature could not call "marriage"—the Legislature has given "explicit official recognition" * . . . to a California right of equal treatment which, because it includes the right to marry, thereby invalidates section 308.5.5.

I cannot join this exercise in legal jujitsu, by which the Legislature's own weight is used against it to create a constitutional right from whole cloth, defeat the People's will, and invalidate a statute otherwise immune from legislative interference. Though the majority insists otherwise, its pronouncement seriously oversteps the judicial power. The majority purports to apply certain fundamental provisions of the state Constitution, but it runs afoul of another just as fundamental—article III, section 3, the separation of powers clause. This clause declares that "[t]he powers of state government are legislative, executive, and judicial," and that "[p]ersons charged with the exercise of one power may not exercise either of the others" except as the Constitution itself specifically provides.

Source: In re Marriage Cases (2008). 43 Cal.4th 757 [76 Cal.Rptr.3d 683, 183 P.3d 384]. Available online at: http://www.courtinfo.ca.gov/opinions/documents/S147999.PDF.

Data

Hate Crime Trends (2001–2006)

The Federal Bureau of Investigation (FBI) annually publishes a summary of hate crime statistics collected from a number of states and local law enforcement agencies. Table 6.1 summarizes the statistics on hate crimes against gay men and women from those reports for the years 2001 through 2006, the latest year for which data are available.

Total "Don't Ask, Don't Tell" Discharges (1994–2006)

Table 6.2 summarizes the number of lesbians and gay men who have been discharged from various branches of the U.S. military service from 1994 to 2006, the most recent year for which data are available.

TABLE 6.1
Hate Crime Trends, 2001–2006

Category	2001	2002	2003	2004	2005	2006
Anti-male	980	825	783	738	621	747
Anti-female	205	172	187	164	155	163
Anti-homosexual	173	222	247	245	195	238
Anti-heterosexual	18	10	14	33	21	26
Anti-bisexual	17	15	8	17	25	21
Total	1,393	1,244	1,239	1,197	1,017	1,195

Source: Federal Bureau of Investigation, annual report, *Crime in the United States.*

Same-Sex Marriages in Massachusetts (2008)

Until 2008, Massachusetts was the only state in the United States to permit same-sex marriages. By that year, the state had accumulated data on the number of same-sex marriages performed over a period of 3.5 years, from May 17, 2004 to the end of 2007. Those data are summarized in Table 6.3.

TABLE 6.2
Total "Don't Ask, Don't Tell" Discharges, 1994–2006

Year	Number of Discharges
1994	617
1995	772
1996	870
1997	1,007
1998	1,163
1999	1,046
2000	1,241
2001	1,273
2002	906
2003	787
2004	668
2005	742
2006	612

Source: Servicemembers Legal Defense Fund, http://www.sldn.org/binary-data/SLDN_ARTICLES/pdf_file/1454. pdf. Based on information obtained from the U.S. Department of Defense, U.S. Army, U.S. Air Force, U.S. Navy, U.S. Marine Corps, U.S. Coast Guard, and unofficial congressional sources.

TABLE 6.3
Same-Sex Marriages in Massachusetts, 2008

Year	Male-to-Female Marriages	Same-Sex Marriages Male-to-Male	Same-Sex Marriages Female-to-Female
2004[a]	27,196 (82%)	2,176 (6.4%)	3,945 (11.6%)
2005	37,447 (95%)	736 (1.9%)	1,324 (3.4%)
2006	36,550 (96%)	543 (1.5%)	899 (2.5%)
2007	19,108 (96%)	356 (1.8%)	511 (2.5%)

Source: Massachusetts Registry of Vital Records and Statistics, by e-mail to author, July 7, 2008.
Note: Percentages may not add to 100 because of rounding.
[a]*May* 17–December 31, 2004.

7

Directory of Organizations

A very large number of organizations now exist with the objective of promoting the expansion of civil rights for gay men, lesbian, bisexuals, and transgendered (LGBT) people. The first section that follows lists some of the most prominent international, national, and regional groups with this objective. Many state and local organizations are also active in promoting lesbian and gay rights. Space prohibits the listing of all or most of these organizations, but an excellent resource for locating these organizations in the United States is the Web site GayRights.org (http://www.gayrights.org), which has an interactive map taking the viewer to organizations located in each of the 50 states and the District of Columbia. Perhaps the most comprehensive single source of gay, lesbian, bisexual, and transgendered persons organizations is the Web site of Alvin Fritz at the University of Washington libraries at: http://faculty.washington.edu/alvin/gayorg.htm. An excellent resource for gay and lesbian rights organizations throughout the world is the Web site Gay Civil Rights. See their Web page at http://www.gaycivilrights.org/gaycivilrights.

It is worth noting that most professional, academic, and governmental organizations today now have subgroups or caucuses of gay men, lesbians, bisexual, and transgendered persons whose objectives include at least to some extent the furtherance of equal rights for all employees and professionals regardless of sexual orientation. See, for example, the entries for the National Lesbian and Gay Journalists Association; Salutaris, the NIH Gay, Lesbian, Bisexual, Transgender Employee Forum; and the Society of Lesbian and Gay Anthropologists. In addition, many

215

nations now have organizations working for gay and lesbian rights in their home country. Space does not permit a complete listing of such organizations, but see Lambda Turkey as an example of such groups.

The successes of the LBGT movement have, at the same time, inspired the founding or increased activity of a number of groups opposed to one or another goal of the LBGT movement. The second section that follows lists a number of these groups. In addition to the groups listed, researchers should also refer to the Web sites for a number of religious organizations, such as the Roman Catholic Church and the Southern Baptist Convention, which oppose equal rights for lesbians and gays and often have active groups working to promote this view.

Organizations Supporting and/or Promoting Lesbian and Gay Rights

ACT-UP
Web site: http://www.actupny.org

ACT-UP is an acronym for AIDS Coalition to Unleash Power. It was founded in March 1987 by a group of New York City activists who were angry that the federal, state, and local governments were taking what they perceived to be inadequate efforts for dealing with the growing HIV/AIDS crisis. The group was convinced that this situation would not improve as long as AIDS funding, research, education, and care remained in the hands of government officials, politicians, academic scientists, and professional health care workers. It originated an aggressive and outspoken campaign to gain more control over AIDS research and care by those who had the disease and were directly threatened by it. While the organization remains focused on health issues confronting gay men and lesbians, by its very existence and actions it has become a powerful force for the promotion of lesbian and gay rights in the United States and throughout the world. It currently has chapters in a number of U.S. and foreign cities, including Paris, Athens, Nairobi, Kathmandu, Los Angeles, East Bay (California), and Austin, Texas.

Publications: ACT-UP has produced a number of brochures, pamphlets, and other publications describing its work, including *Civil Disobedience Manual, The Demonstrator's Manual, ACT-UP Explained, FDA Action Handbook,* and *After 10 Years of ACT UP.*

American Civil Liberties Union (ACLU)

Web site: http://www.aclu.org

The American Civil Liberties Union was founded in 1920 for the purpose of working for the protection of the civil rights of all Americans. The ACLU is arguably the best known, most highly respected, and most successful of all organizations associated with civil rights issues in the United States. Its current areas of concern include the rights of disabled people, free speech, prisoners' rights, reproductive freedom, the rights of the poor, voting rights, and women's rights. In the area of gay and lesbian rights, the organization has led or participated in a number of legal actions, including a lawsuit against the University of Pittsburgh over benefits for gay and lesbian employees, a lawsuit in Texas against the state's sodomy laws, domestic partner benefits for the lesbian survivor of the 9/11 attack, and a number of legal actions involving adoption rights of lesbians and gay men. Most of the ACLU's current activities on behalf of lesbians and gay men are conducted through the organization's Lesbian Gay Bisexual Transgender Project.

Publications: *Too High a Price: The Case against Restricting Gay Parenting, Transgender People and the Law: Frequently Asked Questions, Why We're Asking Courts and Legislatures for Transgender Equality, The Rights of Lesbian, Gay, Bisexual and Transgendered People, Where We Are 2003: The Annual Report of the ACLU's Nationwide Work on LGBT Rights and HIV/AIDS.*

American Veterans for Equal Rights (AVER)

Web site: http://aver.us/aver

Formerly the Gay, Lesbian, and Bisexual Veterans of America (GLBVA), American Veterans for Equal Rights works to eliminate the ban on the right of gay men and lesbians to serve in the U.S. military services. First organized in 1991, the organization currently has local chapters in California, the District of Columbia, Delaware, Florida, Georgia, Hawaii, Illinois, Missouri, Minnesota, New Mexico, New York, Ohio, Texas, and Washington. Both the organization itself and individual members have been active in a number of events designed to promote equality in the military services, including participation in National Coming Out Day; many Memorial Day observances and Veterans Day parades; the 1993 March on Washington; layings of the wreath at the Tomb of the Unknown; the Millennium March On Washington; and presentations before college and university student groups, church groups, civic organizations, and political organizations.

Publications: *LGBT Military News* (online newsletter)

Amnesty International
Web site: http://www.amnesty.org

Amnesty International is a worldwide organization of more than 2.2 million people in over 150 countries working to guarantee the human rights of all people in all countries. The organization was founded in 1961 by British lawyer Peter Benenson. The U.S. chapter is Amnesty International USA, whose Web site is: http://www.amnestyusa.org. Amnesty International USA's priorities include torture and terror, violence against women, Katrina survivors, military contractors, and LGBT (lesbian, gay, bisexual, and transgendered) human rights. One of the organization's most recent publications, "Beyond Stonewalled: Building a Grassroots Alliance to Create Police Accountability," deals with police abuse of LGBT people in the United States.

Publications: Occasional reports on problem issues and problem areas.

Campaign to End Homophobia
Web site: http://www.endhomophobia.org

The Campaign to End Homophobia is a not-for-profit corporation whose purpose it is to bring an end to homophobia and heterosexism through educational efforts. It does so by developing and distributing educational materials, running training institutes, sponsoring conferences, and networking and sharing information with other individuals and organizations. The organization was founded in 1987, largely in response to the U.S. Supreme Court's 1986 decision validating sodomy laws in Georgia.

Publications: Workshop materials and pamphlets, such as "Guide to Leading Introductory Workshops on Homophobia"; "Homosexuality, Heterosexism, and Homophobia"; "Opening Doors to Understanding and Acceptance"; "Speaking Out: A

Manual for Gay, Lesbian, and Bisexual Public Speakers"; and "Hate Crimes and Homophobic Violence."

Canadian Human Rights Commission (CHRC)

Web site: www.chrc-ccdp.ca

The Canadian Human Rights Commission is responsible for carrying out the provisions of the Canadian Human Rights Act of 1977. Its function is to investigate and attempt to resolve issues of discrimination in employment and the administration of justice in Canada. Since 1999, the provisions of the Human Rights Act have been understood to apply to all Canadian citizens, regardless of their sexual orientation and, more recently, their gender identity. The commission's Web site provides an exhaustive supply of publications, legal decisions, governmental policies and regulations, and other documents and actions relating to the rights of gay men, lesbians, bisexuals, and transgendered persons under Canadian law.

Publications: Occasional reports on a variety of topics relating to human rights issues.

Children of Gays and Lesbians Everywhere (COGALE)
Web site: http://www.colage.org

Children of Gays and Lesbians Everywhere is a national program that brings together the children of gays, lesbians, bisexual, and transgendered persons, allowing them to network and share experiences with one another. COGALE provides opportunities for young people to work within the LGBT community, as well as the general community, to achieve social justice for all people. The organization helps introduce pen pals to each other, provides Internet networking, provide training sessions for people within and outside the LGBT community, and offers both scholarship and intern programs.

Publications: The newsletter *Just for Us* comes out two to four times a year.

Egale Canada
Web site: http://www.egale.ca

Egale Canada is Canada's premier organization working to obtain equal rights for lesbian, gay, bisexual, and transgendered persons (LGBT). It has members in every province and territory, and its board of directors includes one male and one female member from every such district. Egale Canada has been involved in every important legal action in Canada aimed at providing civil and legal equality of all citizens, regardless of their sexual orientation. Members of the organization have also testified before parliament a number of times on issues of interest to LGBT persons, such as tax policy, immigration, same-sex marriage and divorce, child custody and adoption, and school safety for LGBT youth.

Publications: *INFO Egale* (quarterly newsletter); *Egale Update* (monthly report); *The Year in Review* (annual report).

Equality Federation (EF)
Web site: http://www.equalityfederation.org

The Equality Federation was formed in 2006 to work for the advancement of equal civil rights for lesbians, gay men, bisexuals, and transgendered (LGBT) persons. The organization focuses its efforts on state and local projects rather than primarily on the federal level. It provides resources and leadership training for state and local groups in the pursuit of these goals. One of its most useful projects is the annual "State of the States" report, which summarizes and analyzes a host of information about the finances, organization, activities, and personnel of state and local LGBT organizations. EF's Web site also provides an interactive map that allows access to equal rights organizations in 40 of the 50 states.

Publications: Occasional online reports on LGBT issues.

Families Like Ours (FLO)
Web site: http://www.familieslikeours.org

Families Like Ours is an organization of adoptive and foster parents offering assistance to other couples who wish to become adoptive or foster parents. FLO focuses its efforts primarily, but not exclusively, on gay and lesbian couples. It offers advice, counseling, and mentoring for couples, from the time they begin to consider fostering or adopting, until that process has been completed. The organization provides a comprehensive guide to adoption and fostering in its publication "Adoption 101: A Family Guide," available on its Web site.

Publications: *Families Like Ours* (monthly newsletter); *Adoption 101: A Family Guide* (online publication); *Becoming a Foster Parent* (online publication).

Family Equality Council (FEC)
Web site: http://www.familyequality.org

Founded originally as the Gay Fathers Coalition in 1979, this organization later changed its name to Gay and Lesbian Parents Coalition International in 1986 and to its current name in 2007. FEC is a national nonprofit organization that works to gain equality not only for those of same-sex couples, but also for those of other nontraditional families, such as single-parent families and mixed-race families whose needs may be ignored by society at large. Family Equality Council operates OUTspoken, a national speaker's bureau that provides speakers on family equality for a wide range of groups and events. As of late 2008, more than 1,000 men and women from 39 states, the District of Columbia, 1 U.S. territory, and 3 foreign countries have volunteered to participate in the OUTspoken program.
Publications: *52 Ways to be OUTspoken; Family Discussions about Political Attacks on Our Families, Talking to Children about Our Families; Interactive Tool: The Rainbow Report Card*; and many other brochures available online.

Freedom to Marry
Web site: http://www.freedomtomarry.org

Freedom to Marry was founded by civil rights attorney and activist Evan Wolfson for the purpose of promoting the rights of all Americans to marry, regardless of their sexual orientation. Through its Voices of Equality program, it draws on a diverse group of prominent Americans who speak out on equality of marriage rights. The group includes individuals such as Rocky Anderson, mayor of Salt Lake City; Christine Chavez, political director of the United Farm Workers of America; Dakota Fine, Washington, D.C., activist; Kim Gandy, president of the National Organization for Women; Congressman John Lewis; and Reverend William G. Sinkford, president of the Unitarian Universalist Association.
Publications: *Why Marriage Matters: America, Equality, and Gay People's Right to Marry* (book); *Candidates' Guide on How to*

Support Marriage Equality and Get Elected(online publication); *Marriage Makes a Word of Difference* (online publication); *The Freedom to Marry: Why Non-Gay People Care and What We Can Do about It* (online publication); *For Richer, For Poorer: The Freedom to Marry as a Matter of Economic Justice* (online publication); *What is Freedom to Marry?* (online publication); *The Time Is Now to Fight for the Freedom to Marry* (online publication); *Stand Up for Our Constitution* (online publication).

Funders for Gay and Lesbian Issues (FGLI)
Web site: http://www.lgbtfunders.org

Funders for Gay and Lesbian Issues was founded as a subgroup of the National Network of Grantmakers (NNG) under the name of the Working Group on Funding Lesbian and Gay Issues. The organization was formed because some members of NNG felt that insufficient attention was being paid to the funding needs of lesbian, gay, bisexual, and transgender (LGBT) groups. The organization's mission is to provide funding for organizations working for "full equality under the law, equal access to services, unconditional respect for difference and the meaningful participation of all communities at tables where decisions are made." In July 2008, FGLI published a report on the way that grant makers integrate racial equity into their policies and practices in supporting LGBT organizations. (The report is available online at: http://www.lgbtfunders.org/files/RE.Reportcard.pdf.)
Publications: *LGBTQ Grantmakers 2008 Report Card on Racial Equity; Key Facts: Policies and Populations in the Midwest; LGBTQ Grantmaking by U.S. Foundations (Calendar Year 2006); Key Facts: New England Policies and Populations; Racial Equity Campaign Overview; Building Communities: Autonomous LGBTQ People of Color Organizations in the U.S.* (all reports).

Gay and Lesbian Advocates and Defenders (GLAD)
Web site: http://www.glad.org

GLAD is one of the oldest gay and lesbian rights organizations in the nation, having been formed in 1978 to fight for an end to discrimination based on sexual orientation, HIV status, and gender identity. Some of the issues about which GLAD has litigated in the past are civil rights, crime and law enforcement, employment, family issues, health care, marriage and civil unions, public accommodations, transgender issues, and gay and lesbian youth and students.

Publications: Legal publications on topics such as *A Legal Q&A for Kids of Trans Parents; Transgender Students' Use of Bathrooms and Locker Rooms; Maine: Joint Adoption Practice and Procedure; New Hampshire Civil Unions; Legal Issues for Non-MA Couples Who Married in MA; Marriage Guide for RI Couples; Rights of LGBTQ Youth in RI; Rights of LGBTQ Youth in ME.*

Gay and Lesbian Alliance against Defamation (GLAAD)
Web site: http://www.glaad.org

Gay and Lesbian Alliance against Defamation works to obtain fair and accurate coverage of lesbians and gay men in the print and electronic media, films and television, and other types of media. The organization strives to confront homophobic defamation, stereotypical portrayal, and heterosexist omission of gay, lesbian, bisexual, and transgendered people from the media. GLAAD makes use of letter writing, telephone "tree" campaigns, demonstrations, panel discussions, and meetings with news, entertainment, education, and business professionals to achieve its objective.

Publications: *GLAAD Media Reference Guide; GLAAD Media Essentials Training Manual; 2006 GLAAD Performance Report; GLAAD Network Responsibility Index; Chinese-Language GLAAD Media Reference Guide; Announcing Equality; GLAAD College Media Reference Guide;* GLAAD News Pops; GLAAD Alerts; GLAAD Calls to Action; GLADD Op-Eds.

Gay, Lesbian, Bisexual, and Transgendered Round Table of the American Library Association (GLBTRT)
Web site: http://www.ala.org/ala/mgrps/rts/glbtrt

The Gay, Lesbian, Bisexual, and Transgendered Round Table was founded in 1970 as the Task Force on Gay Liberation. It was the first organization of gay and lesbian professionals. The mission of the organization is not only to serve the needs of LGBT librarians and library staff members, but also to ensure a free and accurate distribution of information about LGBT issues to the community and to the general public. The organization annually issues Stonewall Book Awards to the best fiction and best nonfiction books on LGBT themes published that year.

Publications: A quarterly newsletter, *GLBTRT Newsletter*, available online at the organization's Web site.

Gender Public Advocacy Coalition (GenderPAC)
Web site: http://www.gpac.org

The Gender Public Advocacy Coalition is a tax exempt 501(c)3 organization that seeks to educate the general public about the nature of discrimination based on gender, sexual orientation, race, class, and age. It works to make educational institutions and workplaces safer for people of all gender and sexual orientation. Its most recent campaigns and reports have dealt with the images portrayed by hip-hop music, how popular images of masculinity lead to hate crimes and violence, and a study of gender equality in the nation's schools and colleges.
Publications: *Hip-Hop: Beyond Beats and Rhymes; 50 Under 30: Masculinity and the War on America's Youth; GENIUS Index (Gender Equality National Index for Universities and Schools)*(all reports).

Gill Foundation
Web site: http://www.gillfoundation.org

The Gill Foundation was established in 1994 by Coloradan Tim Gill in response to a rancorous campaign to limit the rights of gay men and lesbians in that state. Founder of the software company Quark, Inc., Gill was financially able to provide a solid basis for the foundation. Since its creation, the foundation has awarded more than $120 million to support programs and organizations working to ensure equal civil rights for lesbians and gay men in the United States. Much of the foundation's work is currently carried out through two programs, OutGiving and the Democracy Project. OutGiving is an effort to increase philanthropic giving to gay and lesbian organizations, while the Democracy Project is a program to increase the efficient operation of more than 400 groups in the United States working for gay and lesbian rights.
Publications: Annual Reports (available online).

Human Rights Campaign (HRC)
Web site: http://www.hrc.org

The Human Rights Campaign was founded in 1980 to work for the civil rights of all gay men and lesbians in the United States.

The organization currently claims 700,000 members and calls itself the largest organization of its kind in the country. The organization's Center for the Study of Equality works to improve the general understanding of gay and lesbian issues. HRC has published a number of reports on various aspects of the gay and lesbian rights movement, such as "Transgender Inclusion in the Workplace," "Family Matters," "Equality from State to State: Gay, Lesbian, Bisexual and Transgender Americans and State Legislation," and "Small Business Basics."

Publications: *Resource Guide to Coming Out; A Straight Guide to GLBT Americans; Coming Out for African Americans; Guía de Recursos Para Salir del Clóset; Coming Out As Transgender; Living Openly in Your Place of Worship; Buying for Equality 2008; Corporate Equality Index 2008; Healthcare Equality Index 2008.*

Human Rights Watch (HRW)
Web site: http://hrw.org

For many years, Human Rights Watch has included issues of lesbian, gay, bisexual, and transgender rights as one of its primary fields of concern. Each year, it reviews and comments on progress and problems with regard to these issues in various countries around the world. HRW activities span the globe; in 2008 alone, for example, it investigated cases of human rights violation involving lesbians, gay men, bisexuals, and transgendered people in Colombia, Egypt, Gambia, Jamaica, Kyrgyzstan, Morocco, Nigeria, Turkey, Uganda, and the United States. The organization's Web site contains links to organizations working for LGBT rights in more than 100 countries around the world.

Publications (selection only): *Courting History: The Landmark International Criminal Court's First Years; Still Waiting: Bringing Justice for War Crimes, Crimes against Humanity, and Genocide in Bosnia and Herzegovina's Cantonal and District Courts; My Rights, and My Right to Know: Lack of Access to Therapeutic Abortion in Peru; "As If I Am Not Human": Abuses against Asian Domestic Workers in Saudi Arabia; China's Forbidden Zones: Shutting the Media out of Tibet and Other "Sensitive" Stories; United Kingdom: Briefing on the Counter-Terrorism Bill 2008; Preempting Justice: Counterterrorism Laws and Procedures in France; "As If They Fell from the Sky": Counterinsurgency, Rights Violations, and Rampant Impunity in Ingushetia; Neighbors in Need: Zimbabweans Seeking Refuge in South Africa; "We Need a Law for Liberation": Gender,*

Sexuality, and Human Rights in a Changing Turkey; "We Have the Upper Hand": Freedom of Assembly in Russia and the Human Rights of Lesbian, Gay, Bisexual, and Transgender People; Restrictions on AIDS Activists in China.

Immigration Equality (IE)

Web site: http://www.immigrationequality.org

Immigration Equality claims a membership of over 10,000 lesbians, gay men, bisexuals, and transgendered and HIV positive people throughout the United States. The organization was formed in 1994 to work for changes in U.S. immigration law that would allow such individuals to sponsor their partners for immigration benefits, which is not possible under current immigration law. IE works for the passage of the Uniting American Families Act of 2007 to achieve this goal.

Publications: "Family, Unvalued"; "LGBT/HIV Asylum Manual"; "LGBT Immigration Basics"; "HIV Immigration Basics" (Web publications); also available online are archival copies of the organization's earlier newsletters and brochures on specific topics.

International Association of Lesbian and Gay Judges (IALGJ)

Web site: http://home.att.net/ialgj

The International Association of Lesbian and Gay Judges consists of more than 50 members, primarily from the United States and Canada. The organization was founded in 1993 to provide a mechanism by which gay and lesbian judges could meet and exchange information and opinions, increase the visibility of gay and lesbian judges in the judicial system, assist in ensuring the equal treatment of all individuals regardless of sexual orientation in the judicial system, and provide aid and support for gay men and lesbians interested in becoming judges.

Publications: Annual meeting minutes (available online).

International Gay and Lesbian Human Rights Commission (IGLHRC)

Web site: http://www.iglhrc.org/site/iglhrc

The International Gay and Lesbian Human Rights Commission is a New York-based nonprofit corporation whose purpose it is to work for the civil rights of gay men and lesbians in all nations of the world. IGLHRC coordinates its efforts with other social organizations and agencies throughout the world, conducts an active program of education about issues of human sexuality, and provides rapid responses to human rights violations related to issues of sexuality throughout the world. The organization's work is currently organized under six major topics: Africa, Asia, Asylum Documentation, Eastern Europe and Central Asia, HIV/AIDS, and Latin America and the Caribbean.

Publications: Numerous newsletters, annual reports, fact sheets, statements, public presentations, and other resource materials.

International Lesbian and Gay Association (ILGA)
Web site: http://www.ilga.org

The International Lesbian and Gay Association was founded in 1978 to work for achieving equal rights for gay men and lesbians (and now bisexuals and transgendered persons) in all countries throughout the world. Today, it consists of more than 600 member organizations in 90 countries, ranging from small local groups to national organizations with thousands of members. ILGA holds an annual conference and a number of regional conferences. It has produced a number of reports on the status of LGBT people in various countries and regions of the world, as well as on specific topics, such as HIV/AIDS disease, homophobia, same-sex marriage, the worldwide legal status of same-sex relationships, workplace discrimination, and hate music.

Publications: Many reports on topics such as those listed in the previous paragraph.

Lambda Istanbul
Web site: http://www.qrd.org/qrd/www/world/europe/turkey

Lambda Istanbul is typical of many lesbian and gay organizations in countries other than the United States. It was formed in 1993 as the result of a ban by Istanbul police on a planned gay pride celebration. Since that time, the organization has worked to improve the political status of lesbians and gay men in Istanbul and the rest of Turkey. It has also expanded its vision to include health information and support, especially for people with HIV/AIDS; a call-in service for information on gay and lesbian issues; social events at which lesbians and gay men have an opportunity to meet, talk, and socialize; and publication of a bimonthly magazine, *Kaos GL*, available online at http://news.kaosgl.com.

Publication: *Kaos GL* (magazine).

Lambda Legal
Web site: http://www.lambdalegal.org

Lambda Legal is an organization devoted to achieving equal rights for lesbians, gay men, bisexuals, and transgendered (LGBT) persons by litigating cases, promoting public education programs, and advocating for appropriate public policy decisions. The organization has a national office in New York City and regional offices in Los Angeles, Dallas, Chicago, and Atlanta. Lambda Legal has been involved on some level or another in almost every major court case related to LGBT issues since its founding in 1973.
Publications: *Of Counsel; Of Counsel on Campus* (newsletters); *eNews* (online newsletter).

Log Cabin Republicans
Web site: http://online.logcabin.org

Log Cabin Republicans is an organization of gay and lesbian Republicans working to transform the Republican Party on issues of concern to them from inside the party. The organization maintains a full-time staff at its national headquarters in Washington, D.C., and at its western field office in Sacramento, California, and has 44 chapters in 30 states. Log Cabin Republicans describe themselves as "loyal Republicans" who subscribe to traditional party values, such as a strong national defense, individual liberty, individual responsibility, and a free market economy.
Publication: *Inclusion Wins* (electronic newsletter).

Magnus Hirschfeld Centre for Human Rights
Web site: http://come.to/humanrights

The Magnus Hirschfeld Centre for Human Rights was founded in 1986 by activist Bill Courson to help protect and promote the human civil rights of marginal populations, such as gay men, lesbians, those with HIV/AIDS disease, and many kinds of minority groups. Using its own resources or working in conjunction with other human rights organizations, the center provides legal assistance to individuals confronted with discrimination, hate crimes, or other abuses. The organization's Web site lists a number of documents it has produced dealing with human rights violations of gay men and lesbians in many countries around the world. It

also contains an excellent list of international legal resources for lesbians, gay men, bisexuals, and transgendered persons.
Publications: Online reports and cases.

Matthew Shepard Foundation
Web site: http://www.matthewshepard.org

The Matthew Shepard Foundation was founded in 1998 by Dennis and Judy Shepard in memory and honor of their son, Matthew, who was murdered by Russell Arthur Henderson and Aaron James McKinney near Laramie, Wyoming. The foundation has three major goals: to eliminate the kind of hate in our society that resulted in Matthew's murder; working for equal rights for all lesbian, gay, bisexual, and transgendered persons (LGBT); and to educate and provide for the needs of young men and women, especially LGBT individuals. In 2007, the foundation launched an online Youth Lounge, providing an opportunity for young people to interact on issues of concern to them.
Publications: Press releases, news announcements, and media resources online.

National Center for Lesbian Rights (NCLR)
Web site: http://www.nclrights.org

The National Center for Lesbian Rights was founded in 1977 by lesbian attorneys Roberta Achtenberg and Donna Hitchens to work for the rights of lesbians, gay men, bisexuals, and transgendered (LGBT) persons. Each year the center provides legal services for about 5,000 seniors, youth, immigrants, athletes, and other LGBT persons. The organization is also active in public advocacy and educational programs dealing with LBGT issues.
Publications: Press releases, news announcements, and other media resources online.

National Center for Transgender Equality (NCTE)
Web site: http://www.nctequality.org

The National Center for Transgender Equality is a 501(c)3 organization founded in 2003 to work for equality for transgendered persons. The primary issues with which the organization is concerned are discrimination, federal documents, hate crimes, health and medical care, homelessness, immigration, marriage, travel, and military service and veterans' rights.

Publications: *Opening the Door to the Inclusion of Transgender People; 52 Things You Can Do for Transgender Equality; Overcoming Voting Obstacles for Transgender People; Social Security Gender No-Match Letters and Transgender Employees; Making Shelters Safe for Transgender Evacuees; Making Your Voice Heard: A Transgender Guide to Educating Congress* (brochures and pamphlets).

National Coalition of Anti-Violence Programs (NCAVP)
Web site: http://www.ncavp.org

The National Coalition of Anti-Violence Programs is an alliance of programs designed to monitor and document violent crimes against gay men, lesbians, bisexual, and transgendered persons, and people infected with HIV. The six different issues with which NCAVP deals are hate-motivated violence, rape and sexual assault, harassment and discrimination, domestic and partner violence, HIV/AID-related violence, pick-up crimes, police misconduct, and other forms of victimization. The organization focuses on three types of activities: educating the public about violent crimes perpetrated against LGBT people, providing responses to specific cases of violence, and collecting statistics dealing with violent crimes against LGBT persons.

National Conference of State Legislatures (NCSL)
Web site: http://www.ncsl.org

The National Conference of State Legislatures was founded in 1975 to provide support for legislators and staffs of all 50 state legislatures. It provides information, research, and personal support on state and federal issues; sponsors meetings and networking opportunities; lobbies the federal administration and the Congress on issues of interest and importance to the states; and offers print and Internet publications and consulting services to state legislatures. It offers a host of publications on a variety of same-sex issues, such as same-sex marriages, civil unions, and domestic partnerships; state employee health benefit programs; and same-sex youth issues.

Publications: Selection: *State Legislatures* (magazine); *StateConnect* (resource book); *Learning the Game: How the Legislative Process Works* (booklet); *Making your Case: How to Win in the*

Legislature (booklet); *Public Health: A Legislator's Guide* (booklet); *State Budget Update: April 2008* (online resource book); *Protecting Our Critical Infrastructure* (booklet).

National Gay and Lesbian Task Force (NGLTF)
Web site: http://www.thetaskforce.org

The National Gay and Lesbian Task Force focuses on a number of issues of special interest to gay men, lesbians, bisexuals, and transgendered people, including elections and politics, issues of aging, nondiscrimination, parenting and families, hate crimes, and HIV/AIDS disease. In addition to its national office in Washington, D.C., it maintains regional offices in Cambridge, Massachusetts; Miami; New York City; Los Angeles; and Minneapolis. The NGLTF Policy Institute conducts research and issues periodic reports, maps, and fact sheets on a variety of topics related to the civil rights of GLBT people.
Publications: *Opening the Door to the Inclusion of Transgender People: The Nine Keys to Making Lesbian, Gay, Bisexual and Transgender Organizations Fully Transgender-Inclusive* (report); *Living in the Margins: A National Survey of Lesbian, Gay, Bisexual and Transgender Asian and Pacific Islander Americans* (report); *Same-Sex Marriage Initiatives and Lesbian, Gay and Bisexual Voters in the 2006 Elections* (Report); *Policy Priorities in the Lesbian, Gay, Bisexual and Transgender Community* (report).

National Lesbian and Gay Journalists Association (NLGJA)
Web site: http://www.nlgja.org

The National Lesbian and Gay Journalists Association is typical of many organizations of gay men, lesbians, bisexuals, and transgendered persons who combine concerns about their professional interests with those related to special issues involving gay and lesbian rights. NLGJA works both for the professional development of its own members, as well as for the elimination of discrimination against LGBT persons in the workplace. NLGJA has 25 chapters nationwide with members from the print, television, and radio media who work full time and as freelancers for news outlets of all sizes and types.
Publications: *How to Cover LGBT People* (handbook); *Pride Coverage Primer* (handbook); *Stylebook Supplement on LGBT Terminology* (handbook).

National Lesbian and Gay Law Association (NLGLA)
Web site: http://www.nlgla.org

The National Lesbian and Gay Law Association was founded at the 1987 March on Washington for lesbian and gay rights. Within two years, the new organization had adopted a set of bylaws, held its first Lavender Law conference in San Francisco, and added 239 paid members to its roles. In 1992, NLGLA became an official affiliate of the American Bar Association (ABA). Its current activities in promoting equal treatment of all persons regardless of sexual orientation are carried out in cooperation with the ABA's Section on Individual Rights and Responsibilities and its Committee on Sexual Orientation and Gender Identity.
Publications: Monthly electronic newsletter.

Out and Equal Workplace Advocates
Web site: http://www.outandequal.org

Out and Equal Workplace Advocates is the nation's primary organization working to guarantee equal treatment for workers in all types of workplaces. When first formed in 1996, the organization was supported primarily by the United Way. It is now a 501(c)3 nonprofit organization with headquarters in San Francisco. The organization's primary activity is an annual summit in which employers from around the country are invited to meet and discuss issues of gender orientation equity in the workplace. It also offers Building Bridges Diversity Training sessions through regional affiliates in Chicago, Dallas/Fort Worth, New York City, San Francisco, and Chicago; support for employee resource groups; and a national newsletter on workplace issues for gay men, lesbians, bisexuals, and transgendered persons.
Publications: *Working Out* (print newsletter); *eNewsletter* (electronic newsletter).

Parents, Families and Friends of Lesbians and Gays (PFLAG)
Web site: http://community.pflag.org

Parents, Families and Friends of Lesbians and Gays is a nonprofit organization of more than 200,000 members and supporters with more than 500 chapters in the United States. It operates out of a national office in Washington, D.C., and 13 regional offices. PFLAG has six strategic goals that focus on building an organization strong enough to carry out its objectives; creating a world in which young people can grow up without fear of violence or discrimination; ending the isolation of gay men, lesbians, bisexuals, and transgendered people; working for the inclusion of people of all gender orientations in all religious faiths; eliminating prejudice and discrimination in the workplace; and achieving full civil rights and equality for all gay men, lesbians, bisexuals, and transgendered persons.

Publications: The PFLAG Web site lists a number of press releases, "tools for journalists," "hot topics," and articles about PFLAG in the news.

Pride at Work
Web site: http://prideatwork.org

Pride at Work is an official constituency group of the American Federation of Labor and Congress of Industrial Organizations (AFL-CIO), having earned this recognition in 1999. The organization has a two-fold purpose: first, to ensure that all lesbian, gay, bisexual, and transgendered (LGBT) persons receive equal and nondiscriminatory treatment in the workplace; and, second, to make LGBT persons aware of the benefits and advantages of union membership. The issues in which Pride at Work is currently interested are antiwar organizing, domestic partner benefits, farm worker justice, marriage equality, transgender issues, and workers' rights. In addition, the organization is working in support of two major pieces of federal legislation dealing with workplace issues, the Employee Free Choice Act and the Employment Non-Discrimination Act.

Publications: Numerous news stories and press releases online at the Pride at Work Web site.

Religious Action Center of Reform Judaism (RAC)
Web site: http://rac.org

The Religious Action Center was established in Washington, D.C., in 1962 to address legislative and social issues of concern to reform Jews. The center has had a long interest of support for gay and lesbian issues, and maintains an extensive bank of information on such issues on its Web site at: http://rac.org/advocacy/issues/issuegl/index.cfm?#status.

Publications: Selection: *Lirdof Tzedek: A Guide to Synagogue Social Action* (book); *Jewish Dimensions of Social Justice: Tough Moral*

Choices of Our Time (book); *K'hilat Tzedek: Creating a Community of Justice* (discussion guide); *Speak Truth to Power: A Guide for Congregations Taking Public Policy Positions* (manual); *Lirdof Tzedek: A Guide to Synagogue Social Action* (program guide); *Poverty Initiative* (Web site); *For the Sake of the Children: A Synagogue Guide to Public School Partnerships* (booklet).

Salutaris, the NIH Gay, Lesbian, Bisexual, Transgender Employee Forum
Web site: http://www.recgov.org/glef

Salutaris is an organization of gay, lesbian, bisexual, and transgendered persons employed at the National Institutes of Health whose purpose is to promote a work space that is open and accepting of individuals of all gender orientations. The organization is typical of a number of similar groups of federal employees who have organized to provide mutual support and to extend workplace rights to individuals of all sexual orientation and gender identity. Similar organizations include DOJ Pride, the gay, lesbian, bisexual, and transgender employee association of the U.S. Department of Justice (http://www.dojpride.org); NIST GLOBE, an organization of lesbian, gay male, bisexual, and transgender employees, their friends, and supporters at the National Institute of Standards of Technology; Labor GLOBE, a similar organization in the U.S. Department of Labor (http://www.geocities.com/laborglobe); and DOE GLOBE, for gay, lesbian, bisexual, and transgendered employees of the Department of Energy (http://www.goering.net/doeglobe/info.htm).
Publications: none

Scouting for All (SFA)
Web site: http://www.scoutingforall.org

Scouting for All was founded in 1993 by former Boy Scout David Rice and a group of fellow scouts in response to the Boy Scouts of America's (BSA) policy to prohibit gay men and boys, atheists, and others from belonging to their organizations. Although the BSA had long had a policy of discriminating against boys and young men who were not heterosexual and did not believe in God, it took a formal position to this effect only in 2002 when it adopted a resolution indicating that such individuals were unfit to belong to the organization and unacceptable as role models in leadership positions in BSA. Scouting for All consists of large numbers of former Boy Scouts, many of them Eagle Scouts and/or scout leaders who believe that BSA should adopt a less discriminatory policy in dealing with young men who wish to become scouts. Among its many activities, Scouting for All has produced a number of pamphlets and brochures, explaining its position on nondiscrimination in scouting and its attempts to have the BSA change its policies toward gay boys and men, atheists, and other individuals prohibited from joining the Boy Scouts.

Publications: "Reaching Out to All Youth"; "Alliance for Human Rights"; "What You Can Do, Scouting for All's National Campaign"; "Atheists, Other Non-Theists and the Boy Scouts of America"; "Steven's Petition" (pamphlets).

Servicemembers Legal Defense Network (SLDN)
Web site: http://www.sldn.org

Servicemembers Legal Defense Network is a national, non-profit organization whose primary goal is to end the U.S. military's current "don't ask, don't tell" policy for dealing with lesbians and gay men in the military. The policy was adopted by the U.S. Congress and approved by President Bill Clinton in 1993 as a compromise between proponents of a complete ban on having gays and lesbians serve in the military and those who argued for no restrictions of any kind. SLDN currently provides a variety of support activities for those still serving in the military forces and those who have been discharged because of the don't ask, don't tell policy. The organization also works to have that policy revoked and to institute a policy that allows all individuals to serve, regardless of their sexual orientation.

Publications: Many press releases, such as " Openly Gay Army Sergeant Discharged under 'Don't Ask, Don't Tell'"; "Women in Uniform Disproportionately Affected by 'Don't Ask, Don't Tell' Law"; "Servicemembers Legal Defense Network Condemns Presidential Honor for Former Joint Chiefs Chairman Peter Pace"; "First Circuit Rules on 'Don't Ask, Don't Tell' Appeal."

Society of Lesbian and Gay Anthropologists (SOLGA)
Web site: http://www.uvm.edu/~dlrh/solga

Today, virtually every professional association in the United States has a committee, caucus, subgroup, or other organization of lesbians, gay men, bisexuals, and transgendered persons. These groups have a major interest, of course, in the academic field from which they come (such as anthropology, in the case of SOLGA), but they also work to strengthen the bonds among others of the same and similar sexual orientation and gender identity and to ensure equality for all persons within the workplace. SOLGA is a subgroup of the American Anthropological Association (AAA), and membership is open only to members of AAA. It was founded in 1978 as the Anthropology Research Group on Homosexuality (ARGOH) and became an official section of AAA in 1998. Other professional organizations with structures and goals similar to those of SOLGA are the Gay, Lesbian, Bisexual, and Transgendered Round Table of the American Library Association (http://www.ala.org/ala/glbtrt/welcomeglbtround.cfm); Lesbian, Gay, Bisexual and Transgendered Health Science Librarians (http://lgbt.mlanet.org); the National Organization of Gay and Lesbian Scientists and Technical Professionals (http://www.noglstp.org); and Lesbian, Gay, Bisexual, and Transgender Concerns of the American Psychological Association (http://www.apa.org/pi/lgbc).

Publication: "Society of Lesbian and Gay Anthropologists Newsletter" (irregular).

Stonewall

Web site: http://www.stonewall.org.uk

Stonewall is a British organization formed in 1989 in response to the adoption of Section 28 of the Local Government Act, prohibiting the "promotion of homosexuality" in schools. A number of gay men and lesbians were outraged at the stigmatizing of same-sex relationships and decided to create an organization that would work toward overturning this legislation and promoting equal rights of lesbians and gay men in the United Kingdom. Since 1989, the organization has been extraordinarily successful, contributing to changes in the nation's age-of-consent laws, elimination of the ban against gay men and lesbians serving in the military, passage of same-sex adoption legislation, the repeal of Section 28 (in 2003), nondiscrimination in economic transactions (the Equality Act of 2007), and recent passage of domestic partnership legislation. Stonewall currently has offices in England, Scotland, and Wales.

Publications: Ebulletin (online newsletter); numerous press releases.

Stonewall Democrats

Web site: http://www.stonewalldemocrats.org

Stonewall Democrats is a political organization affiliated with the national Democratic party founded by Representative Barney Frank (D-Mass.) in 1998. The organization's name is taken from the famous Stonewall riots of 1969 that mark the beginning of the modern gay and lesbian rights movement. A number of independent gay and lesbian Democratic groups existed throughout the United States prior to 1998, but Frank saw the potential of unifying the efforts of all those groups in a national organization. Today there are nearly 100 affiliates in virtually every state of the union and the District of Columbia. Members of these local clubs are involved in a variety of activities typical of traditional political organizations, including envelope stuffing, door-to-door solicitations, telephone calling, get-out-the-vote campaigns, and running for office.

Publications: Press releases at "Newsroom" page of Web site.

Transgender Law Center (TLC)

Web site: http://www.transgenderlawcenter.org

The Transgender Law Center is an organization working to obtain full civil and legal rights for transgendered persons in the state of California. The organization currently focuses on a number of issues of special concern to transgendered persons, such as economic empowerment; health care access; safe bathrooms; student safety; training for employers, health care workers, business owners, and others; and leadership development. The TLC Web site has an excellent collection of links to resources on a variety of issues of interest to transgendered persons.

Publications: Selection: "Advancements in Federal and California Employment Law Regarding Transgender People"; "Good Jobs NOW!"; "Top 5 Tips for Working with Transgender Clients and Co-Workers"; "Transgender Family Law Facts"; "Family Law 101" (pamphlets).

Unid@s, the National Latina/o Lesbian, Gay, Bisexual, and Transgender Human Rights Organization
Web site: http://www.unidoslgbt.org

Unid@s, the National Latina/o Lesbian, Gay, Bisexual, and Transgender Human Rights Organization, was founded in 2007 as a replacement for an earlier Latino organization, National Latina/o Lesbian Gay, Bisexual, and Transgender Organization, often known as LLEGÓ, which disbanded in 2004. At the time of its founding, Unid@s also consolidated with the National Latino/a Coalition for Justice, an organization working for marriage equality among people of all sexual orientations. In its early phases, Unid@s is developing plans to become a multi-issue organization with strong emphasis on local activism on issues of concern to lesbian, gay, bisexual, and transgendered Latina/os.
Publications: Online news at Web site.

Victory Fund
Web site: http://www.victoryfund.org

Victory Fund was founded in 1991 as the Gay and Lesbian Victory Fund to serve as a nonpartisan federal political action committee with the goal of increasing the number of lesbian, gay, bisexual, and transgendered elected officials at all levels of government. The organization provides strategic, tactical, and financial assistance to candidates whom it chooses to endorse and support. During the first half of 2008, Victory endorsed and supported 35 candidates for local, regional, and state offices, of whom 26 (74 percent) were elected. Victory maintains a list of nearly 700 elected out LGBT officials throughout the world on its Web site at http://www.glli.org/out_officials.
Publications: Annual Reports (available online at website); press releases.

Williams Institute at the University of California at Los Angeles School of Law
Web site: http://www.law.ucla.edu/williamsinstitute/home.html

The Williams Institute is a national think tank concerned with legal aspects of issues of interest to lesbians, gay men, bisexuals, and transgendered persons. The institute carries out its objectives by conducting research; authoring public policy studies and law review articles; providing amicus curiae briefs for important court cases; offering expert testimony at legislative hearings; and training lawyers, judges, and other members of the legal protection as well as the general public. In 2006, the institute absorbed the Institute for Gay and Lesbian Strategic Studies, another think tank with objectives similar to those of the Williams Institute.

Publications: *The Dukeminier Awards Best Sexual Orientation and Gender Identity Law Review Articles of 2008* (monthly journal; date changes annually); *Adoption and Foster Care by Gay and Lesbian Parents in the United States* (report); *The Impact of Extending Marriage to Same-Sex Couples on the New Jersey Budget* (report; similar reports available for California, Iowa, Oregon, New Mexico, Maryland, and other states); *Unequal Taxes on Equal Benefits: The Taxation of Domestic Partner Benefits* (report).

Organizations Opposing Lesbian and Gay Rights

Alliance Defense Fund (ADF)
Web site: http://www.alliancedefensefund.org/main/default.aspx

The Alliance Defense Fund was formed in 1994 by a group of 35 ministers who were concerned about the loss of religious freedom in the United States. The organization's work is currently organized under three major topics: sanctity of life (right-to-life issues), traditional family (same-sex marriage issues), and religious freedom (actions against expression of religious beliefs). The organization has been active in providing funding, legal advice, and leadership training in campaigns against same-sex marriage, civil unions, and domestic partnerships in many states. Some of the fund's work is carried out through subsidary and affiliate organizations, such as the Community Defense Council (formerly the National Family Legal Foundation), the Corporate Research Council, and DOMA Watch,

described as "your legal source for Defense of Marriage Act information."
Publications: Videos and audio clips available online at Web site.

Alliance for Marriage (AFM)
Web site: http://www.allianceformarriage.org

Alliance for Marriage is a 501(c)(3) nonprofit organization working to promote the traditional marriage pattern between one man and one woman. It focuses on efforts to educate the general public, the media, elected officials, and civil society leaders with regard to the benefits of traditional marriage for adults, children, and the society at large. Its current fields of interest are promotion of adoption among heterosexual families, reducing the number of fatherless families, encouragement of stay-at-home parents, improving tax benefits for traditional families, and welfare reform.
Publications: *Not Married to the Job* (report); numerous news clippings, articles, and articles online at Web site.

American Center for Law and Justice (ACLJ)
Web site: http://www.aclj.org

The American Center for Law and Justice was founded in 1990 to work for the constitutional and religious freedom of all Americans. Today, ACLJ has extended its interests to other parts of the world and provides expertise in American Constitutional law, European Union law, and human rights law. It has been active in opposing the extension of marriage and marriage rights to same-sex couples. Attorneys for ACLJ have worked on a number of state cases involving same-sex marriage, have testified before the U.S. Congress on the Federal Marriage Amendment, and have issued a number of press releases and fact sheets on the subject of same-sex marriage.
Publications: Numerous online resources at Web site, including sections on "ACLJ Commentaries"; "ACLJ Spotlight"; "In the Courts"; "In the News"; "On the Issues"; "Trial Notebook"; "Washington Report"; and "Litigation Report."

Christian Coalition of America (CC)
Web site: http://www.cc.org

The Christian Coalition of America was founded in 1989 in order to provide a stronger voice for conservative Christians in the American political system. For many years, it was a powerful voice in shaping the policies of the Republican party, although its influence appears to have waned considerably in the last decade. Although it claims to speak for more than 2 million Americans, some evidence suggests that its current active membership is closer to about 30,000 individuals. Among the issues in which CC is currently most interested are the election and appointment of more conservative judges; ensuring the accessibility of the Internet for groups of all political persuasions, including the Christian Coalition; protecting religious programming on television, preventing approval of the federal government for stem cell research; and advancement of the Federal Marriage Amendment, which prohibits same-sex marriage.

Publications: *Washington Weekly Review* (newsletter); numerous press releases; OneNewsNow.com (online news releases).

Church of Jesus Christ of Latter-day Saints (Mormon Church)
Web site: http://www.lds.org/ldsorg

Although almost all Christian denominations are opposed to same-sex marriage and to many other features of the lesbian and gay rights movement, the Church of Jesus Christ of Latter-day Saints (LDS) has been especially active politically in working against these issues. During the November 2008 initiative on Proposition 8, for example, the Church was the largest single financial donor to the "Yes on 8" (supporting a constitutional ban on same-sex marriage in the state of California) campaign, donating more than $5 million for the campaign. According to one proponent of the ban, the Church also provided between 80 and 90 percent of the volunteers who walked door to door during the campaign (McKinley and Johnson 2008). On June 30, 2008, the First Presidency of the church sent a letter to all LDS members in California, saying that "We ask that you do all you can to support the proposed constitutional amendment by donating of your means and time to assure that marriage in California is legally defined as being between a man and a woman. Our best efforts are required to preserve the sacred institution of marriage" (Preserving traditional marriage, 2008). The Church's Web site contains much more information on its stand on same-sex marriage and related issues.

Publications: A very large selection of books, booklets, pamphlets, and other reading materials, as well as electronic publications on a variety of topics; a number of regular magazines, including *Ensign*, a general publication for adults; *New Era*, a similar publication for youth; *Friend*, a magazine for children; *Liahona*, a publication intended for international readers; and *Church News*, a weekly publication.

Concerned Women for America (CWA)
Web site: http://www.cwfa.org

Concerned Women for America was founded in 1979 by Beverly LaHaye, whose husband, Timothy, was one of the founders of the Christian Coalition. Mrs. LaHaye established the organization in response to pronouncements and activities of the National Organization for Women, which, she felt, did not reflect the views of many women in America. Today, CWA's activities focus on six major areas: family (one man, one woman marriages), sanctity of life (anti-abortion), education (support of private schooling), pornography, religious liberty, and national sovereignty.
Publications: "What Your Teacher Didn't Tell You about Abstinence"; "How to Lobby from Your Home"; "Political Guidelines for Churches and Pastors"; "Pro-Life Action Guide"; "A Painful Choice: Abortion's Link to Breast Cancer"; "Why Children Need Fathers: Five Critical Trends"; "The Grab for Power: A Chronology of the National Education Association" (pamphlets and brochures; available online at Web site).

Family Research Council (FRC)
Web site: http://www.frc.org

The Family Research Council was founded in 1983 to promote the traditional family and traditional marriage. It pursues its work through a number of venues, including books, pamphlets, and other kinds of publications; testimony before a variety of legislative bodies; analysis and review of legal and policy documents with the potential for impacting marriage and the family; and appearances in public debates and discussions.
Publications: Press releases, op-eds, and blogs available online at Web site.

Focus on the Family
Web site: http://www.focusonthefamily.com

Focus on the Family is a Christian organization that attempts to follow Biblical principles in nurturing and defending the (heterosexual) family. It generally tends to oppose any definition of the family other than one consisting of one man, one woman, and one or more children. The guiding principles under which the organization operates is the preeminence of an evangelical interpretation of the Bible, the importance of a permanent marriage between one man and one woman, the value of children to a family, the sanctity of human life, the importance of social responsibility, and the confirmation of clearly defined male and female roles in a family.

Publications: *Citizen* magazine; the organization's primary news and issue analysis outlet is the Web site CitizenLink at: http://www.citizenlink.org/citizenmag.

Heritage Foundation
Web site: http://www.heritage.org

The Heritage Foundation is a conservative think tank founded in 1973 to work for a strong national defense, individual freedom, limited government, traditional American values, and the advancement of free enterprise. As part of its Family and Marriage issues, it has a special interest in working to prevent the spread of same-sex marriage in the United States.

Publications: Commentaries, news releases, and updates on "hot" topics available online at Web site.

Institute for Marriage and Public Policy (IMAPP)
Web site: http://www.marriagedebate.com

The Institute for Marriage and Public Policy is a nonprofit, nonpartisan organization that works to promote discussion on important issues relating to marriage, with the overall goal of strengthening that institution in American society. IMAPP focuses on issues such as adoption, divorce reform, same-sex marriage, tax policy, and unwed pregnancies.

Publications: Articles, policy briefs, community brochures, and model legislation available online at Web site.

Marriage Law Project (MLP)
Web site: http://www.marriagewatch.org

The Marriage Law Project is a program of the Interdisciplinary Program in Law and Religion of Columbus School of Law at the Catholic University of America in Washington, D.C. It works to reaffirm the traditional view of marriage as being between one man and one woman by carrying out research, publishing helpful information, sponsoring conferences, offering pro bono legal advice, taking part in important legal cases, and advising policy makers.

Publications: Headline news; "hot topics"; and background information on many topics available online at Web site.

Traditional Values Coalition
Web site: http://www.traditionalvalues.org

The Traditional Values Coalition was founded in 1980 by Louis P. Sheldon to "empower people of faith through knowledge." The organization currently claims to speak for more than 43,000 churches from virtually every Christian denomination and every racial and socioeconomic status. Among the issues of primary concern to the coalition are same-sex marriage, abortion rights, rights of transgendered persons, abstinence in sex education, and anti-Christian bigotry.

Publications: *50-State Survey of Marriage Protection Amendments; A Gender Identity Disorder Goes Mainstream; A Report on the San Diego "Gay Pride" Parade and Festival in San Diego, July 29, 2006; Abstinence and Fidelity in Marriage Are Keys to Global AIDS Battle* (special reports); press releases, action alerts, editorials, and church bulletin inserts available online at Web site.

References

McKinley, Jesse, and Kirk Johnson. "Mormons Tipped Scale in Ban on Gay Marriage." *New York Times*, November 14, 2008. Available online at: http://www.nytimes.com/2008/11/15/us/politics/15marriage.html. Accessed on December 15, 2008.

"Preserving Traditional Marriage and Strengthening Families." Available online at: http://newsroom.lds.org/ldsnewsroom/eng/commentary/California-and-same-sex-marriage. Accessed on December 15, 2008.

8

Resources

A vast collection of print and electronic resources on gay and lesbian rights issues is currently available. A recent bibliography, for example, lists more than 100 articles, nearly 30 books, and more than a dozen Web sites dealing with the legal aspects of same-sex marriage alone. It is obviously impossible to list every resource on every aspect of the lesbian and gay rights movement in this chapter. Instead, a selection of some of the most widely cited items of interest to the general public are listed and described here. The items are divided into four major sections: historical documents, gay and lesbian civil rights, same-sex relationships and adoption, and international issues. Within each section, resources are divided into four categories: books, articles, reports, and Internet Web sites. Although emphasis is placed on more recent publications, a number of works of historical importance are also included.

An invaluable source of articles on the lesbian, gay, bisexual, and transgendered (LGBT) movement is *The Advocate*, a magazine devoted almost solely to LGBT topics. Having first appeared in 1967, it is the oldest and one of the most respected gay and lesbian publications in the United States. Its Web site is: http://www.advocate.com/, and its ISSN is 0001–8996.

Historical Documents

Books

Adam, Barry D. *The Rise of a Gay and Lesbian Movement,* revised edition. Boston: Twayne Publishers, 1995.

Adam's book is especially strong in its coverage of the international gay and lesbian rights movement. He does a thorough job of reviewing the early movements in Germany and the United States, along with the reactions that developed to those movements. But he also provides sketches of changes taking place in Canada, Mexico, Europe, and other parts of the world. The opening chapter provides a good review of the emergence of the concept of "homosexuality."

Alsenas, Linas. *Gay America: Struggle for Equality.* **New York: Amulet Books, 2008.**

The author reviews some of the most important events in the history of the gay and lesbian rights movement in the United States, from the Colonial period to the present day.

Altman, Dennis. *Homosexual: Oppression and Liberation.* **New York: Outerbridge and Lazarus, 1971.**

One of the best early books on the gay liberation movement, this work describes Altman's own coming-out experience, as well as the development of the early growth of a gay consciousness. The book provides a good historical account of the post-Stonewall period, and also analyzes the political and sociological changes taking place during that period. His final chapter discusses the then-popular notion that a successful gay liberation movement would lead to profound changes in society that, in turn, would result in "The End of the Homosexual."

Bailey, Derrick Sherwin. *Homosexuality and the Western Christian Tradition.* **London: Longman, Green, 1955.**

Bailey was an Anglican clergyman who served on the Royal Committee on Homosexual Offences and Prostitution (generally known as the Wolfenden Commission). The Wolfenden Report is of unusual importance because it provided the best scholarly information on the biblical basis of anti-homosexuality available at the time. Interestingly, it concluded that what the Bible says about homosexual behavior and what the vast majority of clergy and laypeople *think* it says are vastly different.

Bérubé, Allan. *Coming Out under Fire: The History of Gay Men and Women in World War Two.* **New York: The Free Press, 1990.**

Bérubé has written a brilliant, comprehensive, and scholarly study of the role played by lesbians and gay men in World War II, along with the military's policies and attitudes about homosexual behavior. The factual history presented in the book is in startling contrast to the general beliefs that most military and nonmilitary individuals are likely to hold on the subject of gays in the military today.

Boswell, John. *Christianity, Social Tolerance, and Homosexuality.* **Chicago: University of Chicago Press, 1980.**

This book does not deal specifically with the issue of gay liberation or gay and lesbian rights, but it does discuss religious attitudes about homosexuality, probably the most powerful single force in modern society working in opposition to the gay movement. In a tour de force of scholarship, Boswell reviews attitudes about homosexual behavior in the first 12 centuries of Christianity. He concludes that the ancient church was not responsible for the existence of modern antigay attitudes in religion.

Boswell, John. *Same-sex Unions in Premodern Europe.* **New York: Vintage Books, 1995.**

Boswell's exhaustive study of the literature of medieval Europe provides convincing evidence that same-sex unions, especially within religious communities, were widespread and widely accepted by both the church and the lay public.

Bullough, Vern, ed. *Before Stonewall: Activists for Gay and Lesbian Rights in Historical Context.* **New York: Harrington Park Press, 2002.**

This collection of articles tells the story of the gay and lesbian movement in the United States and other countries from its earliest beginnings through biographical sketches of some of the most important individuals involved in the movement.

Bullough, Vern L. *Homosexuality: A History.* **New York: New American Library, 1979.**

Bullough has written extensively on the history of human sexuality. This book covers a wide span of history and includes chapters such as "The Law and Homosexuality," "The Movement," "Out of the Closet," and "Homosexuality Today."

D'Emilio, John. *Sexual Politics, Sexual Communities: The Making of a Homosexual Minority in the United States, 1940–1970.* Chicago: University of Chicago Press, 1983.

Many people think that the modern gay and lesbian movement began with the Stonewall riots of 1969. D'Emilio shows, however, that a small but vigorous movement existed at least two decades before Stonewall. He presents an interesting and thoroughly researched review of the origins of the Mattachine Society, the Daughters of Bilitis, and other early gay and lesbian groups.

D'Emilio, John. *The World Turned: Essays on Gay History, Politics, and Culture.* Durham, NC: Duke University Press, 2002.

D'Emilio writes about the history of the gay and lesbian movement in the United States, emphasizing the special significance of certain individuals (Bayard Rustin, Larry Kramer, and Ken Dawson) and important documents (*Out of the Closet*).

Duberman, Martin. *About Time: Exploring the Gay Past,* revised and expanded edition, 1991.

Distinguished professor of history emeritus at Lehman College and the Graduate School of the City University of New York, Duberman is one of the finest writers on gay topics in the world. This volume collects a number of his own essays along with a selection of historical writings dating to 1826. See especially Part II of the book, containing essays dealing with the gay liberation and gay rights movement.

Duberman, Martin. *Stonewall.* New York: Dutton, 1993.

In this book, Duberman describes and analyzes the events that occurred on June 27 and 28, 1969, during the Stonewall riots in New York City. He uses stories of the lives of four gay men and two lesbians to tell his tale.

Duberman, Martin, Martha Vincus, and George Chauncey Jr., eds. *Hidden from History: Reclaiming the Gay and Lesbian Past.* New York: New American Library, 1989.

This collection of essays surveys the history of homosexual behavior from the ancient world to the late 20th century. Major sections of the book deal with preindustrial societies, the nineteenth century, the early twentieth century, and World War II and the postwar era. The book provides excellent background for the modern gay liberation gay rights movements.

Dugan, Kimberly B. *The Struggle over Gay, Lesbian, and Bisexual Rights: Facing Off in Cincinnati.* **New York: Routledge, 2005.**

Dugan offers a detailed analysis of the 1993 vote in Cincinnati, Ohio, over the legal status of gay men and lesbians as a protected minority. In that election, voters overwhelmingly adopted an ordinance prohibiting the city from extending protection in housing, employment, and public accommodation to gays and lesbians.

Dyer, Kate. *Gays in Uniform: The Pentagon's Secret Reports.* **Boston: Alyson Publications, 1990.**

This book discusses two reports of studies carried out by the Pentagon on the suitability of lesbians and gay men for the armed forces. Both reports concluded that there is no rational justification for the exclusion of gay men and lesbians from the armed forces. Since this conclusion was at variance with existing policy and predilections of the military, the reports were not made public for many years.

Eisenbach, David. *Gay Power: An American Revolution.* **Cambridge, MA: De Capo Books, 2006.**

Eisenbach discusses changes that took place in New York City over the past half century to illustrate the growth and development of the gay and lesbian rights movement. He bases his book on a number of interviews with men and women involved in that movement, as well as on archival materials from the period.

Endean, Steve. *Bringing Lesbian and Gay Rights into the Mainstream: Twenty Years of Progress.* **Edited by Vicki L. Eaklor. New York: Harrington Park Press, 2006.**

Endean was involved in the gay and lesbian rights movement for more than two decades. His memoir provides a comprehensive and powerful review of changes that have taken place in the movement during that period of time.

Eskridge, William N., Jr. *Dishonorable Passions: Sodomy Laws in America, 1861–2003.* New York: Viking Press, 2008.

The debate over gay and lesbian rights has a long history in the United States, dating back to Colonial days. In this book, Eskridge focuses on the issue of antisodomy laws, finally resolved by the U.S. Supreme Court in its 2003 decision in *Lawrence v. Texas.*

Fejes, Fred. *Gay Rights and Moral Panic: The Origins of America's Debate on Homosexuality.* New York: Palgrave Macmillan, 2008.

Some of the seminal battles over gay and lesbian rights took place in the late 1970s, especially in Dade County and Miami, Florida; St. Paul, Minnesota; Eugene, Oregon; and Wichita, Kansas. This book discusses and analyzes these battles and considers their influence on the national discussion about legal issues related to homosexual behavior.

Gallo, Marcia M. *Different Daughters: A History of the Daughters of Bilitis and the Rise of the Lesbian Rights Movement.* Berkeley, CA: Seal Press, 2006.

The author discusses the formation and activities of the earliest lesbian rights movement in the United States, the Daughters of Bilitis.

Goodman, Gerre, George Kaley, Judy Lashof, and Erika Thorne. *No Turning Back: Lesbian and Gay Liberation for the '80's.* Philadelphia: New Society Publishers, 1983.

This book evolved out of a long study on "Gay Oppression and Liberation" commissioned by the Movement for a New Society in 1975. It provides an interesting look back on the leftist orientation of the early gay and lesbian rights movement. The movement's agenda for the 1980s soon proved to be an anachronism as it turned its focus toward civil rights rather than sexual liberation.

Heger, Heinz. *The Men with the Pink Triangle: The True, Life-and-Death Story of Homosexuals in the Nazi Death Camps,* 2nd ed. Translated by David Fernbach. New York: Alyson Books, 1994.

An essential account of the experience of gay men held in Nazi concentration camps during World War II. Because of its extensive personal information, it provides a somewhat different view of this period than many more formal histories of the period.

Lauritsen, John, and David Thorstad. *The Early Homosexual Rights Movement (1864–1935).* **New York: Times Change Press, 1974.**

One of the essential references on the early years of the gay and lesbian rights movement in Germany, Great Britain, and the United States. The authors present a socialist's analysis of the movement, as was common at the time the book was written. The last chapter contains biographies of five pioneers of the movement: Karl Ulrichs, Magnus Hirschfeld, Sir Richard Burton, Walt Whitman, and Edward Carpenter.

Marcus, Eric. *Making Gay History: The Half-century Fight for Lesbian and Gay Equal Rights.* **New York: Harper Perennial, 2002.**

This review of the history of the gay and lesbian rights movements is divided into seven chronological periods: pre-1950, 1950–1961, 1961–1968, 1968–1973, 1973–1981, 1981–1992, and 1992–2001. The author relies on a large number of interviews with gay men, lesbians, and non-gays and non-lesbians who had a part in the movement during each period.

Sears, James T. *Behind the Mask of the Mattachine: The Hal Call Chronicles and the Early Movement for Homosexual Emancipation.* **New York: Routledge Press, 2006.**

The Mattachine Society is generally thought to be the first ongoing organization working for the liberation and rights of gay men. The author discusses in some detail the history of this organization and its long-term impact on the modern gay and lesbian rights movement.

Weeks, Jeffrey. *Coming Out: Homosexual Politics in Britain, from the Nineteenth Century to the Present.* **London: Quartet Books, 1977.**

Although somewhat dated, no better history of the gay political movement in Great Britain exists than this work. Weeks is one of the finest thinkers about gay issues in the world. His book provides not only factual information, but a thoughtful analysis of the changes that occurred from the beginning of the nineteenth century to the late 1970s.

Williams, Walter L., and Yolanda Retter, eds. *Gay and Lesbian Rights in the United States: A Documentary History.* **Westport, CT: Greenwood Press, 2003.**

This invaluable reference book contains a variety of documents dealing with all aspects of the gay and lesbian rights movement dating from the Colonial period to the present day. Among the documents cited are court cases, personal opinion pieces, and laws.

Articles

Loftin, Craig M. "Unacceptable Mannerisms: Gender Anxieties, Homosexual Activism, and Swish in the United States, 1945–1965." *Journal of Social History,* **40 (3, March 2007): 577–596.**

During the early years of the gay and lesbian rights movement in the United States, a tension developed between the aims of its leaders and the rank and file. The former were generally more concerned about the representation of effeminate gay men on social attitudes toward gay men, while the latter were more concerned about the specific effects of such representations in their own jobs and daily lives. This article explores the rise and conflict of these concerns.

Reports

Committee on Homosexual Offences and Prostitution. *The Wolfenden Report: Report of the Committee on Homosexual Offenses and Prostitution.* **New York: Lancer Books, 1964.**

This important report is named after John Wolfenden (1906–1985), formerly headmaster of Uppingham and Shrewsbury schools and then vice chancellor of the University of Reading. A committee of 14 eminent scholars, including physicians, academicians, psychiatrists, and political leaders met for two months and interviewed a number of witnesses, including police officers, psychiatrists, religious leaders, and gay men. The committee eventually concluded and said in their report that "homosexuality cannot legitimately be regarded as a disease, because in many cases it is the only symptom and is compatible with full mental health in other respects." Based on their research, the committee (with one dissent) agreed that "homosexual behaviour between consenting adults in private should no longer be a criminal offence" in Great Britain.

Web Sites

Nash, Carl. "Gay and Lesbian Rights Movements." Encyclopedia of Chicago. URL: http://www.encyclopedia.chicagohistory.org/pages/508.html. Accessed on July 1, 2008.

This short, but very interesting, article presents a review of two early Chicago-based gay rights organizations, Mattachine Midwest and Chicago Gay Liberation.

Gay and Lesbian Civil Rights

Books

Blasium, Mark, ed. *Sexual Identities, Queer Politics*. Princeton, NJ: Princeton University Press, 2001.

This book contains a collection of essays written by political scientists on a variety of issues related to the gay and lesbian movement in the United States, Great Britain, Canada, France, the Netherlands, Latin America, and other parts of the world. It deals with issues such as "outing" of public officials, housing, same-sex marriage, adoption, gay and lesbian think tanks, political action, and economic issues.

Bryant, Anita. *The Anita Bryant Story: The Survival of Our Nation's Families and the Threat of Militant Homosexuality*. Old Tappan, NJ: Revell, 1977.

If the Stonewall riots of 1969 mark the beginning of the modern gay and lesbian rights movement in the United States, the 1977 vote to override gay rights legislation in Dade County, Florida, marks the beginning of the reaction to that movement. The leader of the Dade County fight was Anita Bryant, who tells her story of the battle in this book. She also outlines in some detail the reasons she thinks Americans need to fear the "militant homosexual agenda."

Bull, Chris. *Witness to Revolution: The Advocate Reports on Gay and Lesbian Politics, 1967–1999.* **Los Angeles, CA: Alyson Books, 1999.**

The Advocate is arguably the best-known and most long-lived publication in the United States devoted entirely to gay and lesbian issues. Bull, Washington correspondent for the magazine, has collected articles from the magazine from the first 32 years of its existence, covering virtually every aspect of the gay and lesbian rights movement.

Bunch, Charlotte. *Passionate Politics.* **New York: St. Martin's Press, 1986.**

A collection of essays by one of the leading theorists of the lesbian-feminist movement, this book includes an extensive and interesting introduction describing Bunch's early experiences and involvement in the gay and lesbian rights movement.

Burack, Cynthia. *Sin, Sex, and Democracy: Antigay Rhetoric and the Christian Right.* **Albany: State University of New York Press, 2008.**

The author reviews the recent history of antigay attacks by the Christian right and explains that the philosophy, policy, and methods used in these attacks is more complex than would appear to be the case at first glance.

Burns, Kate, ed. *Gay Rights.* **Farmington Hills, MI: Greenhaven Press/Thomson Gale, 2006.**

This collection of essays for young adult readers deals with a wide variety of topics including gays and lesbians in the military, the history of the gay liberation and gay rights movements, same-sex marriage, hate crimes and violence against gay men and lesbians, and legal issues related to gays and lesbians.

Cain, Patricia A. *Rainbow Rights: The Role of Lawyers and Courts in the Lesbian and Gay Civil Rights Movement.* **Boulder, CO: Westview Press, 2000.**

After an introduction to the history of the gay and lesbian rights movement, the author discusses three aspects of gay and lesbian rights issues: those dealing with privacy, those related to public conduct, and those dealing with issues involving relationships.

Caramagno, Thomas C. *Irreconcilable Differences? Intellectual Stalemate in the Gay Rights Debate.* **Westport, CT: Praeger, 2002.**

The author describes the current debate over gay and lesbian rights as "the new cold war." He explores the long history that has led to the modern confrontation, discussing the role of religion and theology, scientific theories about homosexual behavior, and the politics of pro and antigay rights organizations.

Cruikshank, Margaret. *The Gay and Lesbian Liberation Movement.* **New York: Routledge, Chapman & Hall, 1992.**

Cruickshank discusses the gay and lesbian rights movement from three perspectives: as a movement for sexual freedom, as a political movement, and as a revolution of ideas. She pays particular attention to the interactions of lesbian and feminist thought and to the conflicts that exist within the gay movement between men and women.

Currah, Paisley, Richard M. Juang, and Shannon Price Minter, eds. *Transgender Rights.* **Minneapolis: University of Minnesota Press, 2006.**

The movement for equality based on sexual orientation has expanded from focusing exclusively on gay men and lesbians to also include bisexuals and transgendered persons. The essays that comprise this book review the growth of the transgender equality movement in the United States, reviewing progress in including transgendered persons in nondiscrimination laws that were often intended exclusively for lesbians and gay men.

Curry, Hayden, Denis Clifford, Robin Leonard, and Frederick Hertz. *A Legal Guide for Lesbian and Gay Couples,* **10th ed. Berkeley, CA: Nolo Press, 2007.**

The authors discuss a wide variety of legal issues unique to same-sex couples, such as contracts, housing, finances, real estate, marriage, adoption of children, gay student organizations, estate planning, and medical emergencies.

D'Emilio, John. *Making Trouble*. **New York: Routledge, Chapman & Hall, 1992.**

This book contains a collection of essays on the history and politics of the gay and lesbian movement by one of the most thoughtful and articulate scholars in the field. Chapters include "Capitalism and Gay Identity," "Gay History: A New Field of Study," "The Supreme Court and the Sodomy Statutes: Where Do We Go from Here?" and "You Can't Build a Movement in Anger."

D'Emilio, William B. Turner, and Urvashi Vaid, eds. *Creating Change: Sexuality, Public Policy, and Civil Rights.* **New York: St. Martin's Press, 2000.**

The essays in this collection fall into three major categories: the role of gay men and lesbians in presidential politics and governmental institutions, the gay and lesbian legislative agenda, and the construction of a new and effective advocacy movement for the gay and lesbian movement.

Dynes, Wayne R. *Encyclopedia of Homosexuality.* **New York: Garland, 2 vols., 1990.**

This encyclopedia contains more than 770 articles dealing with every conceivable aspect of homosexuality, including anthropology and ethnology, art and aesthetics, history, economics, gender, literature, the gay and lesbian rights movement, religion, and relationships. The work has been out of print for a decade, but it is still an essential reference on many topics.

Estes, Steve. *Ask and Tell: Gay and Lesbian Veterans Speak Out.* **Chapel Hill: University of North Carolina Press, 2007.**

Based on interviews with more than 50 men and women who served in the U.S. military forces over the previous 65 years, the author discusses the evolution of policy toward gay men and lesbians serving in the U.S. armed forces.

Fetner, Tina. *How the Religious Right Shaped Lesbian and Gay Activism.*

The gay and lesbian rights movement and the religious right movement are seen (correctly) as diametrically opposed to each other in goals and objectives. And yet, the two crusades have a symbiotic relationship with each other, each depending to some extent on the claims, programs, and successes of the other. The author explores this relationship with case studies dating back more than half a century.

Gearhart, Sally, and William R. Johnson. *Loving Women/Loving Men.* **San Francisco: Glide Publications, 1974.**

The authors discuss the specific effects of the gay liberation movement on religion. They talk about religious interpretations of the ban on homosexual behavior and show how the movement brought about changes in various denominations as well as in individual church congregations and church leaders during the early years of the movement.

Holbrook, Sara. *Fighting Back: The Struggle for Gay Rights.* **New York: Lodestar Books, 1987.**

To prepare this young adult book, the author interviewed more than a hundred gay and non-gay individuals and visited many organizations. She explains how gay men and lesbians are denied civil rights and what they are doing in the fight to gain those rights.

Hunter, Nan D., Courtney G. Joslin, and Sharon M. McGowan. *The Rights of Lesbians, Gay Men, Bisexuals, and Transgender People: The Authoritative ACLU Guide to a Lesbian, Gay, Bisexual, or Transgender Person's Rights,* **4th ed. Carbondale: Southern Illinois University Press, 2004.**

Probably the most complete and authoritative book on the rights of gay men, lesbians, bisexuals, and transgendered people, dealing with topics such as nondiscrimination in employment and housing, freedom of speech and association, same-sex marriage, adoption of children, military service, and HIV/AIDS issues.

Koppleman, Andrew. *The Gay Rights Question in Contemporary American Law.* **Chicago: University of Chicago Press, 2002.**

The author reviews legal and moral reasons that gay men and lesbians are entitled to equal civil rights under the U.S. Constitution, but then explains why he believes that the courts will not and should not enforce those rights.

MacKinnon, Catherine A. *Sex Equality: Lesbian and Gay Rights.* New York: Foundation Press, 2003.

This law school casebook includes a discussion of historical, cultural, and linguistic factors related to the debate over gay and lesbian rights, along with a review of legal theory and case studies involving discrimination based on sexual orientation and related topics.

Malone, John. *21st Century Gay.* New York: M. Evans, 2000.

The author provides a broad, general introduction to the history of the gay and lesbian rights movement and assesses its current status in the United States.

Mohr, Richard D. *The Long Arc of Justice: Lesbian and Gay Marriage, Equality, and Rights.* New York: Columbia University Press, 2005.

Mohr analyzes a host of gay and lesbian rights issues, such as same-sex marriage, military service, and HIV/AIDS, from a philosophical and ethical perspective, concluding that gay men and lesbians qualify for equal treatment under the law in our society.

Mucciaroni, Gary. *Same Sex, Different Politics: Success and Failure in the Struggles over Gay Rights.* Chicago: University of Chicago Press, 2008.

The gay and lesbian rights movement has achieved varying degrees of success in different phases of its battle for equality. Mucciaroni analyzes the reason for this fact, examining issues such as gays and lesbians in the military, same-sex marriage, adoption by same-sex couples, civil rights legislation, and legislation on hate crimes.

Murdoch, Joyce, and Deb Price. *Courting Justice: Gay Men and Lesbians v. the Supreme Court.* New York: Basic Books, 2002.

The authors report on their exhaustive review of all cases involving gay and lesbian rights that have come before the U.S. Supreme Court (whether or not the Court has actually agreed to hear and rule on the case) prior to 2001.

Padilla, Yoland C, ed. *Gay and Lesbian Rights Organizing: Community-Based Strategies.* New York: Harrington Park Press, 2004.

This title was published simultaneously as volume 16, number 3/4 of the *Journal of Gay and Lesbian Social Services.* Authors draw on their experiences in a variety of local battles over gay and lesbian rights issues to suggest methods for dealing with social and other problems faced by lesbians and gay men.

Pinello, Daniel R. *Gay Rights and American Law.* New York: Cambridge University Press, 2003.

The author reviews the results of 398 decisions and opinions by 849 appellate judges in all federal jurisdictions and 47 states dealing with same-sex issues, such as marriage, property disputes, adoption and rearing of children, housing, and estate planning and execution. He discusses a number of factors that appear to have been involved in these decisions and opinions. Those factors include not only legal factors, as would be expected, but also personal factors, judicial philosophy, methods of jury selection, and participation in special interest groups.

Raeburn, Nicole C. *Changing Corporate America from Inside Out: Lesbian and Gay Workplace Rights.* Minneapolis: University of Minnesota Press, 2004.

Although the gay and lesbian rights movement has met with limited success in having favorable legislation passed in most city and state entities, the corporate world has moved with surprising speed in extending benefits and recognizing the workplace rights of gays and lesbians. This book presents data dealing with this phenomenon and attempts to explain the logic behind the process.

Ridinger, Robert B., ed. *Speaking for Our Lives: Historic Speeches and Rhetoric for Gay and Lesbian Rights (1892–2000).* New York: Harrington Park Press, 2004.

This anthology collects more than 200 speeches, manifestoes, articles, statements, and other commentaries on all facets of the gay and lesbian rights movement by activists, politicians, academicians, artists, performers, and individuals from many other fields. It provides an invaluable look at the evolution of the gay and lesbian rights movement in the United States over more than a century.

Riggle, Ellen D. B., and Barry L. Tadlock, eds. *Gays and Lesbians in the Democratic Process.* **New York: Columbia University Press, 1999.**

The essays in this volume consider the increasing importance and influence of lesbian and gay political organizations in a number of areas, including the inclusion of gays and lesbians in the U.S. military, the Defense of Marriage Act, the Employment Non-Discrimination Act, funding for HIV/AIDS programs, and public perceptions of gay men and lesbians as political candidates.

Rimmerman, Craig A. *From Identity to Politics: The Lesbian and Gay Movements in the United States.* **Philadelphia: Temple University Press, 2002.**

The author draws on interviews conducted over an eight-year period with activists in the gay and lesbian movement, politicians, legislators, academicians, and journalists. He reviews the successes and failures of the movement over the past century, and considers the relative aims of liberation versus civil rights for the movement.

Rimmerman, Craig A. *The Lesbian and Gay Movements: Assimilation or Liberation?* **Boulder, CO: Westview Press, 2007.**

Gay men and lesbians in the United States have historically debated the relative importance of assimilation—becoming part of the dominant culture—and liberation—identifying themselves as a different and possibly better subculture within the dominant society. This book reviews this conflict and examines its significance for gay men and lesbians of the early twenty-first century.

Sember, Brette McWhorter. *Gay and Lesbian Rights: A Guide for GLBT Singles, Couples and Families,* **2nd ed. Naperville, IL: Sphinx Publishing, 2006.**

The author provides information on a wide range of gay and lesbian legal issues, including discrimination, employment, housing, parenting, estate planning, health and medical issues, and same-sex marriage and civil unions.

Shepard, Curtis F., Felice Yeskel, and Charles Outcalt. *Lesbian, Gay, Bisexual, and Transgender Campus Organizing: A Comprehensive Manual.* **Washington, DC: National Gay and Lesbian Task Force, Fall 1995. Also available online at: http:// www.unco.edu/glbt/forms/LGBTCampusOrgManual.pdf.**

This manual is intended for use by college students attempting to organize gay, lesbian, and related groups on their campuses. Although somewhat dated, the information it provides is extensive and comprehensive and still of considerable value to such individuals. The book includes topics such as goal-setting, a model constitution, management techniques for the group, funding, using the media, educating the campus, nondiscrimination policies, dealing with HIV/AIDS issues, alumni/ae organizing, establishing a resource center, and ROTC discrimination issues.

Smith, Miriam. *Lesbian and Gay Rights in Canada: Social Movements and Equality-Seeking, 1971–1995.* **Toronto: University of Toronto Press, 1999.**

The author draws on archival material, much of which has not yet been studied, and interviews with men and women active in the gay and lesbian movement in Canada to provide a superb history of the movement in the first 25 years of its existence.

Smith, Miriam. *Political Institutions and Lesbian and Gay Rights in the United States and Canada.* **New York: Routledge Press, 2008.**

In many ways, political institutions in the United States and Canada are very much alike. Yet, the response of these institutions to gay and lesbian issues over the past few decades has been very different. This book examines the status of same-sex marriage, sodomy laws, civil rights legislation, military service, and related issues in the two nations.

Stewart, Chuck. *Homosexuality and the Law: A Dictionary.* **Santa Barbara: ABC-CLIO, 2001.**

A collection of more than 100 essays of court cases, legal concepts, historical events, terminology, and organizations dealing with legal issues confronted by lesbians and gay men (primarily). More than 100 pages of appendices provide information on state laws, statutes, cases, resources, and references.

Articles

Berge, W. D. "Is Gay Rights a Civil Rights Issue? Symposium Leaders Debate Same-Sex Marriages and Gay and Lesbian Rights." *Ebony*, 16 (July 2004): 78–84.

A group of African American politicians, religious leaders, and community leaders state their reasons for supporting or opposing the concept that gay rights are a form of civil rights.

Cox, Jason. "Redefining Gender: Hernandez-Montiel v. INS." *Houston Journal of International Law*, 24 (1, September 2001): 187–207.

In the case of *Hernandez-Montiel v. INS*, the Ninth Circuit Court of Appeals granted asylum to Geovanni Hernandez-Montiel, a gay Mexican male, who self-identified as a female, on the basis of harm that might come to him were he repatriated to Mexico from the United States. The case is of special interest because of the potential it holds for redefining the concept of gender, making that determination, as the author says, "less a question of biology and more a determination for the finder of fact."

Garnett, Richard W. "Law Schools and the Military: Don't Ask, Don't Tell, Don't Recruit." *Commonweal*, 132 (January 14, 2005): 8–9.

The author discusses a ruling by the federal court of appeals for the Third District holding that legislation passed by the U.S. Congress requiring law schools to permit recruiters for the U.S. military to solicit candidates on campuses is unconstitutional. He compares the ruling to the U.S. Supreme Court's ruling in *Boy Scouts of America v. Dale*, permitting the Boy Scouts to prohibit gay men from serving as scoutmasters.

McGowan, David. "Making Sense of Dale." *Constitutional Commentary*, 18 (Spring 2001): 121–175.

McGowan reviews and analyzes a decision by the U.S. Supreme Court that the Boy Scouts of America had a right to prohibit gay men from serving as scoutmasters. He points out that the decision is actually more complex than it seems because the Court alluded to the plaintiff's sexual orientation itself as a form of speech (referring to him as a "gay activist"). While correct, McGowan argues, the decision raises some potentially troubling issues about free speech protection in the United States.

Spindelman, Marc. "Sex Equality Panic." *Columbia Journal of Gender and Law*, **13 (2004): 1–47.**

The author reviews the U.S. Supreme Court's decision in *Oncale v. Sundowner Offshore Services, Inc.*, holding that same-sex sexual harassment is illegal under federal antidiscrimination statutes. He argues that the decision marks an important turning point in case law dealing with discrimination against lesbians and gay men.

Reports

Amnesty International. *Stonewalled: Police Abuse and Misconduct against Lesbian, Gay, Bisexual, and Transgender People in the U.S.* **New York: Amnesty International USA, 2005.**

Various parts of this comprehensive report deal with issues such as profiling and selective enforcement; sexual, physical, and verbal abuse; searches and detention; police response to crimes against lesbian, gay, bisexual, and transgendered persons; and training and accountability of law enforcement personnel.

Cox, Gary. *The Streetwatch Report: A Study into Violence against Lesbians and Gay Men.* **Sydney, New South Wales, Australia: Gay and Lesbian Rights Lobby, 1990.**

This study of violence against lesbians and gay men in Sydney has been widely quoted and analyzed in many parts of the English-speaking world. After documenting the number and types of crimes against gay men and lesbians, researchers recommended that a group be established to monitor such ongoing violence. The publication led to the formation of the Lesbian and Gay Anti-Violence Project in New South Wales, which is still active.

Dang, Alain, and Cabrini Vianney. *Living in the Margins: A National Survey of Lesbian, Gay, Bisexual and Transgender Asian and Pacific Islander Americans.* Washington, DC: National Gay and Lesbian Task Force, 2007.

This report summarizes the results of a survey of 860 gay and lesbian Asian Americans and Pacific Island Americans living in 38 states and the District of Columbia. It provides extensive data on demographic characteristics, discrimination, verbal and physical harassment, political activity, and policy involvement among respondents.

Egan, Patrick J., Murray S. Edelman, and Kenneth Sherrill. *Findings from the Hunter College Poll of Lesbians, Gays and Bisexuals: New Discoveries about Identity, Political Attitudes, and Civic Engagement.* New York: Hunter College, 2008.

The study reported here consists of findings from 25-minute interviews with 768 lesbians, gay men, and bisexuals (LGBs). Among the study's findings are that LGBs tend to be more liberal and more politically active than non-LGBs. Political issues of highest priorities tend to be elimination of workplace discrimination, provision for federal partner benefits, and laws against hate crimes. Same-sex marriage is an issue of greater concern among younger LBGs than it is among the older colleagues.

Gates, Gary. *Gay Men and Lesbians in the U.S. Military: Estimates from Census 2000.* Washington, DC: The Urban Institute. URL: http://www.urban.org/UploadedPDF/411069_GayLesbianMilitary.pdf. Posted September 28, 2004.

This study attempts to estimate the number of gay men and lesbians serving in the U.S. active military, national guard, and reserves at the time of the study. It also provides an extensive array of demographic characteristics of those individuals. The study makes no attempt to recommend policy choices based on these data, but points out that existing policies have developed with almost no information on the characteristics reported in this study.

Human Rights Campaign Foundation. *Corporate Equality Index 2008.* Washington, DC: Human Rights Campaign Foundation, 2007.

This annual report ranks 519 companies on the basis of their treatment of gay men, lesbians, bisexuals, and transgendered people. The 2008 report found that 195 companies (a 41 percent increase over the previous report) received a perfect score. Three companies—ExxonMobil, Meijer grocery stores, and Perot Systems—received scores of zero. The average rating for the companies surveyed was 81 percent.

Human Rights Campaign Foundation. *Equality from State to State: Gay, Lesbian, Bisexual and Transgender Americans and State Legislation.* **Washington, DC: Human Rights Campaign Foundation, December 2007.**

This annual report summarizes the status of state legislation on topics such as same-sex marriage, child adoption, hate crimes, and nondiscrimination in housing and employment.

Human Rights Watch. *Family, Unvalued Discrimination, Denial, and the Fate of Binational Same-Sex Couples under U.S. Law.* **URL: http://hrw.org/reports/2006/us0506/. Posted May 2006.**

This report describes the legal status of same-sex couples in the United States in which one member of the couple is not an American citizen. The study finds that such couples have essentially no rights under existing laws.

Human Rights Watch. *Hatred in the Hallways: Violence and Discrimination against Lesbian, Gay, Bisexual, and Transgender Students in U.S. Schools.* **URL: http://www.hrw.org/reports/2001/uslgbt/toc.htm. Posted May 2001.**

Researchers conclude from their extensive study of American schools that gay, lesbian, bisexual, and transgendered children face constant physical and emotional threats in their daily lives from their peers. They say that the U.S. government has demonstrated an "abject failure" to deal with this problem.

Web Sites

About.com. "Gay Life." **URL: http://gaylife.about.com/od/ samesexmarriage/Marriage.htm. Accessed on July 15, 2008.**

This Internet resource includes articles on a number of issues related to gay and lesbian rights, such as civil unions, domestic partnerships, same-sex marriage, tax issues for same-sex couples, estate planning, a review of gay and lesbian rights in other nations, benefits of legalized marriage, arguments against same-sex marriage, and the Federal Marriage Amendment.

American Civil Liberties Union. "Lesbian Gay Bisexual Transgender Project." URL: http://www.aclu.org/lgbt/index. html. Accessed on July 1, 2008.

A rich source of information on all legal issues related to the gay, lesbian, bisexual, and transgendered (LGBT) movement. The Web site contains an exhaustive review of current and past LGBT-related court cases.

Boutcher, Steven. "The Symbolic Effects of Losing Litigation: Gay and Lesbian Rights in the Aftermath of Bowers." URL: http://www.allacademic.com/meta/p17669_index.html. Posted on June 27, 2008.

This paper, presented at the annual Law and Society convention in Las Vegas, Nevada, reviews the U.S. Supreme Court decision in *Bowers v. Hardwick* in 1986, in which the court upheld the state of Georgia's sodomy laws. Boutcher points out the importance of the decision as a motivating factor for the gay and lesbian community in working more aggressively to have the nation's sodomy laws overturned.

CNN.com. "Hospital Ratings Set by Gay-Rights Groups." URL: http://m.cnn.com/cnn/archive/archive/detail/111244/1. Posted on May 13, 2008.

Two groups, the Human Rights Campaign and the Gay and Lesbian Medical Association, have combined to develop a system for rating hospitals in terms of their openness and accessibility to same-sex couples. The groups found that 45 of the 88 hospitals who participated in the survey got perfect marks for services such as patient nondiscrimination, visitation and decision-making rights for partners, diversity training for staff, and nondiscriminatory employment practices. The report itself can be found at: http://www.hrc.org/documents/Healthcare_ Equality_Index_2008.pdf.

Donahue, Dave. "Lesbian, Gay, Bisexual, and Transgender Rights: A Human Rights Perspective." URL: http://www.hrea. org/erc/Library/display_doc.php?url=http%3A%2F%2Fwww1. umn.edu%2Fhumanrts%2Fedumat%2Fhreduseries%2FTB3%2 Ftoc.html&external=N. Accessed on July 5, 2008.

This Web site contains a curriculum for high school students on lesbian, gay, bisexual, and transgendered issues. It consists of nine activities dealing with topics such as issues of language and terminology, are gay rights "special," homophobia, and same-sex marriage.

DoSomething.org. "Gay Rights." URL: http://www.dosometh-ing.org/node/27917. Accessed on July 1, 2008.

This Web site provides access to information and discussions about more than three dozen important social issues, gay and lesbian rights being one. The Web site offers background information, a list of organizations, and an opportunity for discussion by those who access the site.

FindLaw. "Gay and Lesbian Rights/Sexual Orientation Discrimination." URL: http://public.findlaw.com/civil-rights/more-civil-rights-topics/gay-lesbian-civil-rights-more/. Accessed on July 5, 2008.

This Web site is an extraordinary resource on the legal rights of gay men and lesbians, with information on federal, state, and local legislation, corporate policies, hate crimes, civil rights, and many other important topics.

Fitzpatrick, Brian. "Media Ignore Impending Collision: Gay Rights vs. Religious Liberty." URL: http://www.cultureand mediainstitute.org/articles/2008/20080610145004.aspx. Posted on June 10, 2008.

The author presents a somewhat different take on the gay and lesbian rights movement, arguing that it is not really a civil rights movement at all, but, instead, "a war against Western civilization's Judeo-Christian moral order." He discusses the evolution of attitudes toward same-sex relationships in Canada as evidence for this position.

"Gay Library." URL: http://www.gaylibrary.com/. Accessed on July 1, 2008.

Gay Library is an all-purpose resource for topics such as gay civil rights organizations, gay film festivals, gay community centers, gay sports and recreation activities, and other gay- and lesbian-related topics.

"Gay Rights Watch." URL: http://www.gayrightswatch.com/. Accessed on July 1, 2008.

This Web site contains an extensive collection of news stories on the gay and lesbian rights movement, with comments available from viewers on these stories.

Peters, Jeremy, and Danny Hakim. "How Governor Set His Stance on Gay Rights." *New York Times.* URL: http://www. nytimes.com/2008/05/30/nyregion/30paterson.html. Posted on May 30, 2008.

In May 2008, Governor David A. Paterson issued a directive indicating that the state of New York would hence recognize same-sex marriages consummated in other states. The authors discuss Paterson's own experience and attitudes about gay men and lesbians and review the provision of his directive.

Pinello, Daniel R. "Casebook on Sexual Orientation and the Law." URL: http://www.danpinello.com/Family2.htm. Accessed on July 5, 2008.

This Web site contains information extracted from the author's book *Gay Rights and American Law.* It contains links to about three dozen important appellate cases dealing with same-sex issues such as marriage, property disputes, wills and estates, domestic violence, and legal rights of same-sex partners.

Public Agenda. "Gay Rights." URL: http://www.publicagenda. org/issues/frontdoor.cfm?issue_type=gay_rights. Accessed on July 1, 2008.

Public Agenda is a highly regarded impartial source for information on a variety of important political, economic, and social issues. Its Web site provides relevant facts on issues, discussion guides, additional resources, existing and proposed legislation, public opinion summaries, and additional resources for understanding the issues.

"Queer Resources Directory." URL: http://www.qrd.org/qrd/. Last updated on July 11, 2008.

This invaluable Web site has links to 25,488 files on virtually every aspect of lesbian, gay, bisexual, and transgendered topics, including same-sex marriage and parenting; gay and lesbian youths; religion; health-and-safety issues; electronic resources; gay media culture and events; international information; business and workplace issues; organizations; and politics and activism.

Robinson, Bruce A. "Homosexuality and Bisexuality: All Viewpoints." Ontario Consultants on Religious Tolerance. URL: http://www.religioustolerance.org/homosexu.htm. Accessed on July 1, 2008.

This Web site provides a great deal of unbiased information about homosexual and bisexual behavior, with detailed discussions on topics such as the impact of religion on beliefs and attitudes about homosexuality and bisexuality; same-sex unions and civil unions; challenges faced by gay men, lesbians, and bisexuals; hate crimes; reparative therapies; laws affecting gay men, lesbians, and bisexuals; and essays, comments, sermons, and other resources.

SpeakOut.com. "Gay Rights." URL: http://www.speakout. com/activism/gayrights/. Accessed on July 1, 2008.

This Web site provides basic information on a number of gay-related issues, such as gays and lesbians in the military, antidiscrimination laws, hate crimes, same-sex marriage, civil unions, and social issues. It also offers links to a number of related Internet sites.

Yahoo! News. "Gay and Lesbian Issues." URL: http://news. yahoo.com/fc/US/Gays_and_Lesbians. Accessed on July 5, 2008.

This Web site contains a number of news articles, editorials, statements of opinion, and links dealing with many aspects of the gay and lesbian rights movement. New items are no longer being added to the site, but those currently there will not be removed (according to Yahoo!) and are of some historical interest. More recent articles can be found at: http://news.search.yahoo.com.

Same-Sex Relationships and Adoption

Books

Andryszewski, Tricia. *Same-Sex Marriage: Moral Wrong or Civil Right?* Minneapolis, MN: Twenty First Century Books, 2007.

The author attempts to present a balanced view of same-sex marriage for young adult readers. She opens with a review of the gay and lesbian rights movement in the United States, and then talks about political developments in the 1990s, the adoption of same-sex marriage in Massachusetts, and some features of gay and lesbian family life.

Chauncey, George. *Why Marriage?: The History Shaping Today's Debate over Gay Equality.* New York: Basic Books, 2005.

The author places the current controversy over same-sex marriage within the context of the historical development of antigay attitudes in the United States (beginning primarily in the mid-twentieth century) and pressures brought to bear on the gay and lesbian communities as a result of the HIV/AIDS crisis in the United States.

Gerstmann, Evan. *Same-Sex Marriage and the Constitution,* 2nd ed. New York: Cambridge University Press, 2008.

Gerstmann argues that the U.S. Constitution provides a fundamental right of marriage in the United States, a right that includes marriage between two people of the same sex. He asks why that right, which now extends to almost all classes of people who are otherwise marginalized in our society, has still not been expanded to include gay men and lesbians.

Myers, David G., and Letha Dawson Scanzoni. *What God Has Joined Together?: A Christian Case for Gay Marriage.* New York: HarperSanFrancisco, 2005.

The authors present an analysis from the standpoint of Christian theology in support of same-sex marriage, pointing out that Jesus had nothing to say about same-sex relationships, and the Bible also has no comment on long-term, committed relationships between two people of the same sex. They also present arguments that same-sex marriages can be in the best interest of families and of children in such relationships.

Polikoff, Nancy D. *Beyond (Straight and Gay) Marriage: Valuing All Families under the Law.* **Boston: Beacon Press, 2008.**

The author argues that the meanings of marriage and family have, for a number of years, been changing, both in the United States and other parts of the world. She reviews this history and examines the social, economic, political, and legal significance of these changes for many types of families, including those of gay men, lesbians, bisexuals, and transgendered individuals.

Rauch, Jonathan. *Gay Marriage: Why It Is Good for Gays, Good for Straights, and Good for America.* **New York: Times Books/Henry Holt and Company, 2004.**

Rauch argues that current efforts to provide "separate-but-equal" arrangements for same-sex couples (such as domestic partnerships) can only harm the traditional institution of heterosexual marriage itself, as well as the best interests of same-sex couples.

Sullivan, Andrew. *Same-Sex Marriage: Pro and Con,* **revised and updated edition. New York: Vintage Books, 2004.**

The more than six dozen essays that make up this anthology have been taken from a wide variety of sources, from the Bible and other ancient literature to modern-day court decisions, laws, and polemics on both sides of the same-sex marriage debate.

Wolfson, Evan. *Why Marriage Matters: America, Equality, and Gay People's Right to Marry.* **New York: Simon & Schuster, 2005.**

Attorney Wolfson defends the right of same-sex couples to marry as a matter of civil rights, one that he calls "one of the first important civil rights campaigns of the 21st century." The book has been discussed widely and is one of the most important works on same-sex marriage in the United States.

Articles

Allen, Douglas W. "An Economic Assessment of Same-Sex Marriage Laws." *Harvard Journal of Law and Public Policy.* 29 (2006): 949–980.

The author argues that the debate over same-sex marriage often omits consideration of the economic issues involved. He points out that such costs could be enormous and, for that reason, society might consider the possibility of having two types of marriage, homosexual marriage and heterosexual marriage. Although not an ideal solution, he believes that the two-marriage model would have fewer harmful economic effects than a one-marriage-for-all model.

Brooks Devon, and Sheryl Goldberg. "Gay and Lesbian Adoptive and Foster Care Placements: Can They Meet the Needs of Waiting Children?" *Social Work*, 46 (2, April 2001): 147–157.

The authors review the demographics of the adoption problem in the United States today, find that there are far more children waiting for adoption than potential adoptive parents, and suggest that laws and regulations be eased to permit same-sex couples to adopt more easily. They review policy implications and changes in practice necessitated by this recommendation.

"Can Anyone Show Just Cause Why These Two Should Not Be Lawfully Joined Together?" *New England Law Review*, 38 (2003–2004): 487–688.

The 15 articles in this issue deal with a variety of issues relating to same-sex marriage, such as Constitutional issues, evolving patterns in the United States and other countries of the world, estate planning for same-sex couples, adoption by same-sex couples, issues for grandparents, and religious issues involved in the approval of same-sex marriages.

Committee on Psychosocial Aspects of Child and Family Health. American Academy of Pediatrics. "Coparent or Second-Parent Adoption by Same-Sex Parents." *Pediatrics*, 109 (2, February 2002): 339–340.

A special committee of the American Academy of Pediatrics appointed to study same-sex adoptions recommends that pediatricians support legislative and legal efforts to recognize such adoptions.

Coolidge, David Orgon, and William C. Duncan. "Reaffirming Marriage: A Presidential Priority." *Harvard Journal of Law and Public Policy,* **24 (Spring 2001): 623–651.**

The authors present arguments for maintaining the definition of a marriage as a union between one man and one woman, explain how some activists are trying to break down that traditional definition through civil unions and same-sex marriages, and propose actions by the incoming administration of George W. Bush to retain and enforce the traditional definition of marriage.

Duncan, William C. "Avoidance Strategy: Same-Sex Marriage Litigation and the Federal Courts." *Campbell Law Review,* **29 (2006): 29–46.**

The author points out that advocates for same-sex marriage nearly always bring suit in state, and not federal, courts. He suggests that the reason for this pattern is that the U.S. Constitution provides no basis for endorsing same-sex marriage, and he cites a number of past rulings to confirm this view. He argues that the adoption of same-sex marriages nationwide through actions by individual state courts will have a "sorry legacy," not only for traditional marriage, but also for the law.

"Editors' Symposium: The Meaning of Marriage." *San Diego Law Review,* **42 (2005): 821–1149.**

This issue consists of 22 articles dealing with almost every conceivable aspect of the so-called Federal Marriage Amendment, a proposed amendment to the U.S. Constitution defining marriage as the union of one man and one woman. Some issues discussed include the meaning of marriage, the effects of same-sex marriage on children, the amendment and polygamy, and lessons from natural law and tradition.

Franke, Katherine M. "The Politics of Same-Sex Marriage Politics." *Columbia Journal of Gender and Law,* **15 (2006): 236–248.**

After the decriminalization of same-sex sex practices by the U.S. Supreme Court in *Lawrence v. Texas*, many members of the lesbian and gay community chose to raise the political ante by pushing for same-sex marriage. The author explores the history of this evolution of political goals and some problems that it raises for both the gay and lesbian community and the society at large.

Goldberg, Suzanne B. "A Historical Guide to the Future of Marriage for Same-Sex Couples." *Columbia Journal of Gender and Law*, **15 (2006): 249–272.**

The author notes that most decisions about same-sex marriage include references to the history of such relationships, but that those references are flawed for two reasons. First, historical precedence is an insufficient basis on which to make such decisions, and, second, the historical analyses that are made are typically based on inaccurate readings of historical documents.

Katz, Pamela S. "The Case for Legal Recognition of Same-Sex Marriage." *Journal of Law and Policy*, **8 (1999): 61–106.**

Katz argues for same-sex marriage on the basis of two legal principles: due process law and discrimination based on gender and/or sexual orientation. She says that there is no legitimate reason for suspecting that the existence of same-sex marriages will represent a threat to the stability of society.

Koppelman, Andrew. "Interstate Recognition of Same-Sex Marriages and Civil Unions: A Handbook for Judges." *University of Pennsylvania Law Review*, **153 (2005): 2143–2194.**

As legal same-sex arrangements (marriages, civil unions, domestic partnerships, etc.) become more common, the legal question as to whether states must recognize such arrangements from other states becomes more important. Koppelman reviews four kinds of same-sex arrangements, "evasive," "migratory," "visitor," and "extraterritorial" marriages (depending on the relationship of the couple to the state in which they are married), and the legal consequences of each for the question of recognition.

Kurtz, Stanley. "Beyond Gay Marriage." *The Weekly Standard*, **8 (August 4–11, 2003): 26–33.**

Kurtz argues that legalization of same-sex marriage raises some serious questions about the nature of marriage itself that need to be discussed on a broad and open front in American society. He suggests that approval of the practice will lead to a variety of other kinds of nontraditional relationships, such as polygamy and three-person marriages.

Lipkin, Robert Justin. "The Harm of Same-Sex Marriage: Real or Imagined?" *Widener Law Review*, **11 (2005): 277–308.**

Conservatives argue that permitting same-sex marriage will harm society, and liberals suggest they cannot imagine how such harm can occur. Lipkin says that conservatives are right, but that the real question is how any harm that may occur is balanced by providing a segment of the population (gay men and lesbians) with a legitimate civil right.

"Same-Sex Couples: Defining Marriage in the Twenty-First Century." *Stanford Law and Policy Review*, **16 (2005): 1–232.**

The eight articles in this special symposium issue deal with legal, religious, economic, and moral issues related to the increasing popularity of same-sex marriages.

Stewart, Monte Neil. "Judicial Redefinition of Marriage." *Canadian Journal of Family Law*, **21 (2004): 11–132.**

The author examines four judicial decisions dealing with same-sex marriage, two in the United States and two in Canada, from the standpoint of their judicial quality. He finds that all four decisions were "materially defective" in that they failed to deal adequately with basic issues raised by opponents of same-sex marriage, such as the importance of a couple's being able to reproduce. He concludes that "courts did an unacceptable job with their performance of the very tasks that lie at the heart of judicial responsibility in virtually every case."

Volokh, Eugene. "Same-Sex Marriage and Slippery Slopes." *Hofstra Law Review*, **33 (2005): 1155–1201.**

Critics of same-sex marriage often offer the "slippery-slope" argument: Such relationships may be without harm at the moment, but they may lead to serious problems at some time in the future. Volokh analyzes the logic of this argument and concludes that it is inappropriately used to argue against same-sex marriages. He also reviews a number of reasons that same-sex marriages are good not only for the individuals involved, but also for society as a whole.

Wardle, Lynn D. "A Critical Analysis of Constitutional Claims for Same-Sex Marriage," *Brigham Young University Law Review*, 1 (1996): 96–100.

A listing of law review articles dealing with same-sex marriage dating from 1970 to 1975 and from 1990 to 1995. The articles are categorized as in favor of or opposed to same-sex marriage.

Weiser, Jay. "Foreword: The Next Normal: Developments Since Marriage Rights for Same-Sex Couples in New York." *Columbia Journal of Gender and Law*, 13: 48–69.

The author provides a comprehensive and exhaustive introduction to the subject of same-sex marriage, with special focus on circumstances in the state of New York. The article is an introduction to a 2000 report issued by a number of committees of the Association of the Bar of the City of New York, "A Report on Marriage Rights for Same-Sex Couples in New York," reprinted on pages 70–99 of the same issue of the journal.

Wilkins, Richard G. "The Constitutionality of Legal Preferences for Heterosexual Marriage." *Regent University Law Review*, 16 (2003/2004): 121–137.

Wilkins suggests that the traditional definition of marriage as being between one man and one woman is under attack from a number of forces, same-sex unions being one. He asks if "the various legal preferences conferred on traditional marriage [must] be extended to alternative partnership arrangements?" and decides that the answer is "no." He offers both constitutional and social issues for reaching this decision.

Reports

The Beckett Fund for Religious Liberty. "Scholars' Conference on Same-Sex Marriage and Religious Liberty." URL: http://www. becketfund.org/index.php/article/494.html. Posted on May 4, 2006.

This report summarizes the proceedings of a conference sponsored by the Beckett Fund on the consequences of the legalization of same-sex marriages on religious freedom. The Web site has links to seven papers presented at that conference, along with the text of three amicus curiae briefs based on the presentations made and filed by the fund in related cases heard by courts in Connecticut, Iowa, and Maryland.

Brodzinsky, David M., and the staff of the Evan B. Donaldson Adoption Institute. *Adoption by Lesbians and Gays: A National Survey of Adoption Agency Policies, Practices, and Attitudes.* [New York: Evan B. Donaldson Adoption Institute]. URL: http://www.adoptioninstitute.org/whowe/Lesbian% 20and%20Gay%20Adoption%20Report_final.doc [October 29, 2003].

Researchers report on a study of policies and practices of 307 private and public adoption agencies in all 50 states and the District of Columbia. The study shows that, in general, adoption agencies are increasingly willing to place children with same-sex couples. About two of five responding agencies have already placed children with couples known to be gay or lesbian, and 60 percent of respondents indicate a willingness to accept applications for adoptions from same-sex couples.

Gates, Gary J., M. V. Lee Badgett, Jennifer Ehrle Macomber, and Kate Chambers. *Adoption and Foster Care by Gay and Lesbian Parents in the United States.* URL: http://www.urban. org/UploadedPDF/411437_Adoption_Foster_Care.pdf. Posted March 2007.

The four researchers from the Williams Institute at the University of California at Los Angeles School of Law and the Urban Institute in Washington, D.C., summarize demographic data about an estimated 65,500 children living in families headed by a same-sex couple or a single gay or lesbian parent in the United States, and they compare those data with information about comparable heterosexual families. They point out ways in which same-sex and opposite-sex families are alike and different and conclude that, in general, bans on adoptions by same-sex couples are likely to have more negative than positive results for children, adoptive parents, and the general community.

Web Sites

aardvarc.org. "Domestic Violence in Gay and Lesbian Relationships." URL: http://www.aardvarc.org/dv/gay.shtml. Last updated on January 10, 2008.

aardvarc.org (An Abuse, Rape and Domestic Violence Aid and Resource Collection) provides information on personal, social, and legal aspects of domestic violence within same-sex relationships. The Web site points out that the rate of domestic violence among same-sex couples is probably about the same as it is in opposite-sex couples, but obtaining help from outside sources is often much more difficult because of professionals' unfamiliarity and unwillingness to deal with same-sex violence.

"Alternative Family Matters." URL: http://www.alternative families.org/. Accessed on July 1, 2008.

Operated by Jenifer Firestone, social worker, community activist, and lesbian mother, this Web site provides information and advice on the adoption of children by lesbian, gay, bisexual, and transgendered (LGBT) persons. It provides articles and other resources on the topic and links to other Web sites dealing with adoption by LBGT persons.

Axel-Lute, Paul. "Same-Sex Marriage: A Selective Bibliography of the Legal Literature." URL: http://law-library.rutgers. edu/SSM.html. Last updated on December 12, 2007.

This Web site provides a superb bibliography of books, articles, and Internet resources on the subject of same-sex marriage.

Bidstrup, Scott. "Gay Marriage: The Arguments and the Motives." URL: http://www.bidstrup.com/marriage.htm. Accessed on July 1, 2008.

The author, a proponent of same-sex marriage, presents stated and the *real* arguments against the practice, along with some valuable material related to this debate.

"Marriage Project Hawaii." URL: http://members.tripod.com/ ˉMPHAWAII/. Last updated on September 3, 2001.

The first major event in the modern U.S. debate over same-sex marriage occurred in 1993 when the Hawaii Supreme Court ruled that laws denying the right of same-sex couples to marry violated the state constitution. That decision was eventually nullified when the state legislature later passed laws limiting marriage to heterosexual couples. Over time, however, the legislature also passed a number of laws creating the condition of *reciprocal beneficiary* to same-sex couples, a status that carries many of the same benefits enjoyed by heterosexual couples. This Web site, now moribund, contains some extremely useful information about the original battle over same-sex marriages and the provisions of the reciprocal beneficiary laws.

National Center for Lesbian Rights. "Adoption by Lesbian, Gay and Bisexual Parents: An Overview of Current Law." URL: http://www.nclrights.org/site/DocServer/adptn0204.pdf? docID=1221. Posted in January 2004.

This publication provides a comprehensive, well-documented, and detailed review of the current legal status of adoption by lesbians, gay men, and bisexuals in the United States.

Stanton, Glenn T. "Is Marriage in Jeopardy?" URL: http:// www.family.org/socialissues/A000000646.cfm and http://www. family.org/socialissues/A000000647.cfm.

This two-part article appears on the Web site of Focus on the Family (FoF), an organization that opposes same-sex marriage. The articles pose a number of questions that readers might have about the same-sex-marriage debate, and answers for those questions from the FoF point of view. The author provides extensive lists of additional readings for both essays, although, of course, they present only one side of the debate.

International Issues

Books

Badgett, Lee. *Sexual Orientation Discrimination: An International Perspective*. New York: Routledge, 2007.

The author analyzes the economic consequences of discrimination against lesbians and gay men in a number of countries throughout the world. The book includes sections on wages and jobs; discrimination in various types of institutions, such as education, religion, and sports; and discrimination through laws, regulations, and other expressions of public policies.

Hunt, Gerald, ed. *Laboring for Rights: Unions and Sexual Diversity across Nations.* Philadelphia: Temple University Press, 1999.

The articles in this anthology discuss issues of sexual diversity for labor unions in the United States, Canada, Australia, Great Britain, South Africa, and other countries.

Articles

Whitaker, Brian. "Pink Planet. The New Global Gay Politics, from China and Iraq to South America." *New Statesman*, 136 (4854, July 19, 2007): 32–33.

The author provides a brief, but excellent, review of the status of the gay and lesbian rights movement in various parts of the world, pointing out that activists have made considerable progress, but that, in response, opposition to the movement has also become better organized and more aggressive.

Web Sites

Fuentes, Federico, and Kiraz Janicke. "Struggling for Gay and Lesbian Rights in Venezuela." URL: http://www.venezuel analysis.com/analysis/1512. Posted on December 5, 2005.

A very interesting article on the battle for gay and lesbian rights in Venezuela, a country about which very little has been written with regard to sexual-orientation issues. The authors suggest that as part of the new revolutionary philosophy in Venezuela, many people are beginning to question traditional beliefs about sexual and gender orientation.

Jara, Mazibuko. "Gay and Lesbian Rights; Forcing Change in South Africa." URL: http://www.africafiles.org/article.asp?ID=3804. Originally posted in the May 1998 issue of *South Africa Report.*

The author provides a brief review of the young gay and lesbian rights movement in South Africa beginning in 1996 with a review of its accomplishments over the next two years.

Valente, Marcela. "Argentina: The 'Final Battle' for Gay and Lesbian Rights." URL: http://ipsnews.net/news.asp?idnews= 30038. Posted on August 26, 2005.

The author provides background on efforts to legalize same-sex marriages in Argentina. As of late 2008, those efforts have still not been successful.

Glossary

accomodationism   The belief that anyone who is considered an "outsider" in society should make such adaptations as will allow society to be more likely to accept that person as a "normal" part of the culture.

antidiscrimination legislation   Any law that makes it illegal to treat any class of citizens in any regard than the way the majority of citizens is treated.

antimiscegenation law   A law that prohibits the marriage of two people of different races. Antimiscegenation laws in the United States were considered to be constitutional until 1967.

bisexual   A term that refers to acts, fantasies, or feelings that involve individuals of either sex. People who call themselves bisexual experience an erotic interest in both men and women, although not necessarily to an equal extent.

civil rights   Personal rights guaranteed to all citizens, usually as the result of some defining document, such as the U.S. Constitution.

civil union   A legally sanctioned relationship between two individuals of the same or opposite sex who are not otherwise allowed to marry under laws of the state. *See also* **domestic partnership**; **registered partnership**.

coming out   The act by which a person acknowledges his or her homosexual orientation. Gay men and lesbians often acknowledge various levels of coming out, including coming out to oneself; to one's relatives, neighbors, friends, and coworkers; and acknowledging the social and political implications of a homosexual orientation in the general society.

consensual sexual act   Any sexual act to which both (or all) parties agree.

decriminalization   The removal of a law or laws prohibiting certain types of behavior.

domestic partners   Two individuals who are not legally married to each other, but who do live together and share their lives together, sometimes in a legally sanctioned relationship known as a civil union, domestic partnership, or registered partnership.

domestic partnership   A legally sanctioned relationship between two individuals of the same or opposite sex who are not otherwise allowed to marry under laws of the state. The term is used most commonly in the United States. *See also* **civil union; registered partnership.**

don't ask, don't tell (DADT)   The official policy of the U.S. government regarding the right of lesbians and gay men to serve in the military. Such individuals are allowed to be a part of the military provided they do not disclose their sexual orientation. In addition, the armed services promise not to pursue investigations of a person's sexual orientation.

entrapment   An act by a law officer that induces a person to take part in a crime that he or she might not otherwise have committed.

Full Faith and Credit Clause   Section 1 of the Fourth Amendment to the U.S. Constitution says that all states must accept and honor all legal decisions made by another state. One of the very few situations in which that clause has been ignored in U.S. history has been same-sex marriage, in which nearly all states have decided not to honor same-sex marriages conducted in another state.

gay   A term that has come to be associated with individuals, organizations, acts, events, or other phenomena involving two individuals of the same gender, most commonly, two men.

gay bashing   Any activity in which individuals—most commonly, young men—beat up gay men, lesbians, or other individuals whom they judge to be of a sexual orientation to which they object, usually without any apparent rational basis, often "just for the fun of it."

gay liberation   A movement whose goals it was to free lesbians and gay men from long-standing prejudices, fears, and hatreds of non-gays, and, in many cases, to make issues of sexuality more open and free for all people whatever their sexual orientation.

gay rights legislation   Any law, executive order, administrative rule, or other legal action that specifically provides for the protection of some civil liberty (such as employment or housing) for lesbians and gay men.

gender   A term that refers to a person's social identity as a man or a women. The concept of gender includes not only one's biological sex (male or female), but also the social constructs created by a culture that tend to be associated with one or the other sex.

gender identity   The perception that a person has as to whether he or she is a man or a woman. Gender identity and gender or gender identity and sex are not always the same. An individual who is biologically male and who may assume all the characteristics of a man may feel that he is actually "a woman trapped in a man's body."

hate crime   Any criminal act that is based solely or primarily on prejudice against some group of individuals, such as women, blacks, Hispanics, or gay men and lesbians.

heterosexual   Any feeling, fantasy, or act that involves two people of the opposite sex.

homophile   A term by which many early gay rights activists (and some gay men and lesbians since then) referred to themselves. The suffix -*phile* from the Greek for "love," was thought to have a less clinical implication than did the earlier term *homosexual*.

homophobia   The irrational fear of gay men and lesbians.

homosexual   A term that should probably best be used as an adjective, referring to any feeling, fantasy, or act that involves two people of the same sex. Historically, the word has also been used to refer to an individual or group of individuals. It is less successful in that context because it tends to define individuals and groups of individuals solely on the basis of their erotic interests.

intermediate sex   A term used by some early students of human sexuality to describe men and women with homosexual interests.

invert   A term used by some early social scientists to refer to gay men and lesbians.

lesbian   A women whose primary erotic interest involves other women.

mutual adoption   The process by which each member of a couple legally adopts the children of his or her partner. The term usually, but not inevitably, applies to same-sex couples.

partner   A term that has become increasingly popular in describing one member of a same-sex couple.

pedophilia   The condition of being erotically attracted to children. Although pedophilia is sometimes associated with homosexuality, most studies suggest that the vast majority of pedophiliacs are heterosexual men or men with a troubled heterosexual orientation who are attracted to young girls or to all young children of either sex.

psychosocial   A term that refers to an individual's personal health and development within the general context of social standards and mores.

public accommodation   Facilities or services that are available to the general public, such as hotels, restaurants, libraries, stores, public transportation systems, and government services.

queer   A derogatory word used to describe gay men and lesbians. The term has now been adopted by many gay men and lesbians as an act of defiance against those who would use the term in a disparaging manner.

registered partnership A legally sanctioned relationship between two individuals of the same or opposite sex who are not otherwise allowed to marry under laws of the state. The term is used most commonly in Europe. *See also* **civil union; domestic partnership.**

second-parent adoption A process by which the partner of a child's parent legally adopts the child, as in step-parent adoption.

sex The genetic and biological characteristic of maleness or femaleness, usually characterized by the presence or absence of certain sex organs, such as a penis and a vagina.

sexual orientation The tendency of a person to be erotically attracted to someone of the same gender, the opposite gender, or both genders. The term *orientation* usually suggests that this tendency is not consciously chosen by a person, but is determined by some genetic or biological factor. *See also* **sexual preference.**

sexual preference The tendency of a person to be erotically attracted to someone of the same gender, the opposite gender, or both genders. The term *preference* usually suggests that this tendency is consciously selected by a person rather than being the result of a genetic or biological factor.

slippery slope argument An argument that claims that taking one action inevitably leads to other actions, which, in turn, lead to even more actions, so that the significance of the first action is much greater than it might otherwise seem. For example, some people believe that allowing two people of the same sex to become legally married will eventually lead to: (1) three-person marriages, (2) marriages between a human and an animal, and/or (3) marriages between nonhuman animals.

sodomy An ambiguous term that at one time referred to the sexual act in which one man inserts his penis into a second man's anus. Over many decades, the term has come to have a much wider range of meanings, including anal sex between a man and a woman, oral sex between any two genders, and even cunnilingus, masturbation, and bestiality.

transgendered person A person who has undergone one or more steps in the process of changing one's sex, from male to female or from female to male.

transvestite A person (almost always a man) who enjoys dressing in the clothing of someone of the opposite sex and, often, takes on the social characteristics of that sex. A man who enjoys dressing as a women and then going shopping in that attire is a transsexual. The great majority of transvestites are heterosexual males.

uranian A term suggested by Karl Ulrichs for individuals erotically attracted to someone of their own gender.

Index

287

About the Author

David E. Newton holds an associate's degree in science from Grand Rapids (Michigan) Junior College, a BA in chemistry (with high distinction) and an MA in education from the University of Michigan, and an EdD in science education from Harvard University. He is the author of more than 400 textbooks, encyclopedias, resource books, research manuals, laboratory manuals, trade books, and other educational materials. He taught mathematics, chemistry, and physical science in Grand Rapids, Michigan, for 13 years; was professor of chemistry and physics at Salem State College in Massachusetts for 15 years; and was adjunct professor in the College of Professional Studies at the University of San Francisco for 10 years. Previous books for ABC-CLIO include *Global Warming: A Reference Handbook* (1993), *The Ozone Dilemma: A Reference Handbook* (1995), *Environmental Justice* (1996, 2009), *Encyclopedia of Cryptology* (1997), and *Social Issues in Science and Technology: An Encyclopedia* (1999).